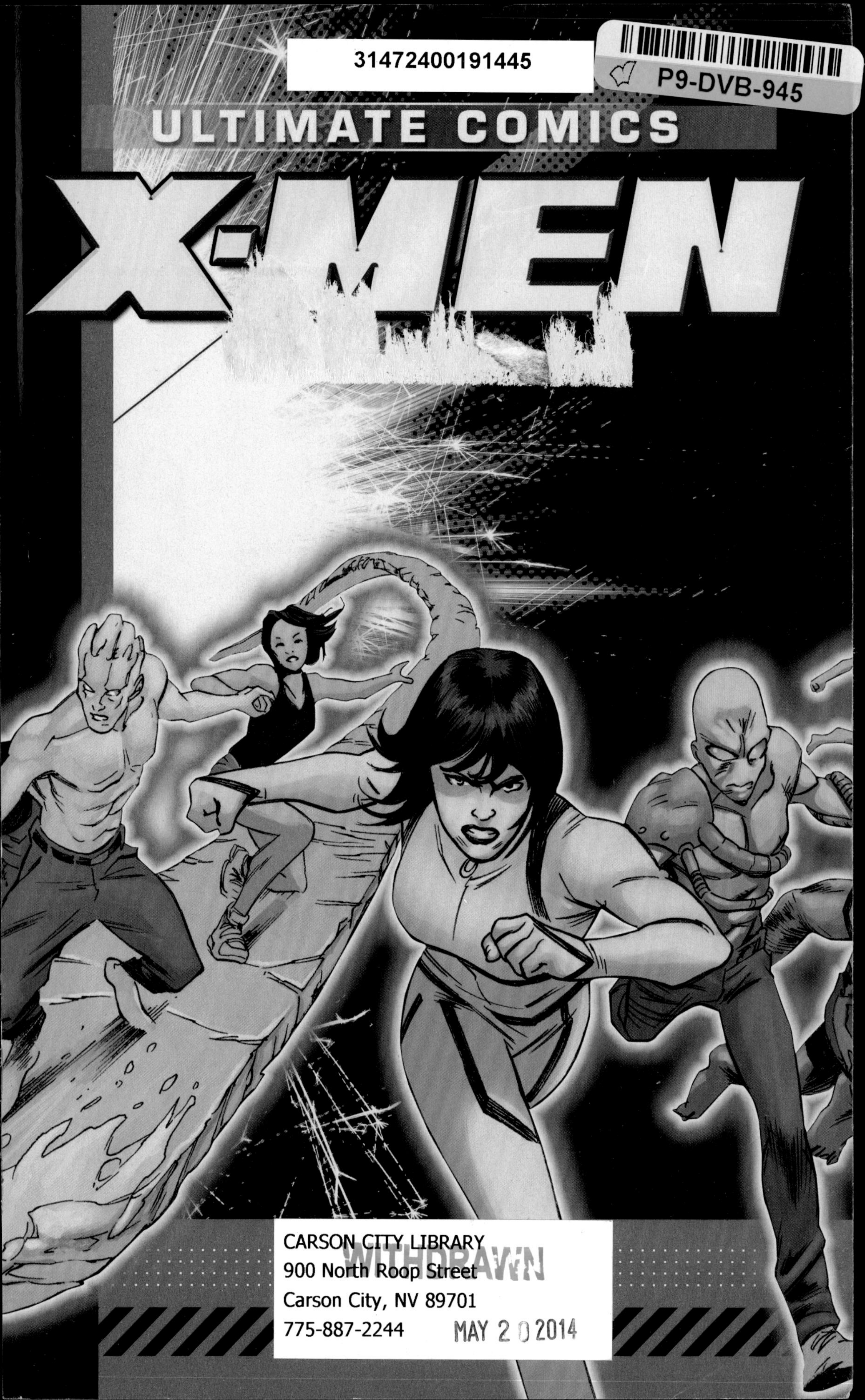

ULTIMATE COMICS
X-MEN

ULTIMATE COMICS

X-MEN

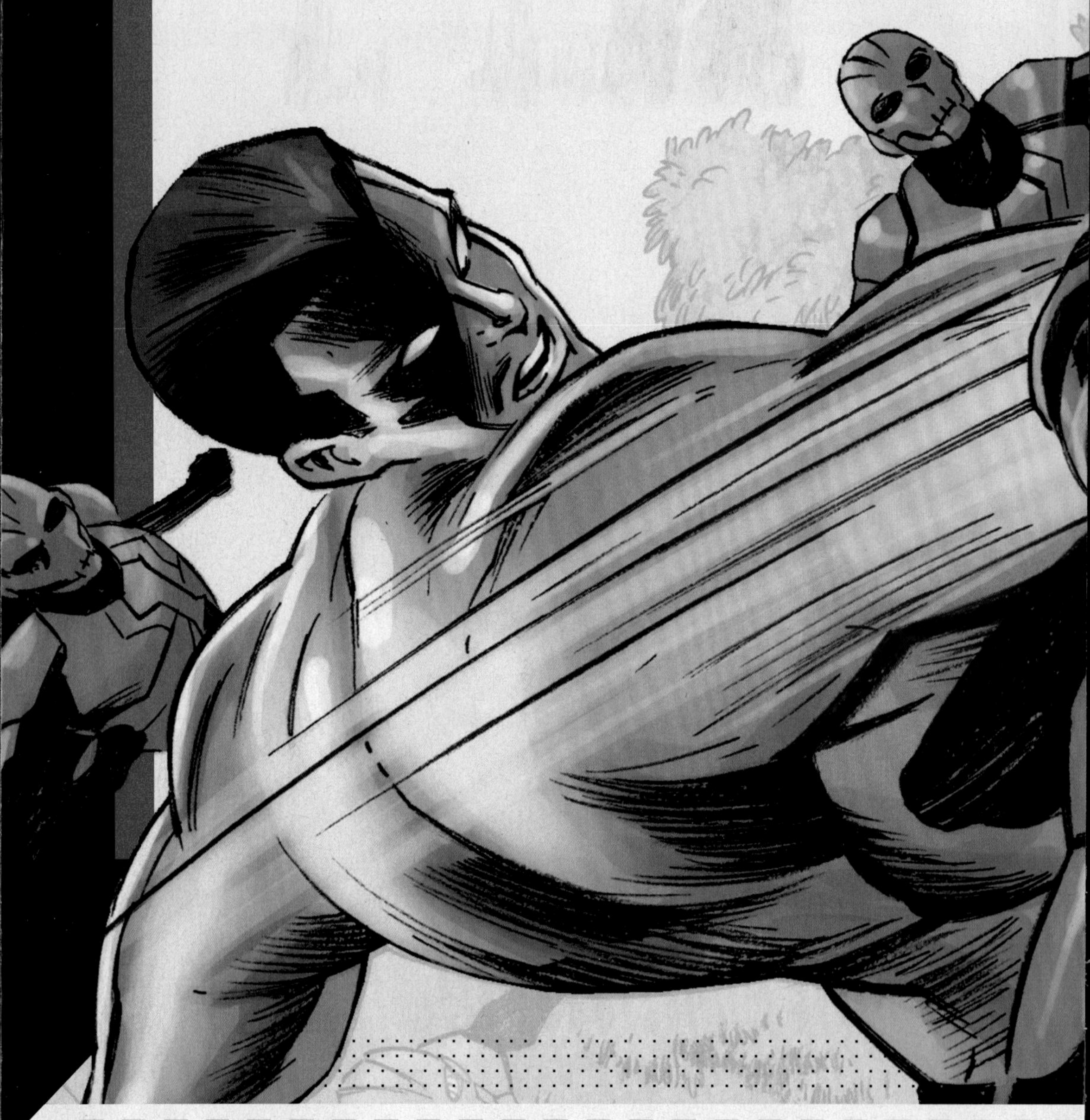

WRITER: **BRIAN WOOD**

PENCILER: **ALVARO MARTINEZ**

INKER: **JOHN LUCAS**

COLORIST: **CHRIS SOTOMAYOR**

LETTERER: **VC'S JOE SABINO**

COVER ART: **GABRIEL HARDMAN** WITH

ELIZABETH BREITWEISER (#29 & #31-33)

& **JORDIE BELLAIRE** (#30)

ASSISTANT EDITOR: **EMILY SHAW**

EDITOR: **MARK PANICCIA**

COLLECTION EDITOR: **JENNIFER GRÜNWALD**
ASSISTANT EDITORS: **ALEX STARBUCK** & **NELSON RIBEIRO**
EDITORS, SPECIAL PROJECT: **MARK D. BEAZLEY**
SENIOR EDITOR, SPECIAL PROJECTS: **JEFF YOUNGQUIST**
LAYOUT: **JEPH YORK**
SVP PRINT, SALES & MARKETING: **DAVID GABRIEL**
BOOK DESIGNER: **JOE FRONTIRRE**

EDITOR IN CHIEF: **AXEL ALONSO**
CHIEF CREATIVE OFFICER: **JOE QUESADA**
PUBLISHER: **DAN BUCKLEY**
EXECUTIVE PRODUCER: **ALAN FINE**

ULTIMATE COMICS X-MEN BY BRIAN WOOD VOL. 3. Contains material originally published in magazine form as ULTIMATE COMICS X-MEN #29-33. First printing 2014. ISBN# 978-0-7851-6721-1. Published by MARVEL WORLDWIDE, INC., a subsidiary of MARVEL ENTERTAINMENT, LLC. OFFICE OF PUBLICATION: 135 West 50th Street, New York, NY 10020. Copyright © 2014 Marvel Characters, Inc. All rights reserved. All characters featured in this issue and the distinctive names and likenesses thereof, and all related indicia are trademarks of Marvel Characters, Inc. No similarity between any of the names, characters, persons, and/or institutions in this magazine with those of any living or dead person or institution is intended, and any such similarity which may exist is purely coincidental. **Printed in CANADA.** ALAN FINE, EVP - Office of the President, Marvel Worldwide, Inc. and EVP & CMO Marvel Characters B.V.; DAN BUCKLEY, Publisher & President - Print, Animation & Digital Divisions; JOE QUESADA, Chief Creative Officer; TOM BREVOORT, SVP of Publishing; DAVID BOGART, SVP of Operations & Procurement, Publishing; C.B. CEBULSKI, SVP of Creator & Content Development; DAVID GABRIEL, SVP of Print & Digital Publishing Sales; JIM O'KEEFE, VP of Operations & Logistics; DAN CARR, Executive Director of Publishing Technology; SUSAN CRESPI, Editorial Operations Manager; ALEX MORALES, Publishing Operations Manager; STAN LEE, Chairman Emeritus. For information regarding advertising in Marvel Comics or on Marvel.com, please contact Niza Disla, Director of Marvel Partnerships, at ndisla@marvel.com. For Marvel subscription inquiries, please call 800-217-9158. **Manufactured between 12/27/2013 and 2/3/2014 by SOLISCO PRINTERS, SCOTT, QC, CANADA.**
1 0 9 8 7 6 5 4 3 2

29

WORLD WAR X

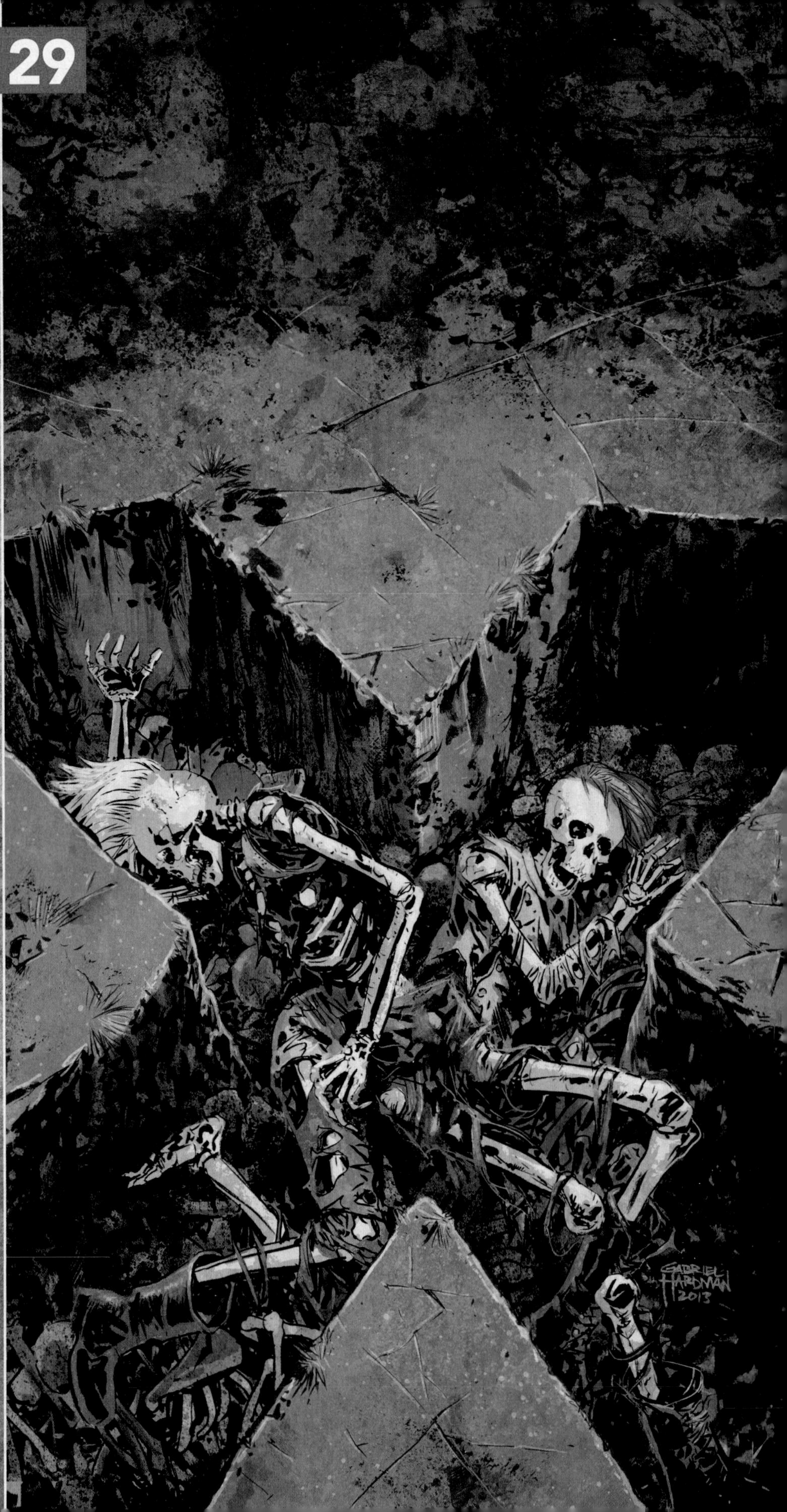
GABRIEL HARDMAN 2013

LIVING IN A WORLD WHERE MUTANTS ARE HATED AND FEARED MORE THAN EVER, ONE GROUP OF YOUNG HEROES HAS BANDED TOGETHER TO FIGHT BACK.

ULTIMATE COMICS X-MEN

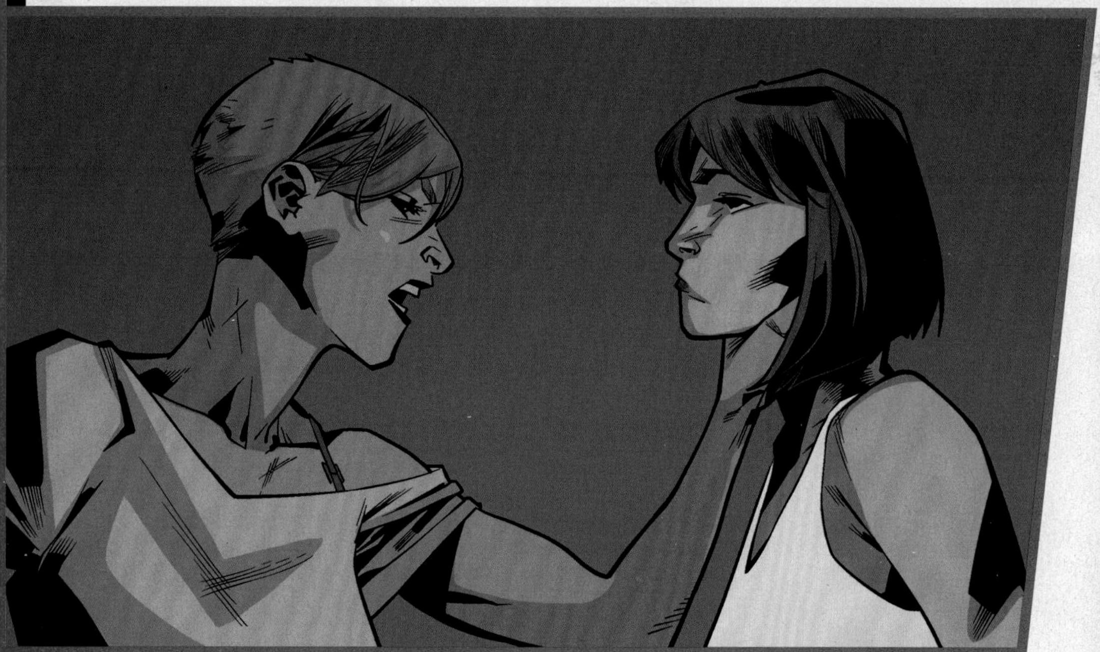

PREVIOUSLY:

The war against the humans is over. But the war between the mutants is just beginning...

The mutants of the newly founded mutant nation, Utopia, defended themselves victoriously against the Army's unwarranted attack.

At the end of the battle, Kitty Pryde and Jean Grey came to a stand-off where the leader of Utopia dismissed the leader of Tian — the mutant paradise that floats among the clouds. With her mental powers blocked by the Sentient Seed, Jean reluctantly complied, but not before she sent her servant Farbird back to Tian to begin preparations for "Project Supersonic."

Will the second Mutant Nation, in its infancy, be able to escape the violence that has plagued mutants for so long or will the next seed of terror come from within?

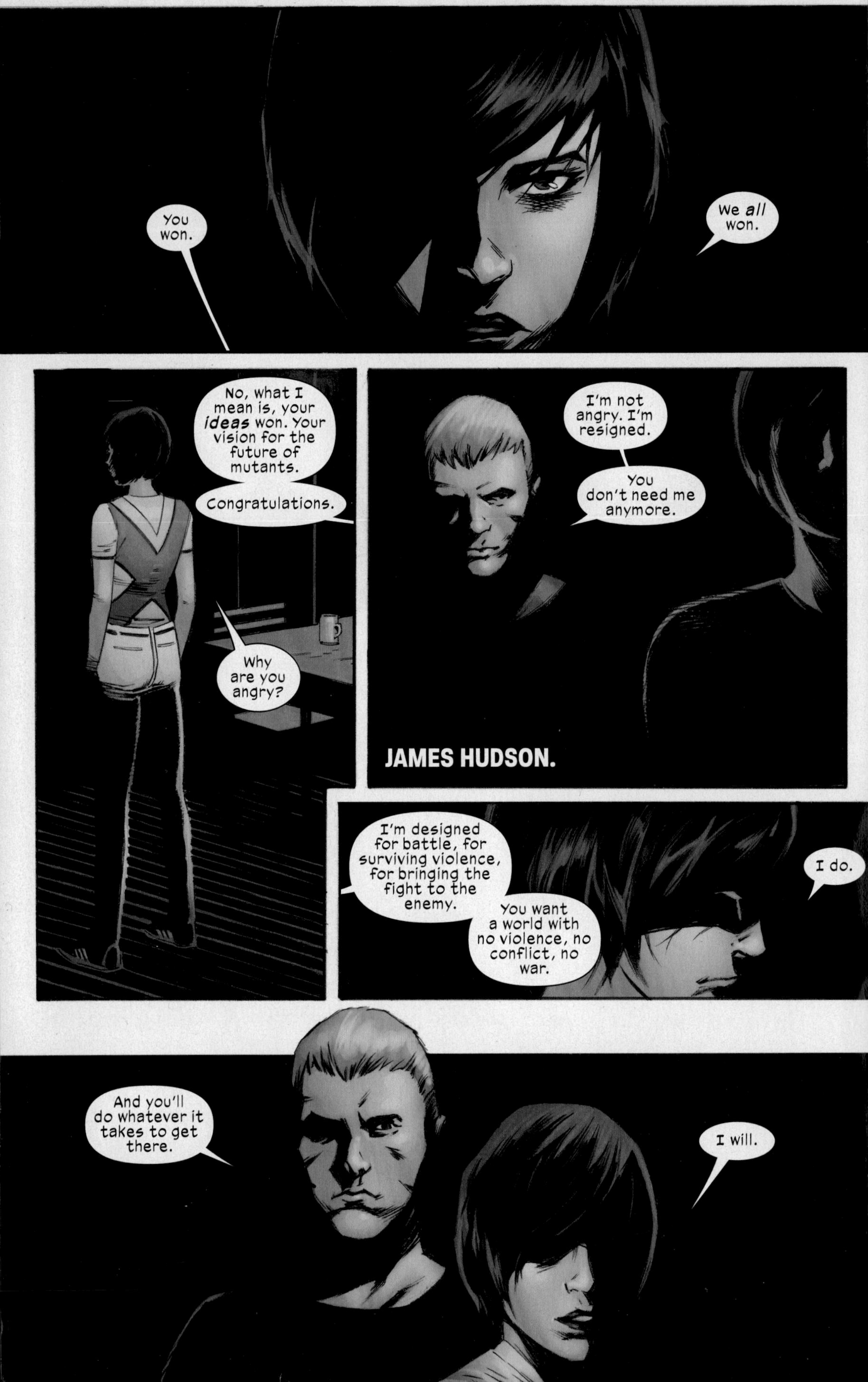

You won.
We *all* won.
No, what I mean is, your *ideas* won. Your vision for the future of mutants.
Congratulations.
Why are you angry?
I'm not angry. I'm resigned.
You don't need me anymore.
JAMES HUDSON.
I'm designed for battle, for surviving violence, for bringing the fight to the enemy.
You want a world with no violence, no conflict, no war.
I do.
And you'll do whatever it takes to get there.
I will.

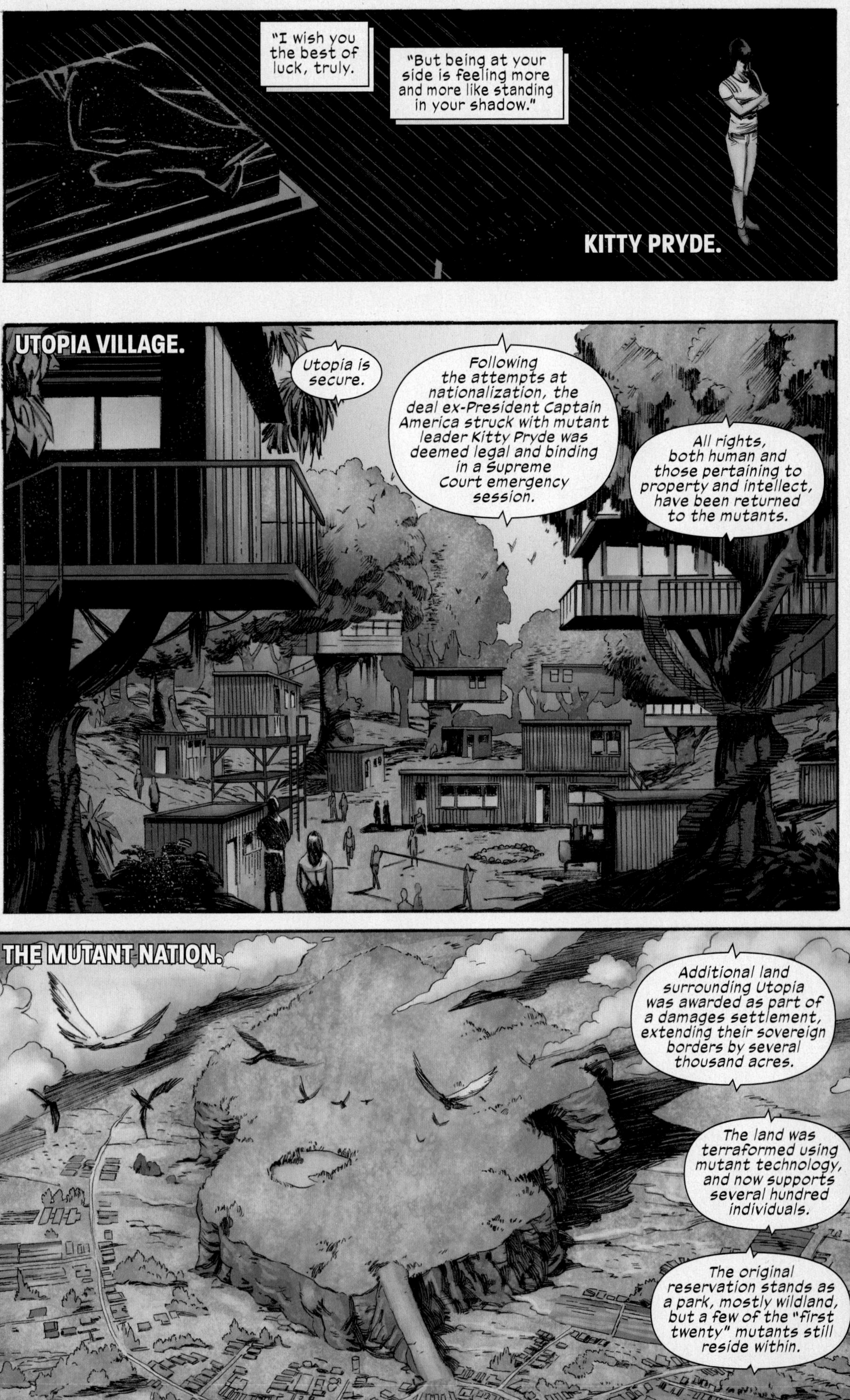
"I wish you the best of luck, truly.
"But being at your side is feeling more and more like standing in your shadow."
KITTY PRYDE.
UTOPIA VILLAGE.
Utopia is secure.
Following the attempts at nationalization, the deal ex-President Captain America struck with mutant leader Kitty Pryde was deemed legal and binding in a Supreme Court emergency session.
All rights, both human and those pertaining to property and intellect, have been returned to the mutants.
THE MUTANT NATION.
Additional land surrounding Utopia was awarded as part of a damages settlement, extending their sovereign borders by several thousand acres.
The land was terraformed using mutant technology, and now supports several hundred individuals.
The original reservation stands as a park, mostly wildland, but a few of the "first twenty" mutants still reside within.

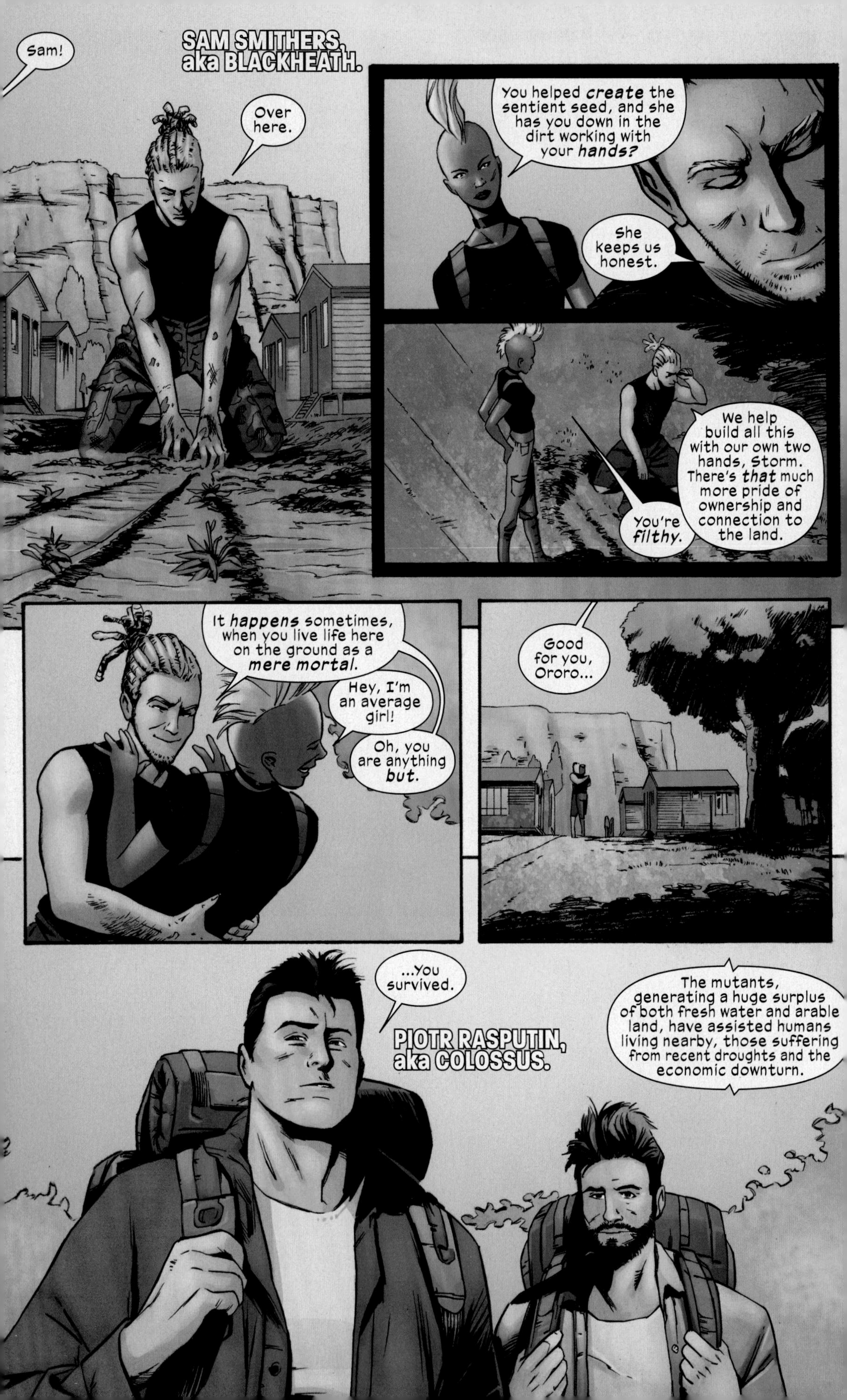

Sam!
SAM SMITHERS, aka BLACKHEATH.
Over here.
You helped *create* the sentient seed, and she has you down in the dirt working with your *hands?*
She keeps us honest.
You're *filthy.*
We help build all this with our own two hands, Storm. There's *that* much more pride of ownership and connection to the land.
It *happens* sometimes, when you live life here on the ground as a *mere mortal.*
Hey, I'm an average girl!
Oh, you are anything *but.*
Good for you, Ororo...
...You survived.
PIOTR RASPUTIN, aka COLOSSUS.
The mutants, generating a huge surplus of both fresh water and arable land, have assisted humans living nearby, those suffering from recent droughts and the economic downturn.

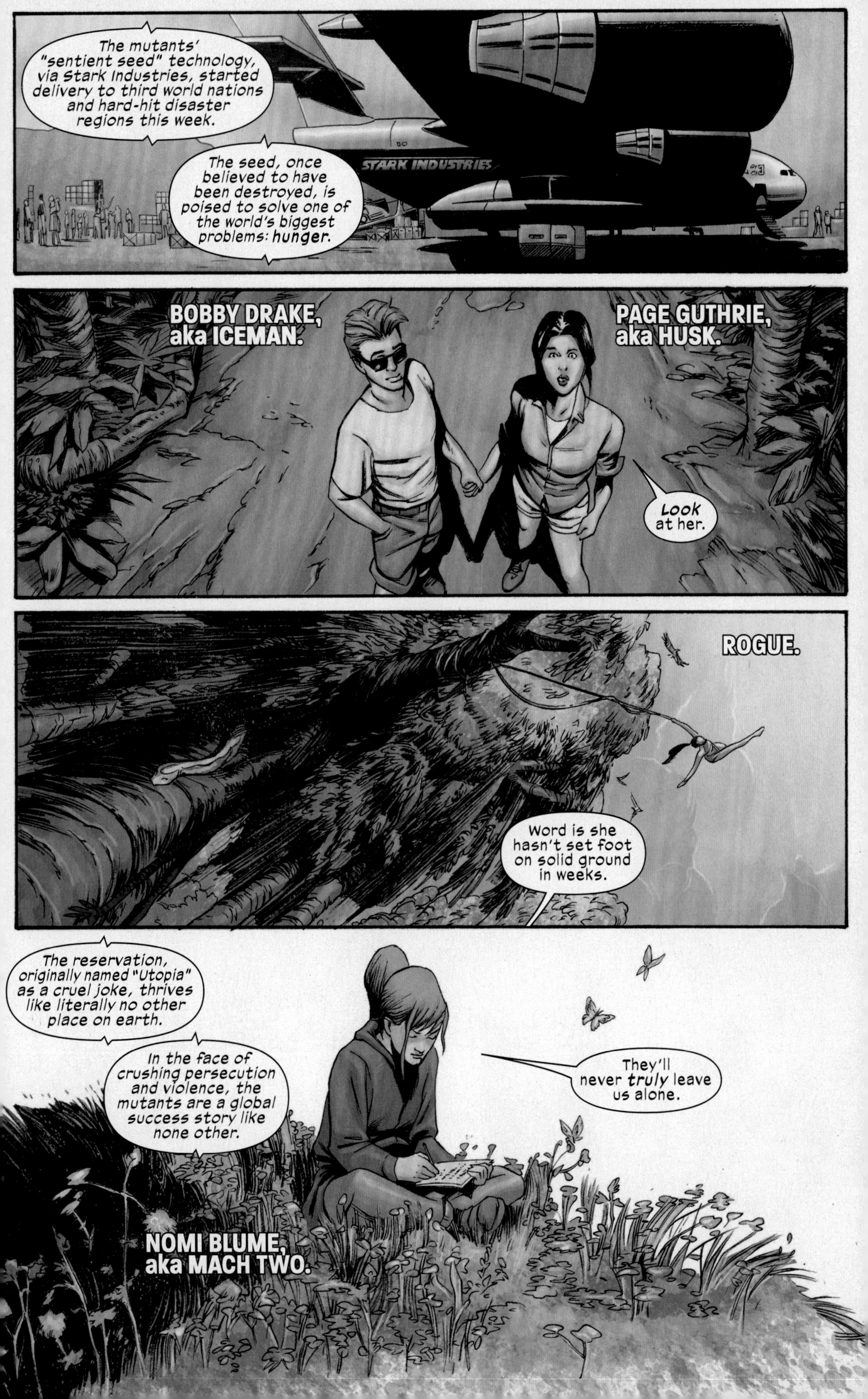
The mutants' "sentient seed" technology, via Stark Industries, started delivery to third world nations and hard-hit disaster regions this week.
STARK INDUSTRIES
The seed, once believed to have been destroyed, is poised to solve one of the world's biggest problems: hunger.
BOBBY DRAKE, aka ICEMAN.
PAGE GUTHRIE, aka HUSK.
Look at her.
ROGUE.
Word is she hasn't set foot on solid ground in weeks.
The reservation, originally named "Utopia" as a cruel joke, thrives like literally no other place on earth.
In the face of crushing persecution and violence, the mutants are a global success story like none other.
They'll never truly leave us alone.
NOMI BLUME, aka MACH TWO.

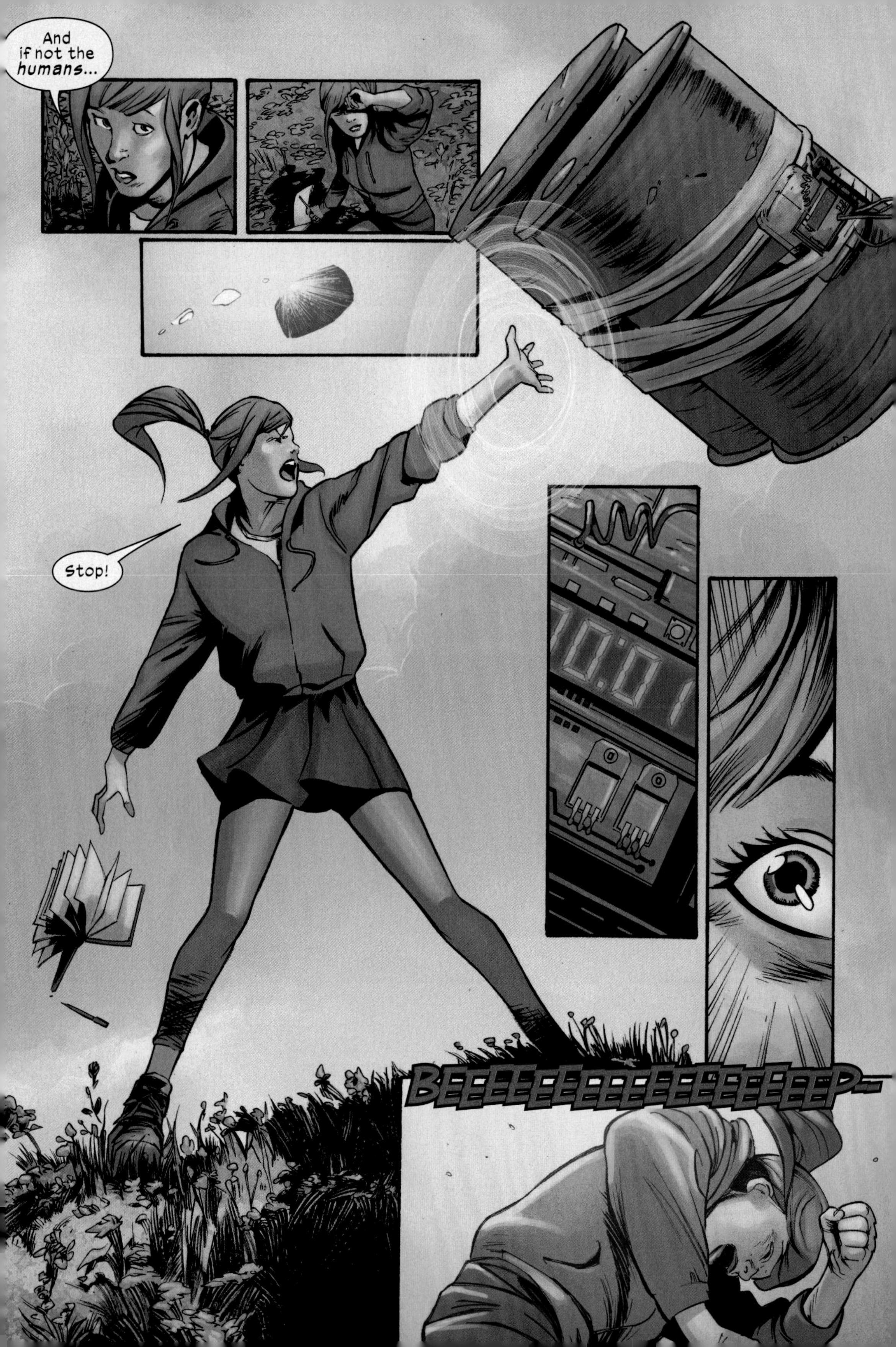
And if not the *humans*...
Stop!
BEEEEEEEEEEEEEEEEEEP--

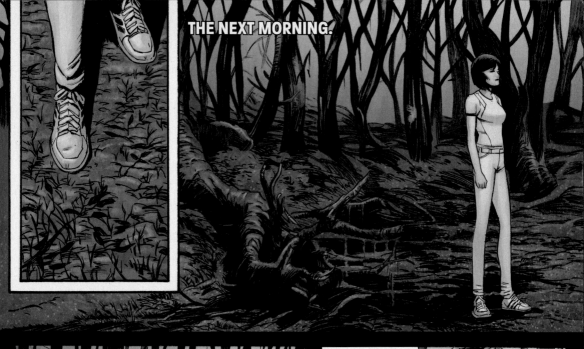

She's dying, Kitty.

It's a nasty herbicide, all right. Aerosol detonation, powerful enough to have spread it hundreds of meters.

Whatever this is, it's military-grade, other-level bio-warfare. There might be a bit of sentience in it, too.

At the very least, it's adaptive.

But she's not dead yet. She's fighting it.

Who *did* this?

Kitty...

Come see for yourself.

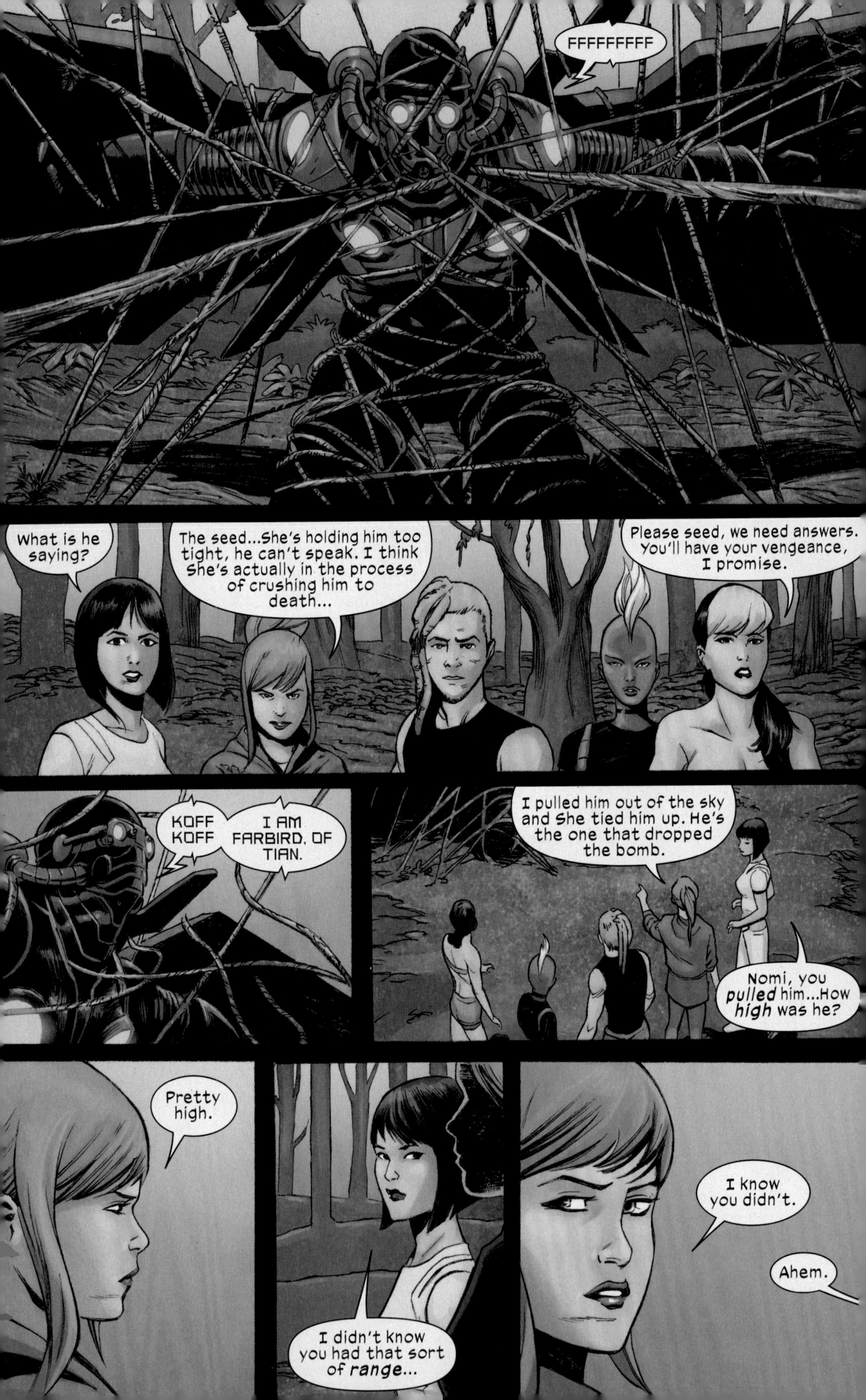
FFFFFFFFF
What is he saying?
The seed...She's holding him too tight, he can't speak. I think She's actually in the process of crushing him to death...
Please seed, we need answers. You'll have your vengeance, I promise.
KOFF KOFF
I AM FARBIRD, OF TIAN.
I pulled him out of the sky and She tied him up. He's the one that dropped the bomb.
Nomi, you *pulled* him...How *high* was he?
Pretty high.
I didn't know you had that sort of *range*...
I know you didn't.
Ahem.

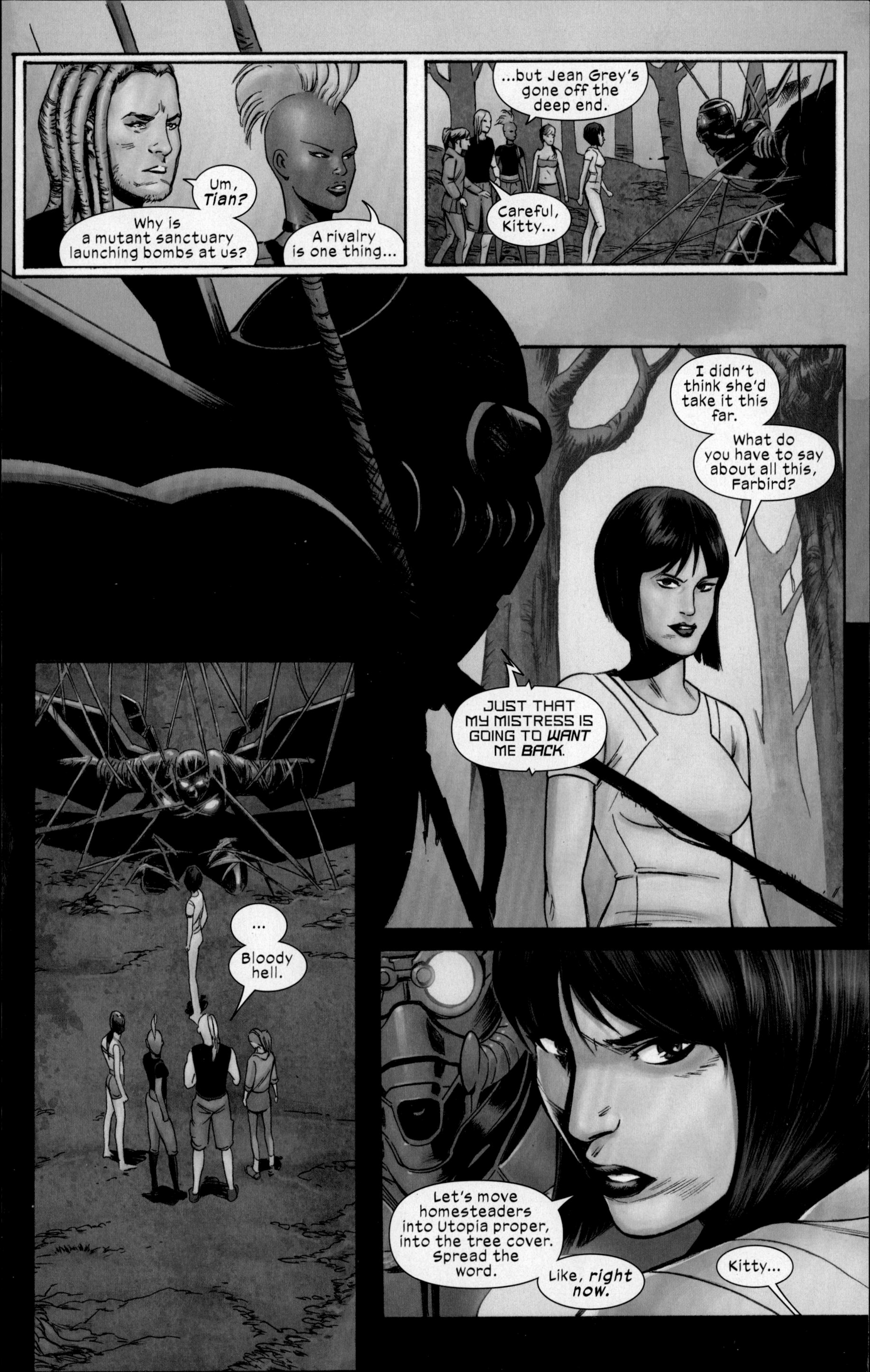
Um, *Tian?*
Why is a mutant sanctuary launching bombs at us?
A rivalry is one thing...
...but Jean Grey's gone off the deep end.
Careful, Kitty...
I didn't think she'd take it this far.
What do you have to say about all this, Farbird?
JUST THAT MY MISTRESS IS GOING TO *WANT* ME *BACK*.
...
Bloody hell.
Let's move homesteaders into Utopia proper, into the tree cover. Spread the word.
Like, *right now.*
Kitty...

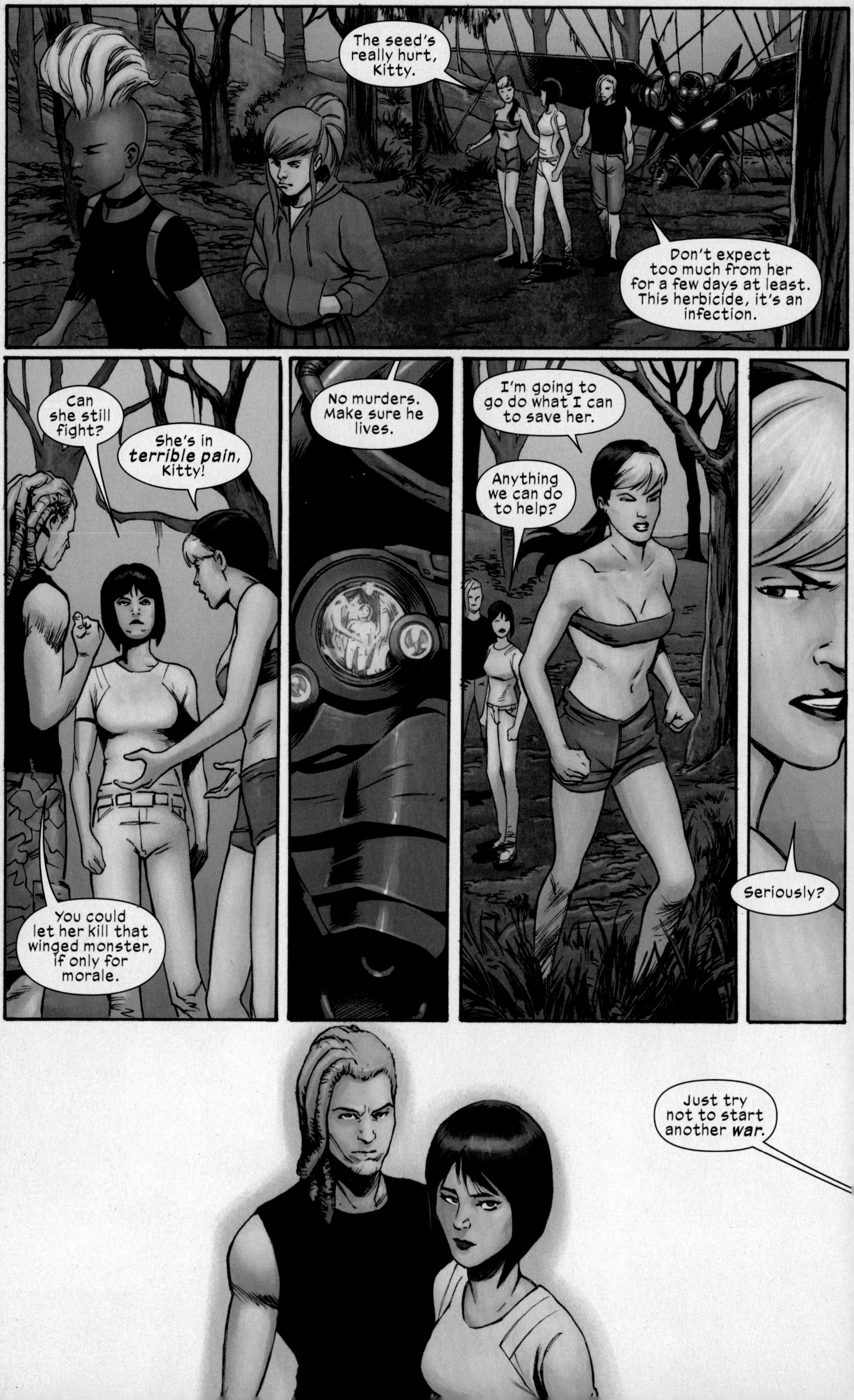

The seed's really hurt, Kitty.
Don't expect too much from her for a few days at least. This herbicide, it's an infection.
Can she still fight?
She's in *terrible pain*, Kitty!
You could let her kill that winged monster, if only for morale.
No murders. Make sure he lives.
I'm going to go do what I can to save her.
Anything we can do to help?
Seriously?
Just try not to start another *war*.

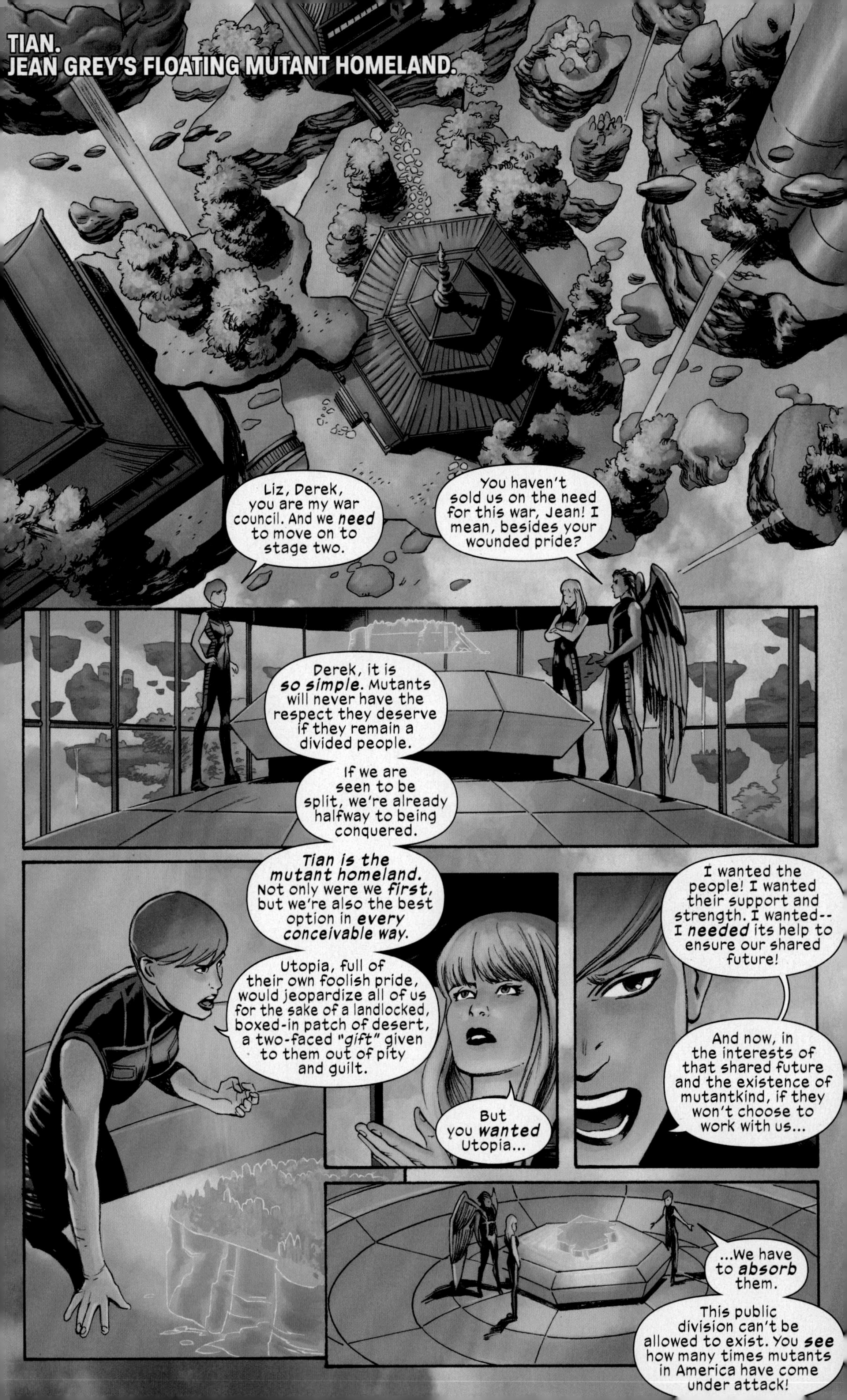
TIAN.
JEAN GREY'S FLOATING MUTANT HOMELAND.
Liz, Derek, you are my war council. And we need to move on to stage two.
You haven't sold us on the need for this war, Jean! I mean, besides your wounded pride?
Derek, it is so simple. Mutants will never have the respect they deserve if they remain a divided people.
If we are seen to be split, we're already halfway to being conquered.
Tian is the mutant homeland. Not only were we first, but we're also the best option in every conceivable way.
Utopia, full of their own foolish pride, would jeopardize all of us for the sake of a landlocked, boxed-in patch of desert, a two-faced "gift" given to them out of pity and guilt.
But you wanted Utopia...
I wanted the people! I wanted their support and strength. I wanted-- I needed its help to ensure our shared future!
And now, in the interests of that shared future and the existence of mutantkind, if they won't choose to work with us...
...We have to absorb them.
This public division can't be allowed to exist. You see how many times mutants in America have come under attack!

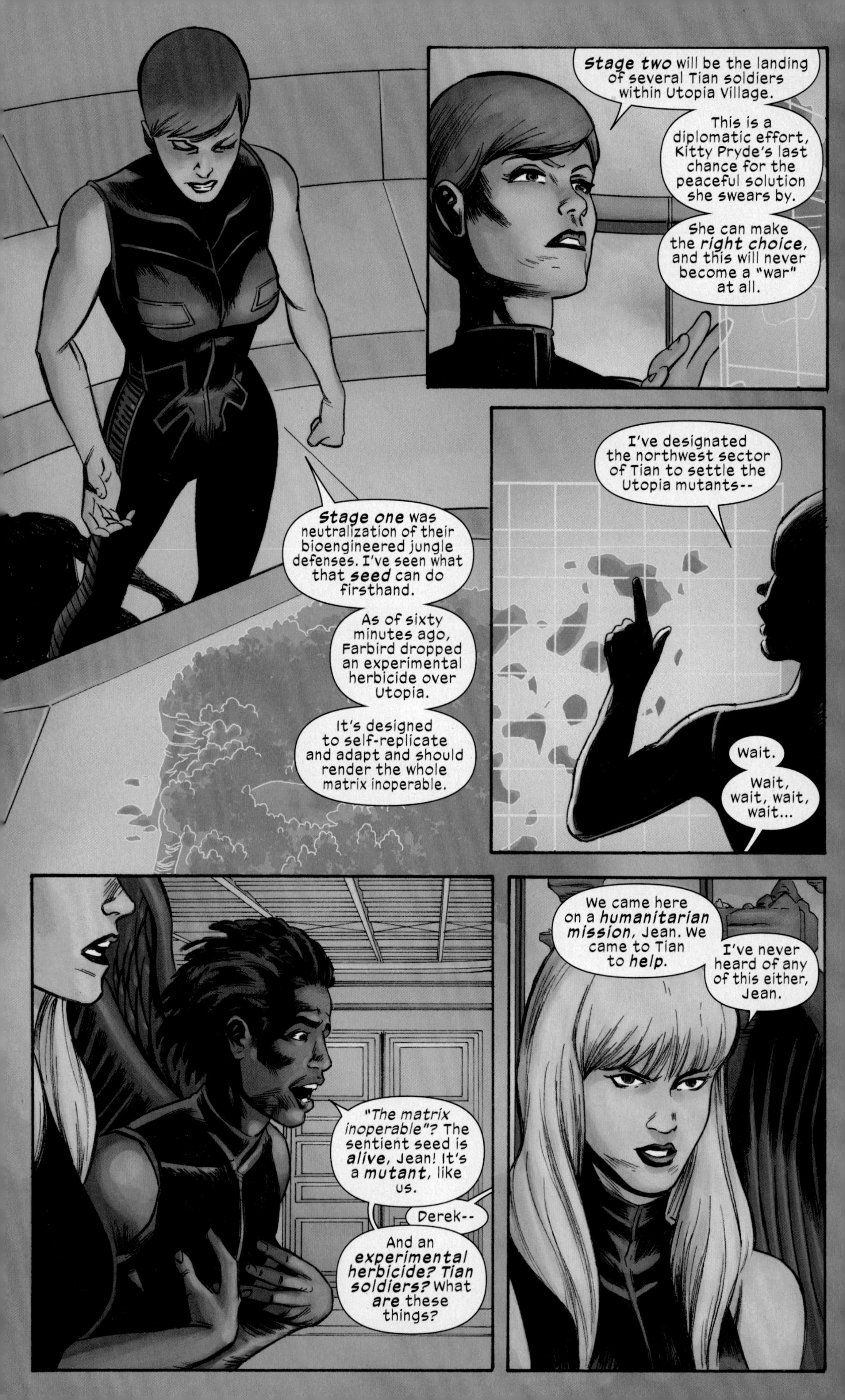
Stage two will be the landing of several Tian soldiers within Utopia Village.
This is a diplomatic effort, Kitty Pryde's last chance for the peaceful solution she swears by.
She can make the right choice, and this will never become a "war" at all.
Stage one was neutralization of their bioengineered jungle defenses. I've seen what that seed can do firsthand.
As of sixty minutes ago, Farbird dropped an experimental herbicide over Utopia.
It's designed to self-replicate and adapt and should render the whole matrix inoperable.
I've designated the northwest sector of Tian to settle the Utopia mutants--
Wait.
Wait, wait, wait, wait...
"The matrix inoperable"? The sentient seed is alive, Jean! It's a mutant, like us.
Derek--
And an experimental herbicide? Tian soldiers? What are these things?
We came here on a humanitarian mission, Jean. We came to Tian to help.
I've never heard of any of this either, Jean.

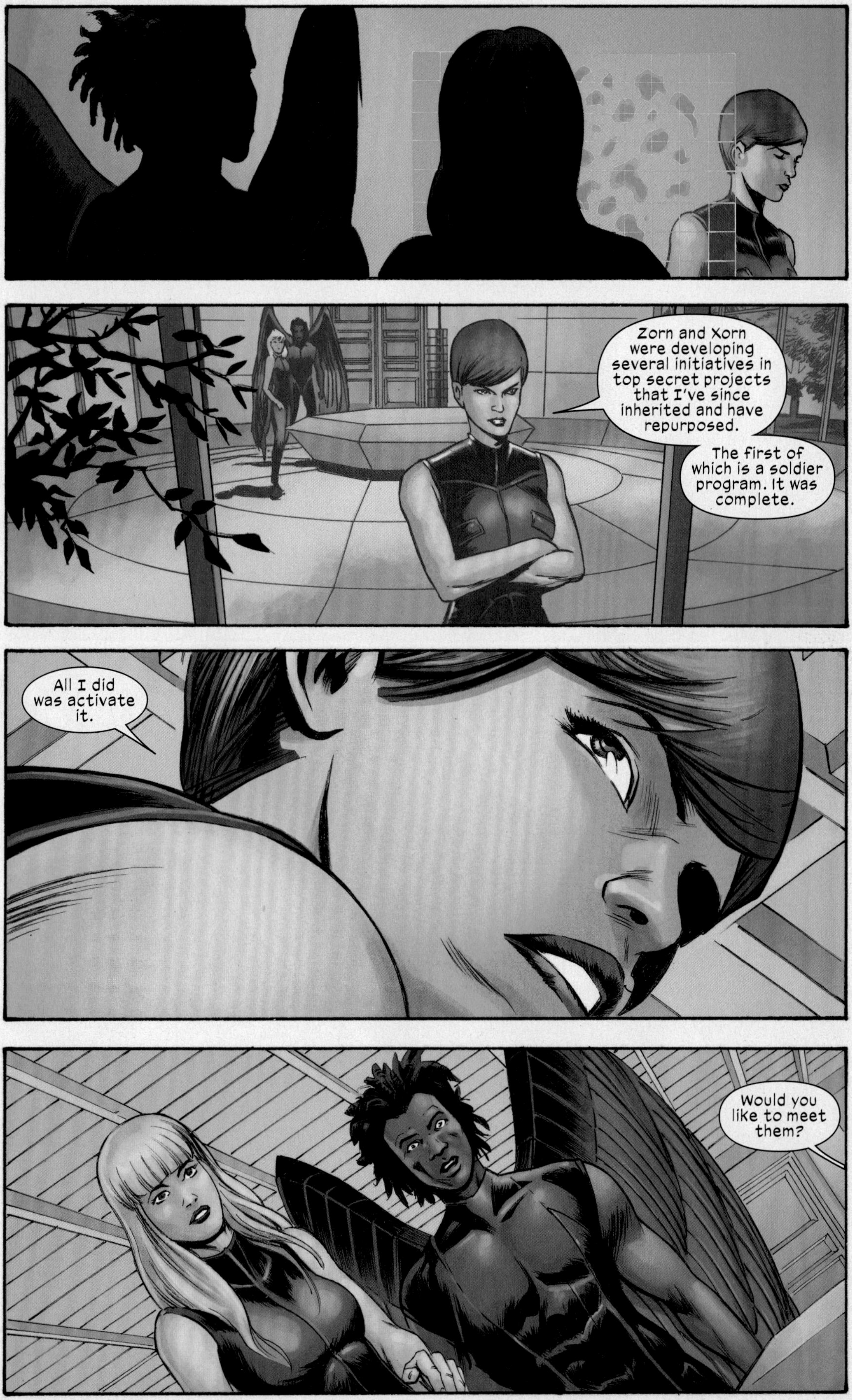
Zorn and Xorn were developing several initiatives in top secret projects that I've since inherited and have repurposed.
The first of which is a soldier program. It was complete.
All I did was activate it.
Would you like to meet them?

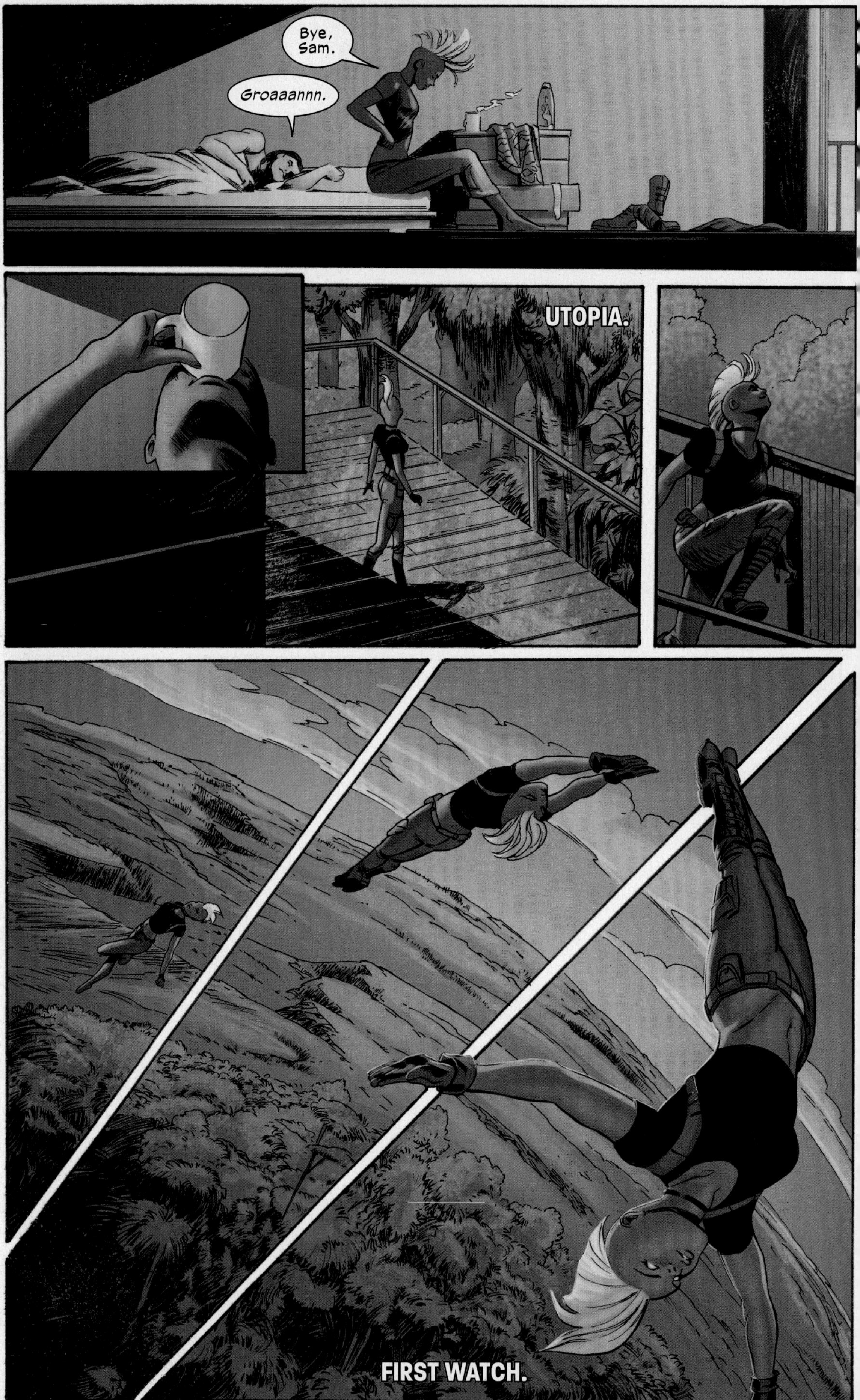
Bye, Sam.
Groaaannn.
UTOPIA.
FIRST WATCH.

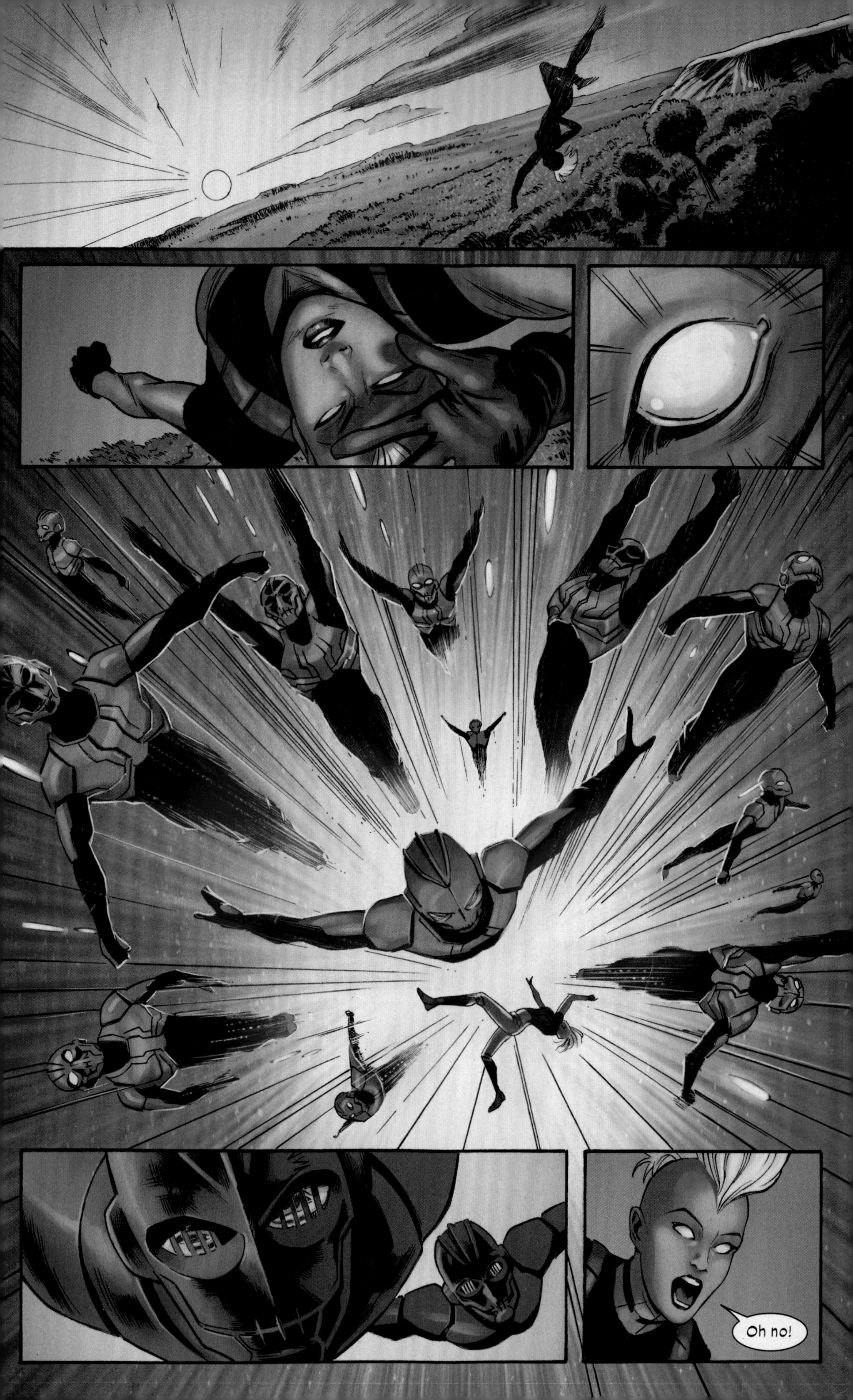
Oh no!

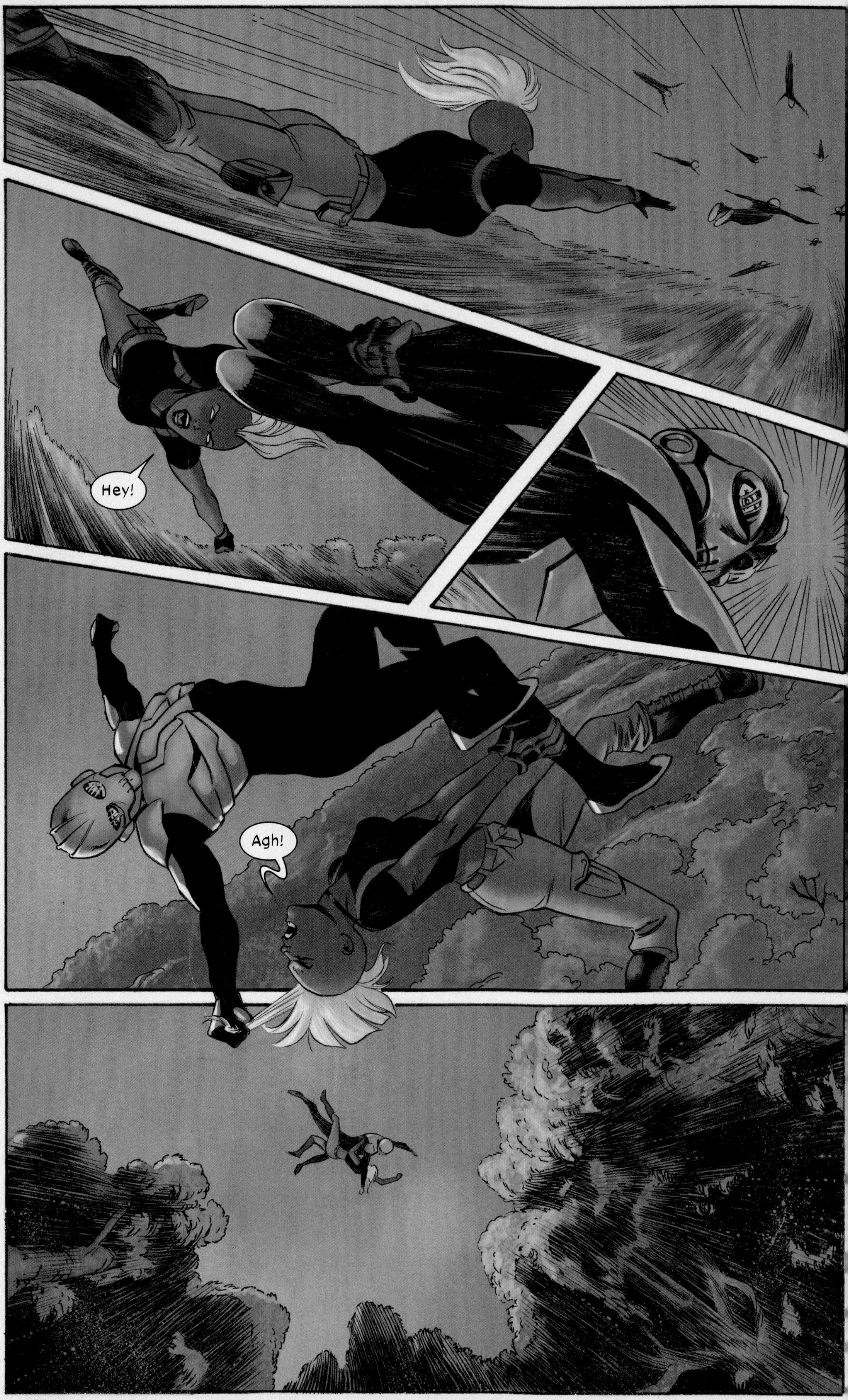
Hey!
Agh!

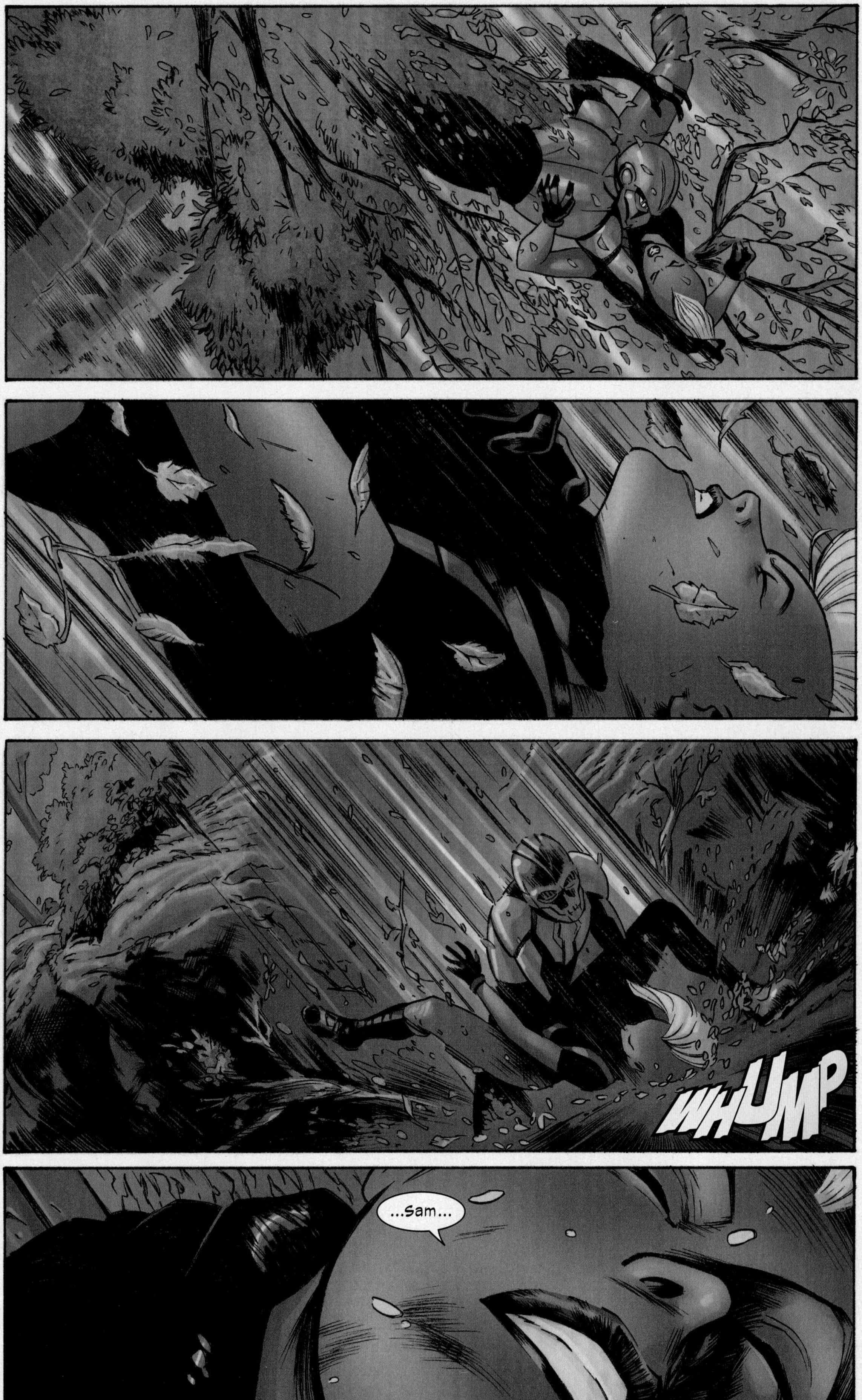
WHUMP
...Sam...

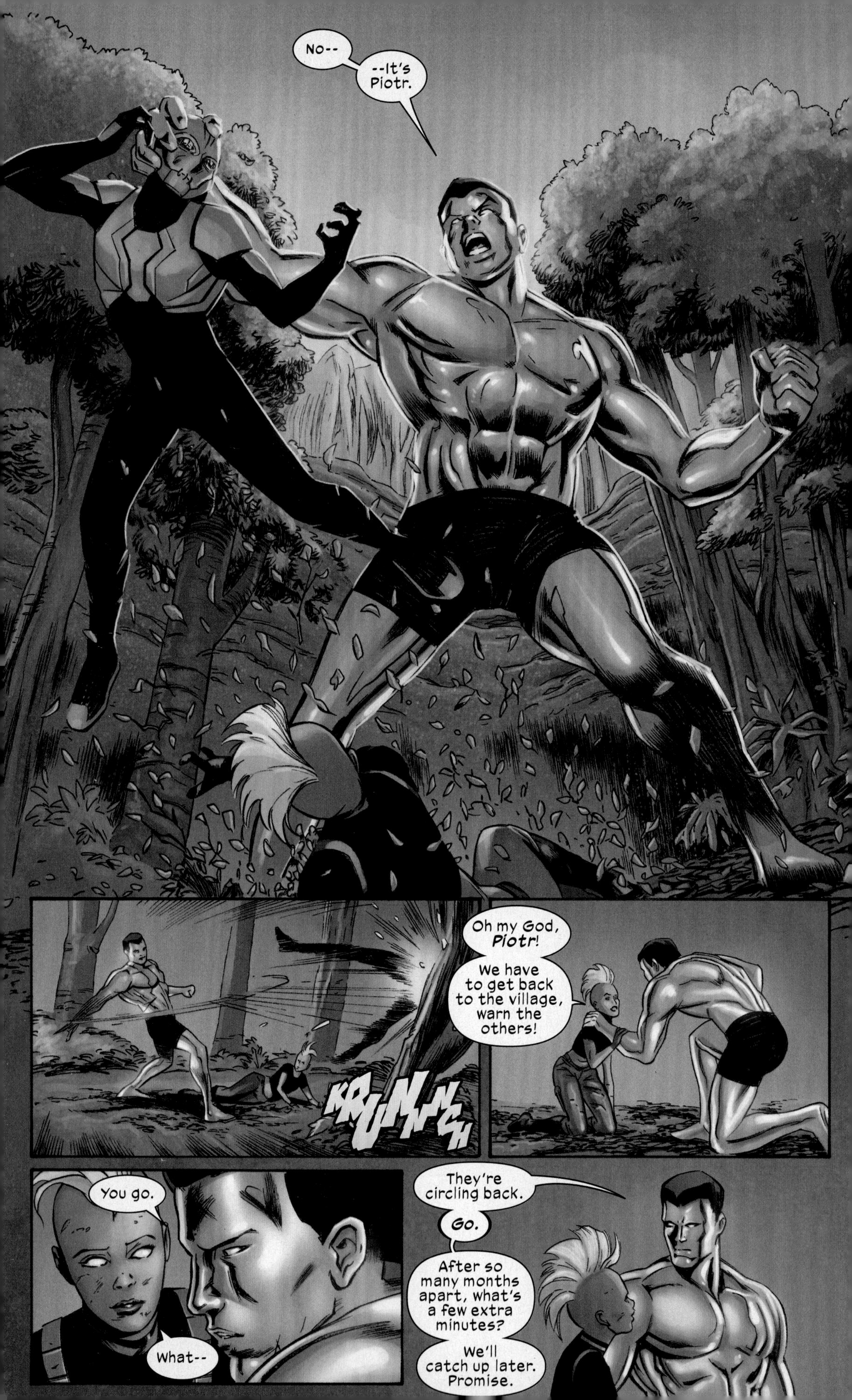
No--
--It's Piotr.
Oh my God, Piotr!
We have to get back to the village, warn the others!
KRUNNNCH
You go.
What--
They're circling back.
Go.
After so many months apart, what's a few extra minutes?
We'll catch up later. Promise.

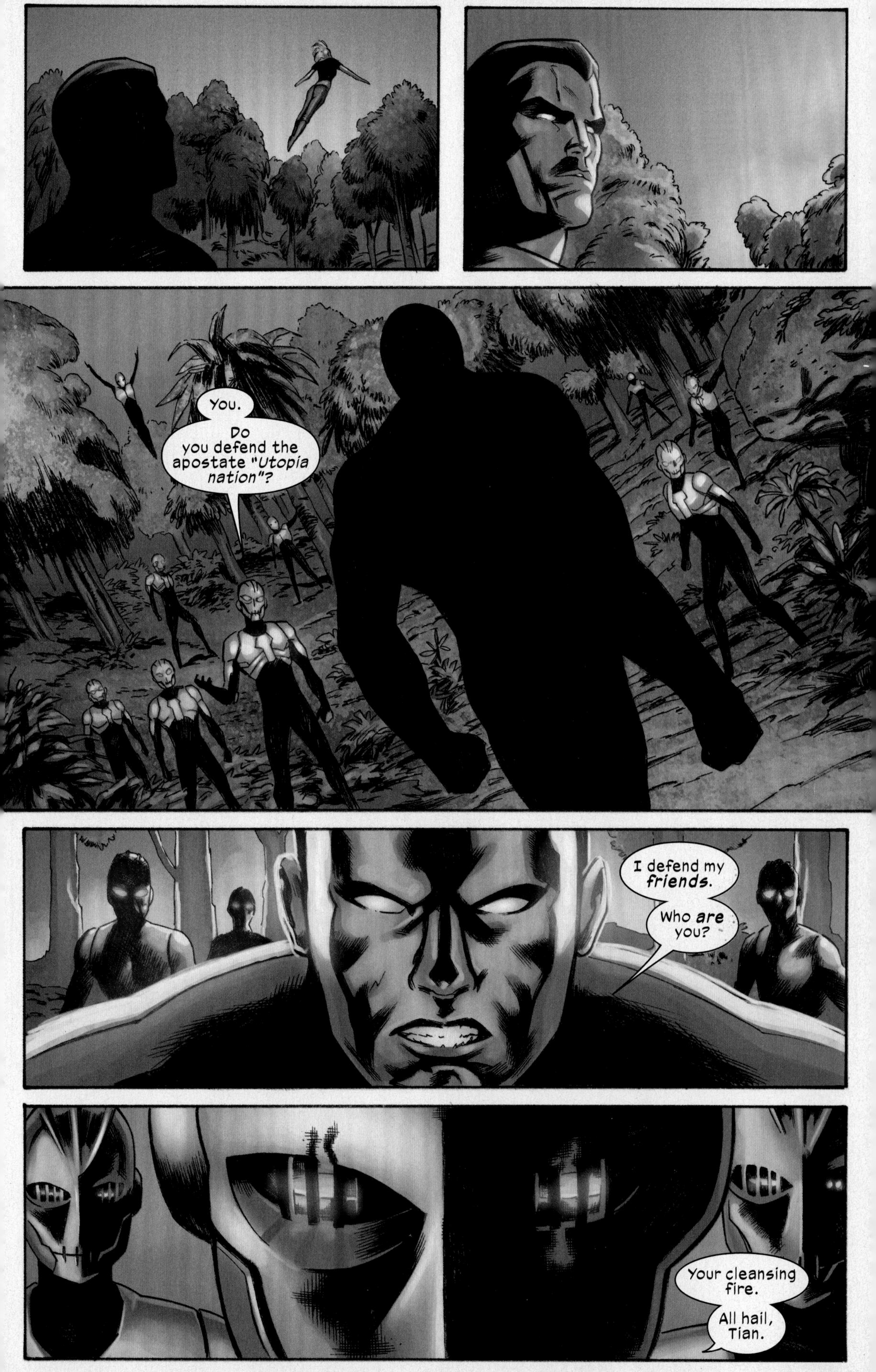
You.
Do you defend the apostate "*Utopia nation*"?
I defend my ***friends.***
Who ***are*** you?
Your cleansing fire.
All hail, Tian.

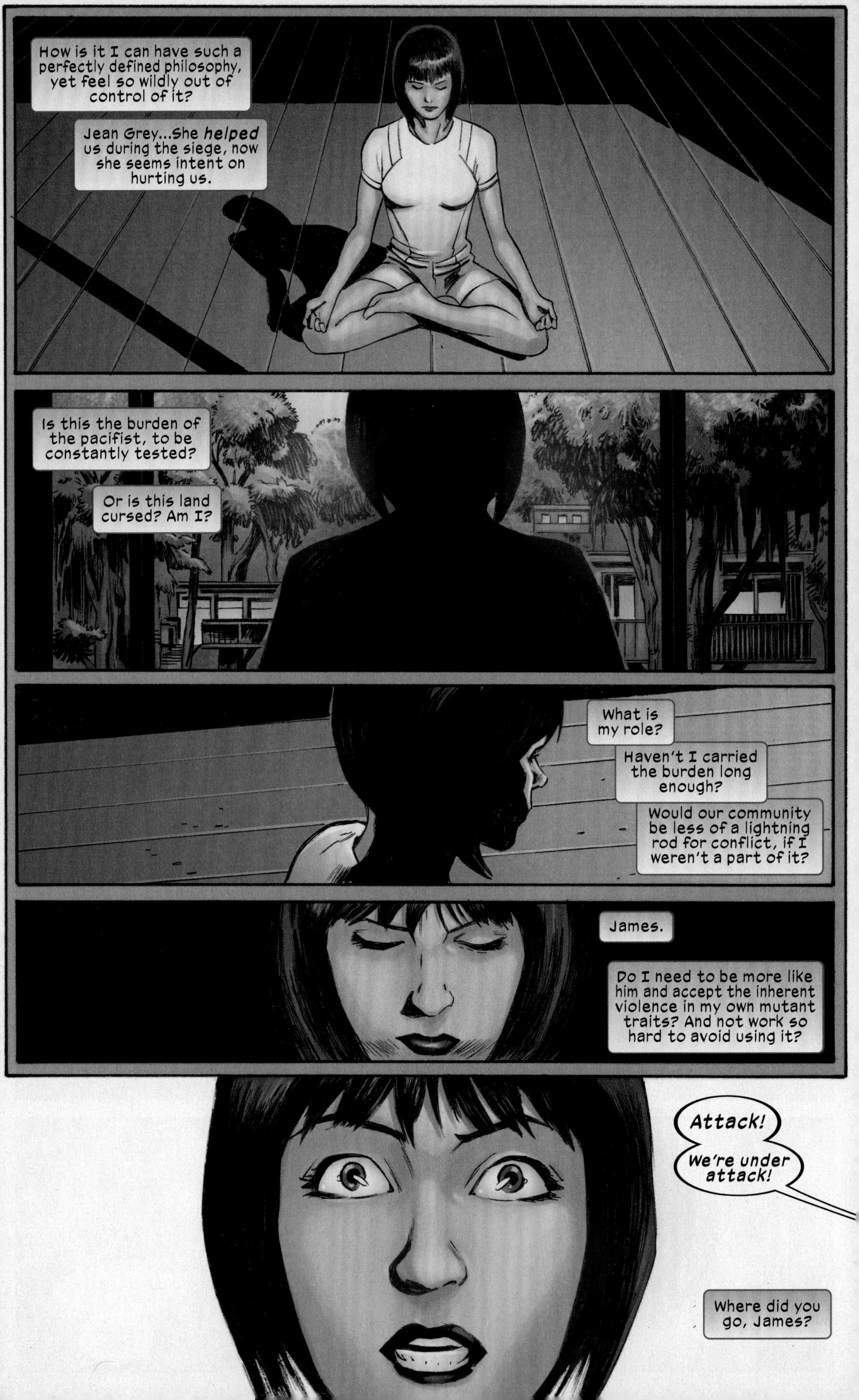
How is it I can have such a perfectly defined philosophy, yet feel so wildly out of control of it?
Jean Grey...She *helped* us during the siege, now she seems intent on hurting us.
Is this the burden of the pacifist, to be constantly tested?
Or is this land cursed? Am I?
What is my role?
Haven't I carried the burden long enough?
Would our community be less of a lightning rod for conflict, if I weren't a part of it?
James.
Do I need to be more like him and accept the inherent violence in my own mutant traits? And not work so hard to avoid using it?
Attack!
We're under attack!
Where did you go, James?

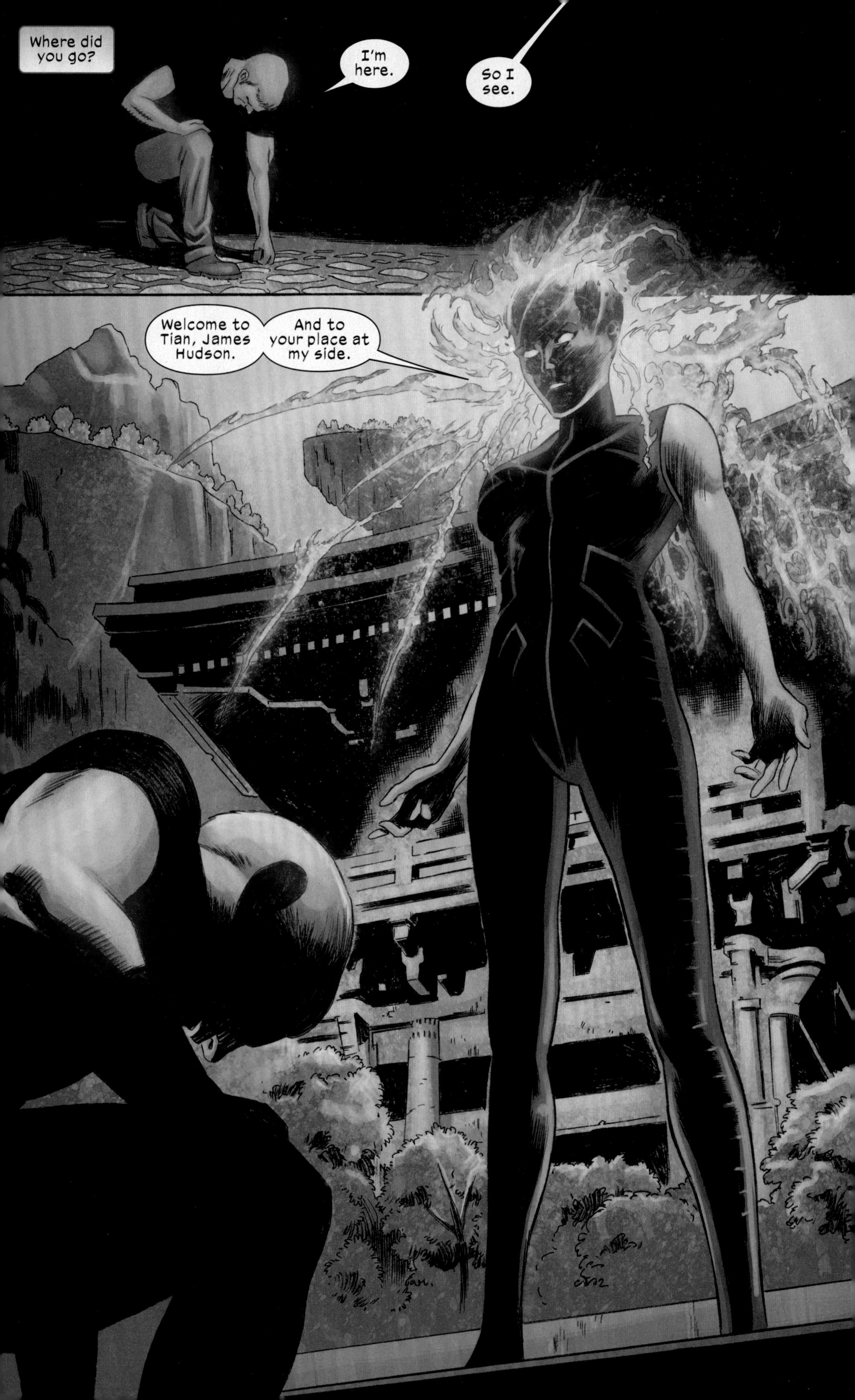
Where did you go?
I'm here.
So I see.
Welcome to Tian, James Hudson.
And to your place at my side.

30

WORLD WAR X

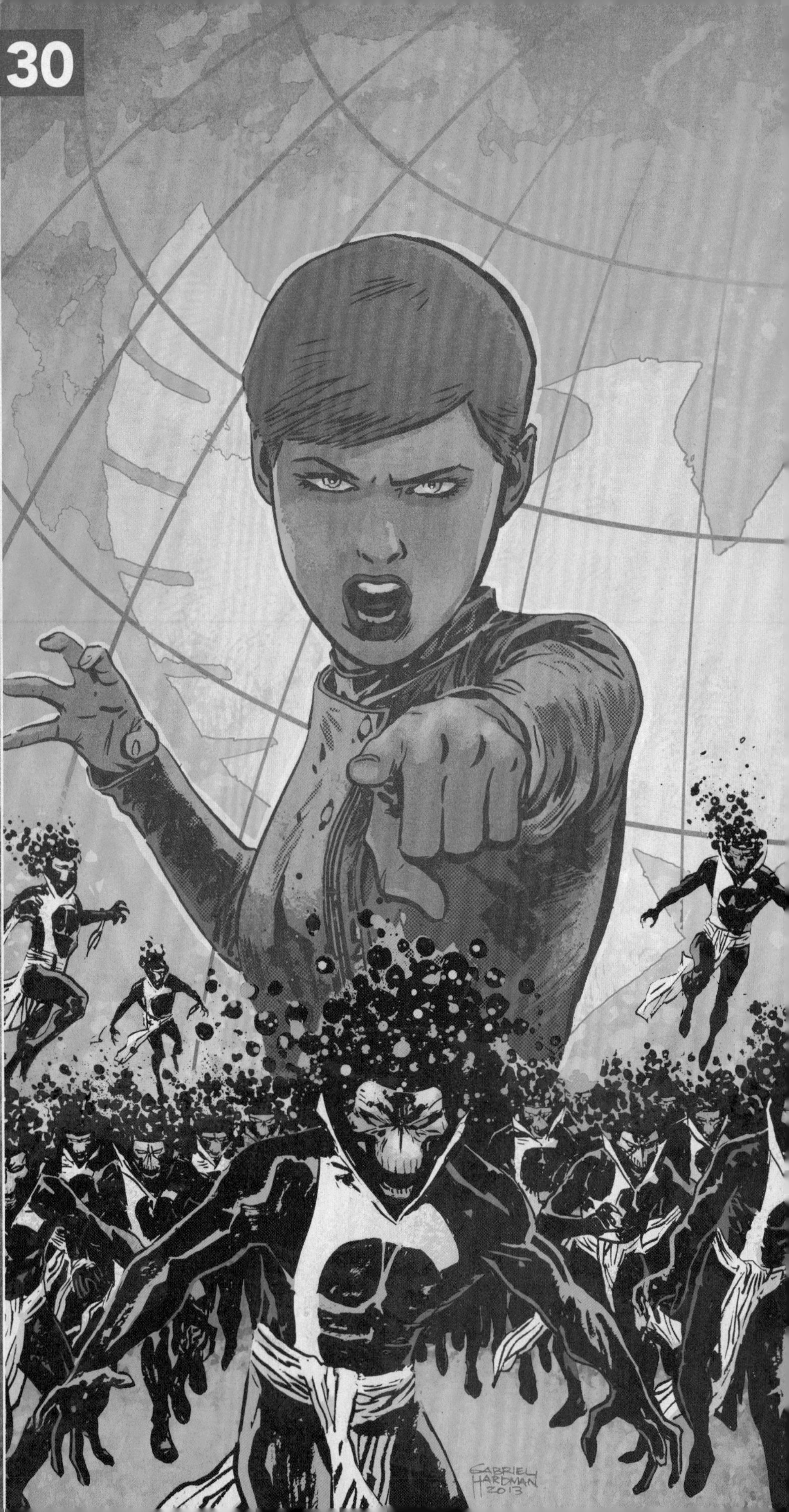

GABRIEL HARDMAN 2013

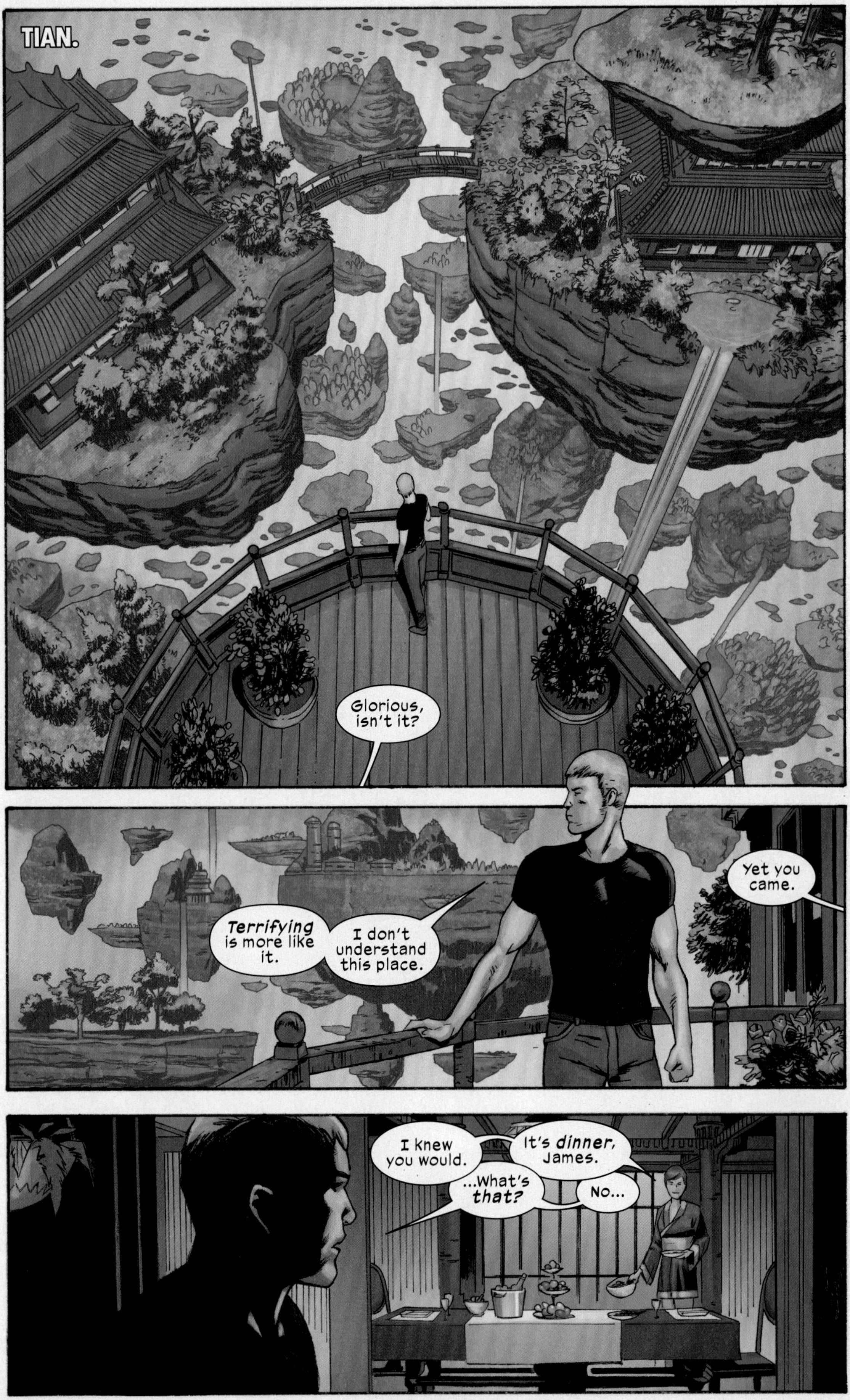
TIAN.
Glorious, isn't it?
I don't understand this place.
Terrifying is more like it.
Yet you came.
I knew you would.
It's *dinner*, James.
...What's *that?*
No...

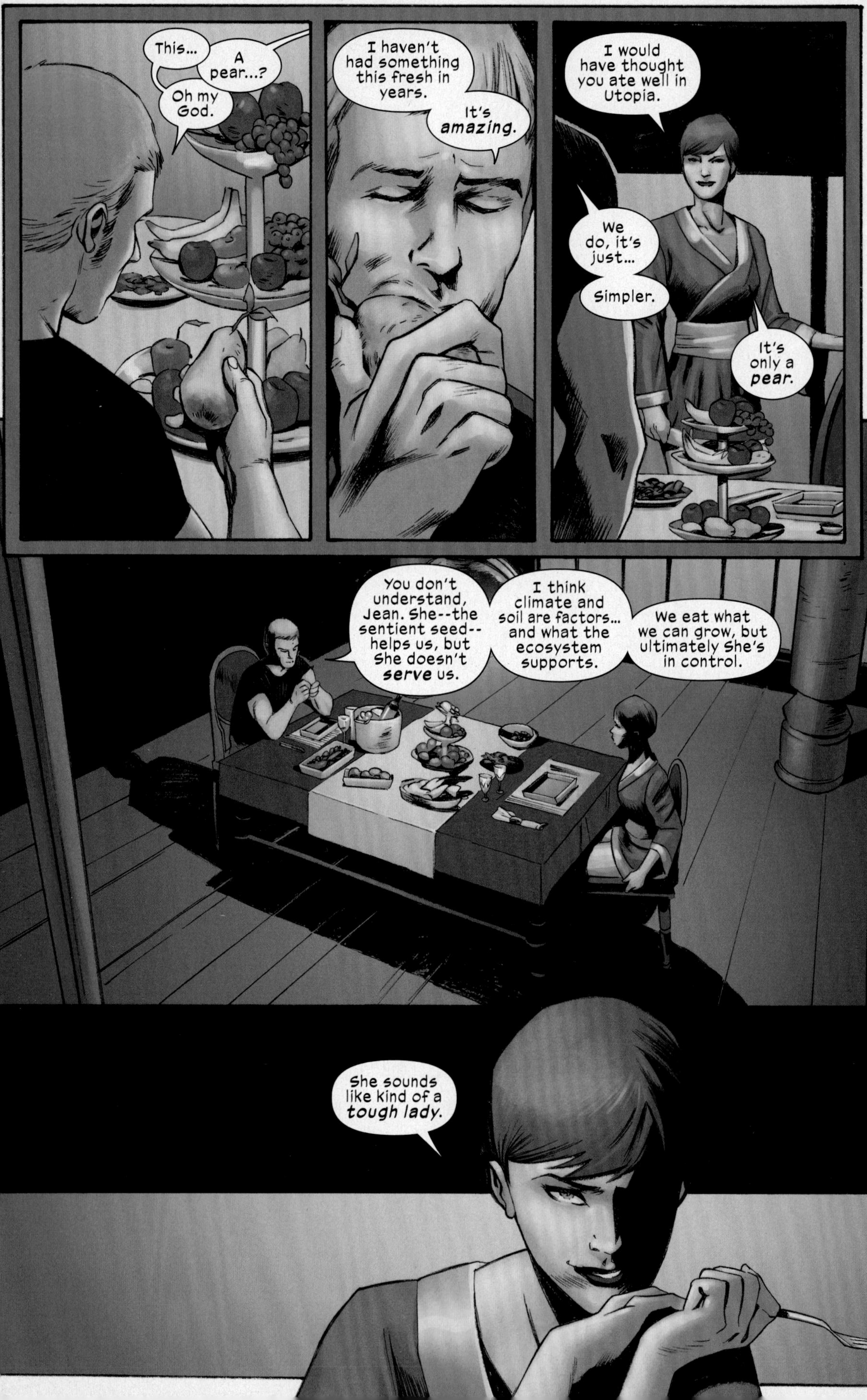
This...
A pear...?
Oh my God.
I haven't had something this fresh in years.
It's *amazing*.
I would have thought you ate well in Utopia.
We do, it's just...
Simpler.
It's only a *pear*.
You don't understand, Jean. She--the sentient seed--helps us, but She doesn't *serve* us.
I think climate and soil are factors... and what the ecosystem supports.
We eat what we can grow, but ultimately She's in control.
She sounds like kind of a *tough lady*.

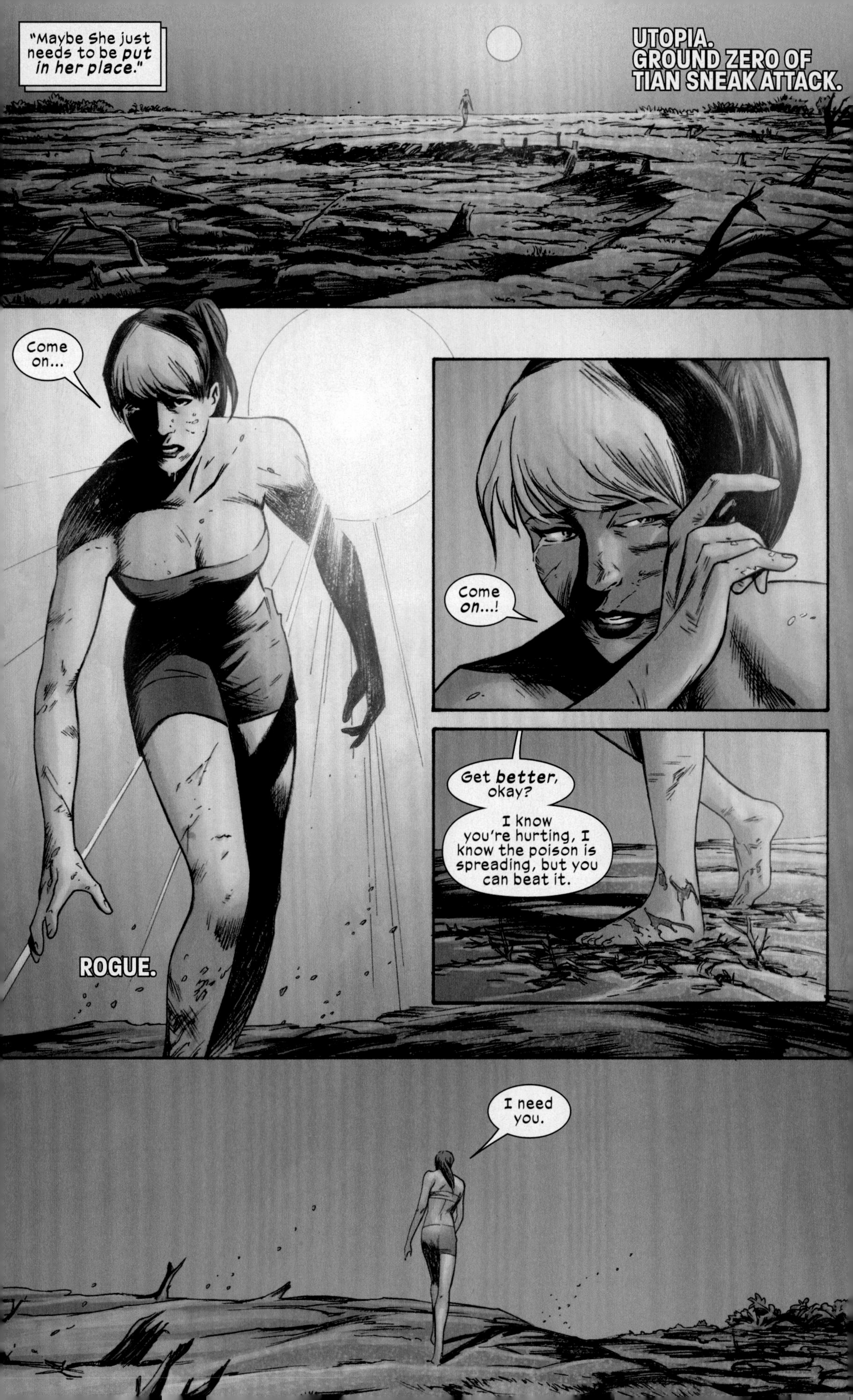
"Maybe she just needs to be put in her place."
UTOPIA. GROUND ZERO OF TIAN SNEAK ATTACK.
Come on...
ROGUE.
Come on...!
Get better, okay?
I know you're hurting, I know the poison is spreading, but you can beat it.
I need you.

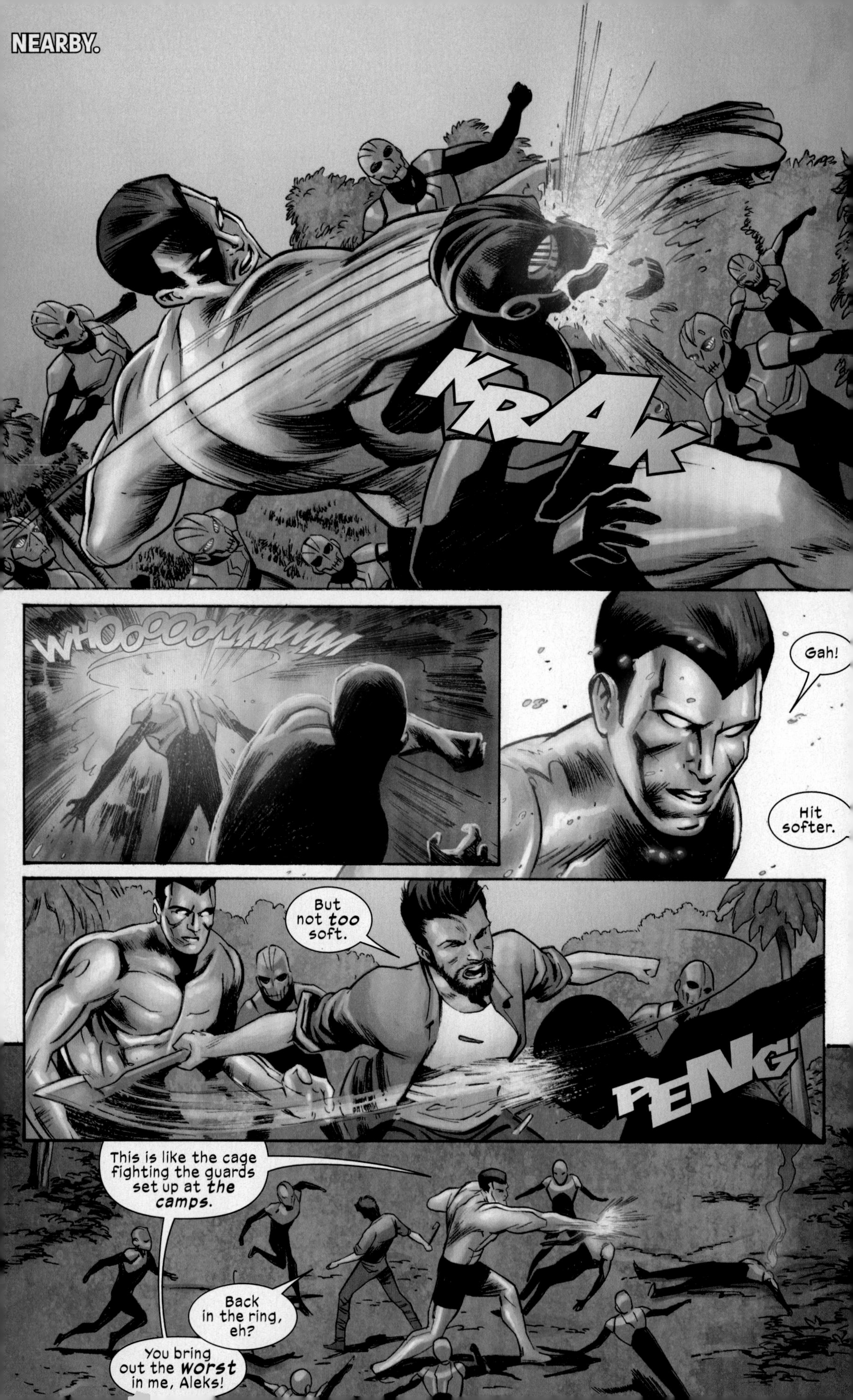

NEARBY.
KRAK
WHOOOOOMMMM
Gah!
Hit softer.
But not too soft.
PENG
This is like the cage fighting the guards set up at the camps.
Back in the ring, eh?
You bring out the worst in me, Aleks!

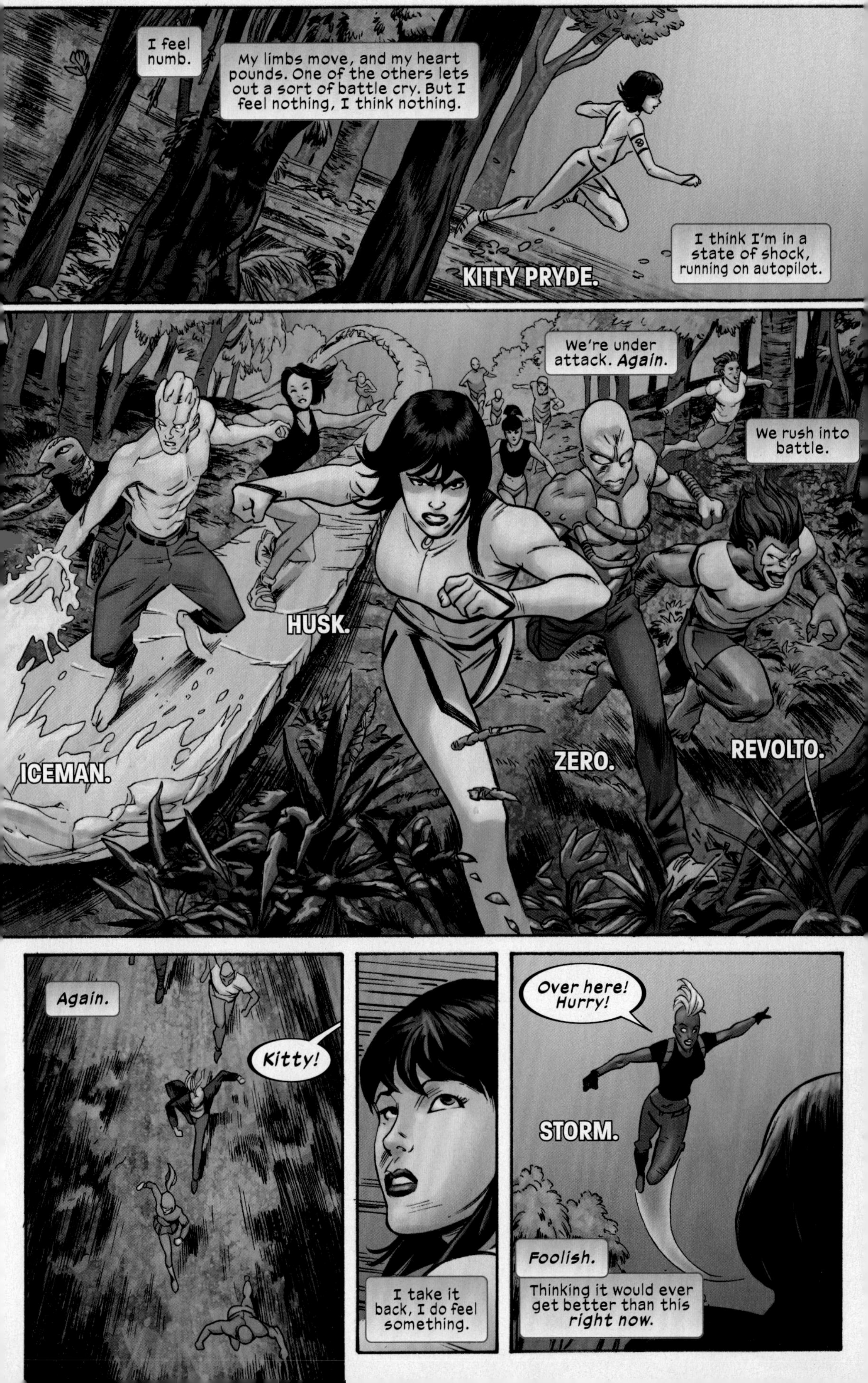
I feel numb.
My limbs move, and my heart pounds. One of the others lets out a sort of battle cry. But I feel nothing, I think nothing.
KITTY PRYDE.
I think I'm in a state of shock, running on autopilot.
We're under attack. *Again.*
We rush into battle.
HUSK.
ICEMAN.
ZERO.
REVOLTO.
Again.
Kitty!
I take it back, I do feel something.
Over here! Hurry!
STORM.
Foolish.
Thinking it would ever get better than this *right now.*

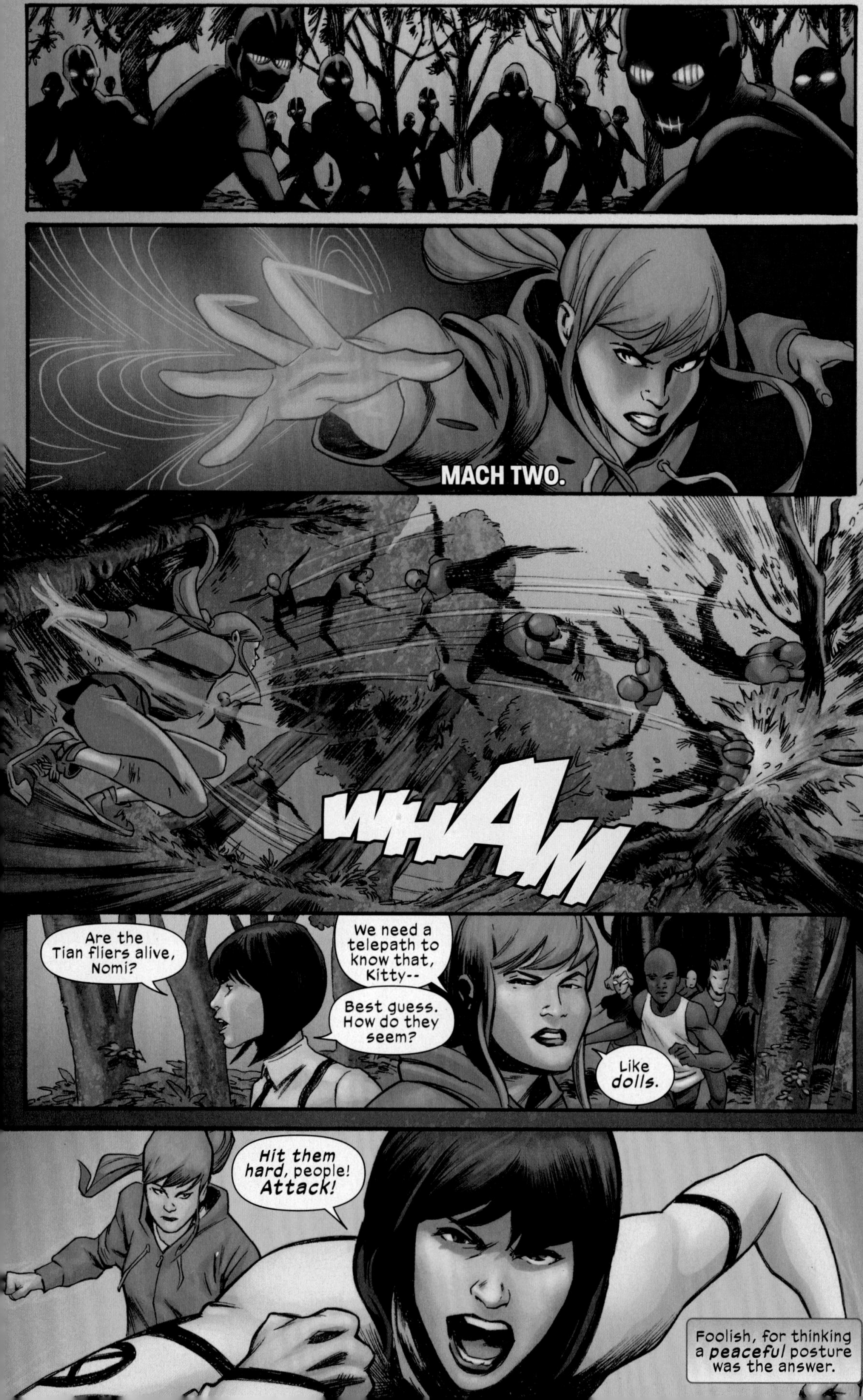
MACH TWO.
WHAM
Are the Tian fliers alive, Nomi?
We need a telepath to know that, Kitty--
Best guess. How do they seem?
Like dolls.
Hit them hard, people! Attack!
Foolish, for thinking a peaceful posture was the answer.

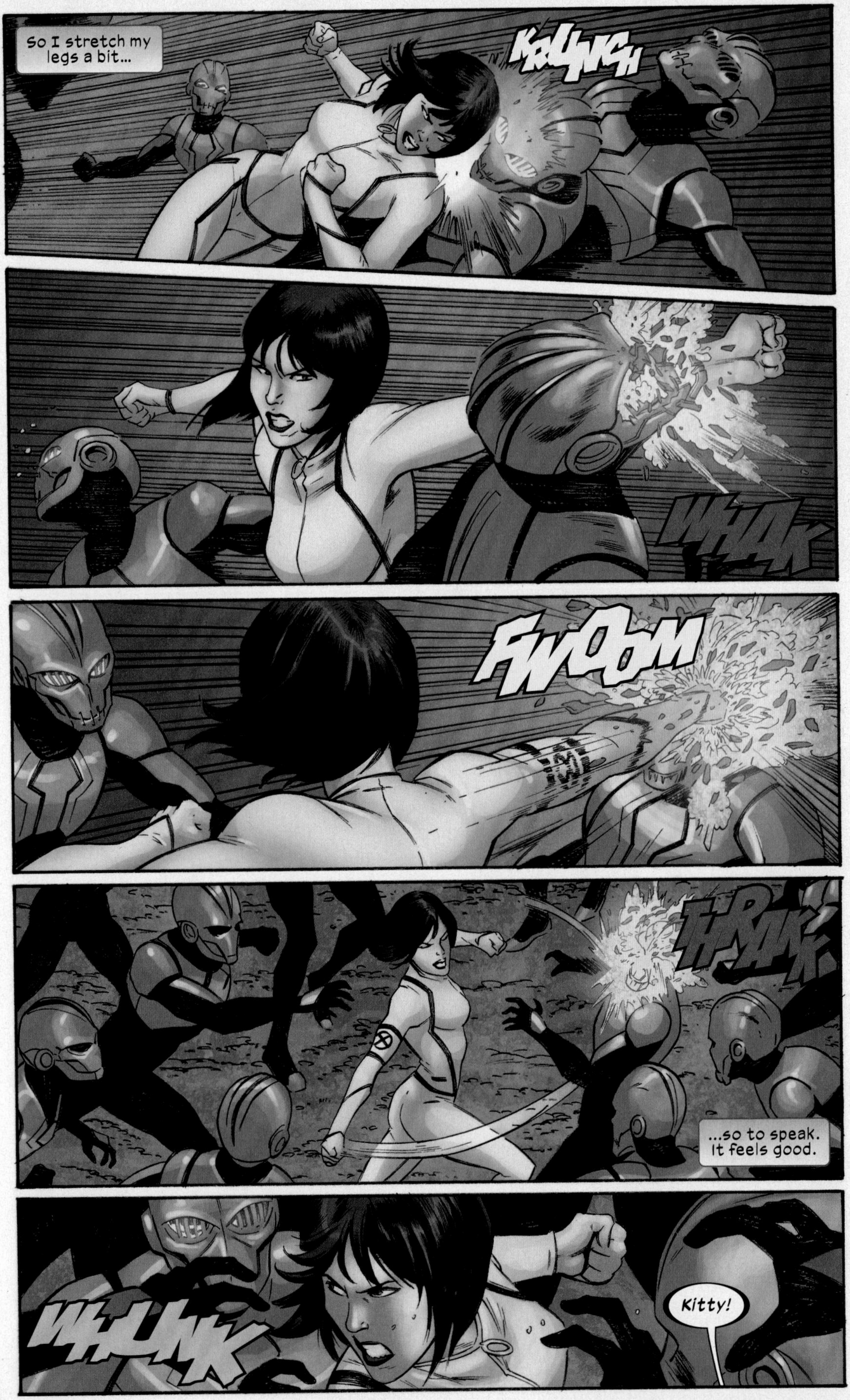

So I stretch my legs a bit...
KRUNCH
WHAK
FWOOM
THRAK
...so to speak. It feels good.
WHUNK
Kitty!

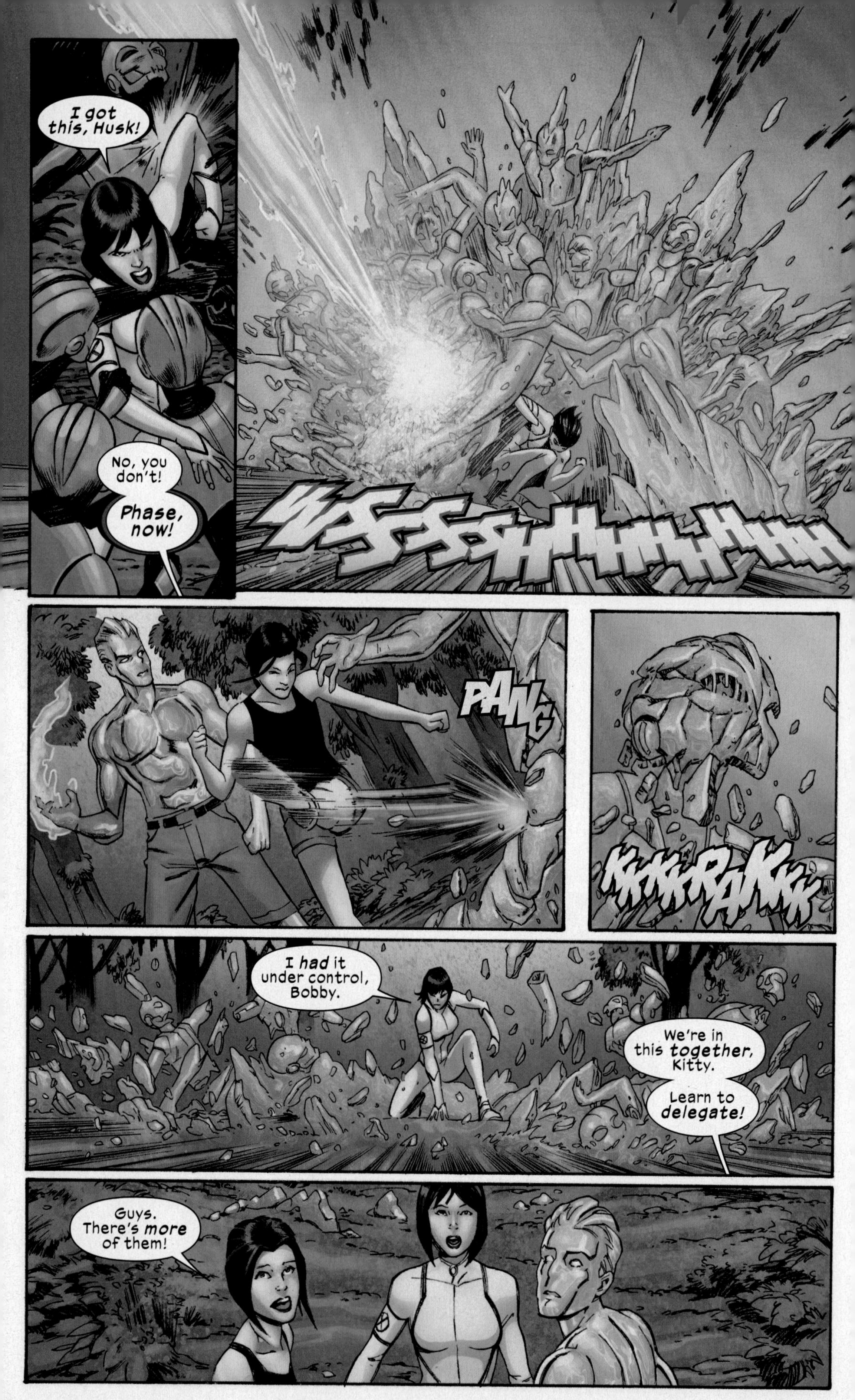
I got this, Husk!
No, you don't!
Phase, now!
WSSSHHHHHHHHH
PANG
KKKRAKKK
I had it under control, Bobby.
We're in this together, Kitty.
Learn to delegate!
Guys. There's more of them!

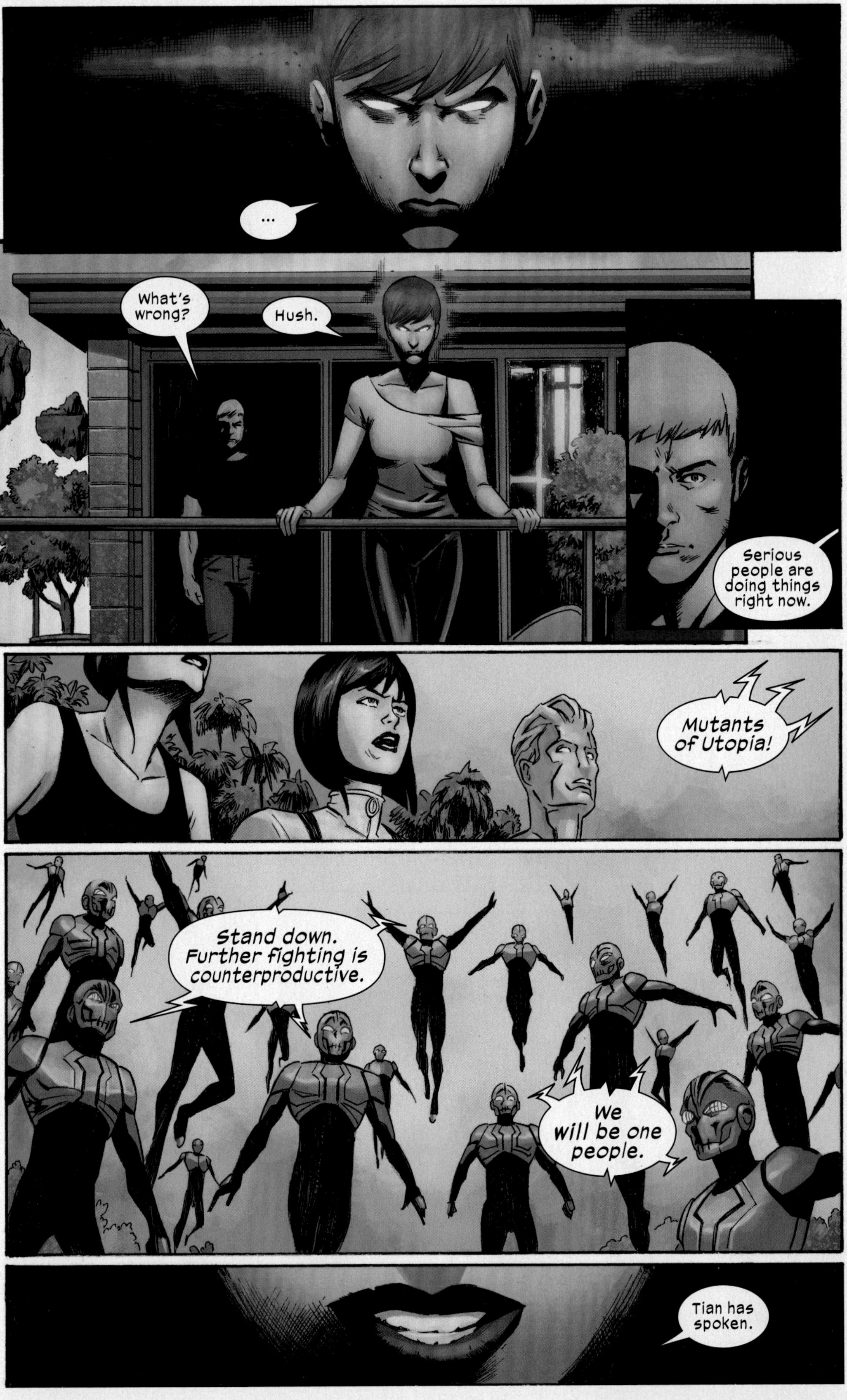
...
What's wrong?
Hush.
Serious people are doing things right now.
Mutants of Utopia!
Stand down. Further fighting is counterproductive.
We will be one people.
Tian has spoken.

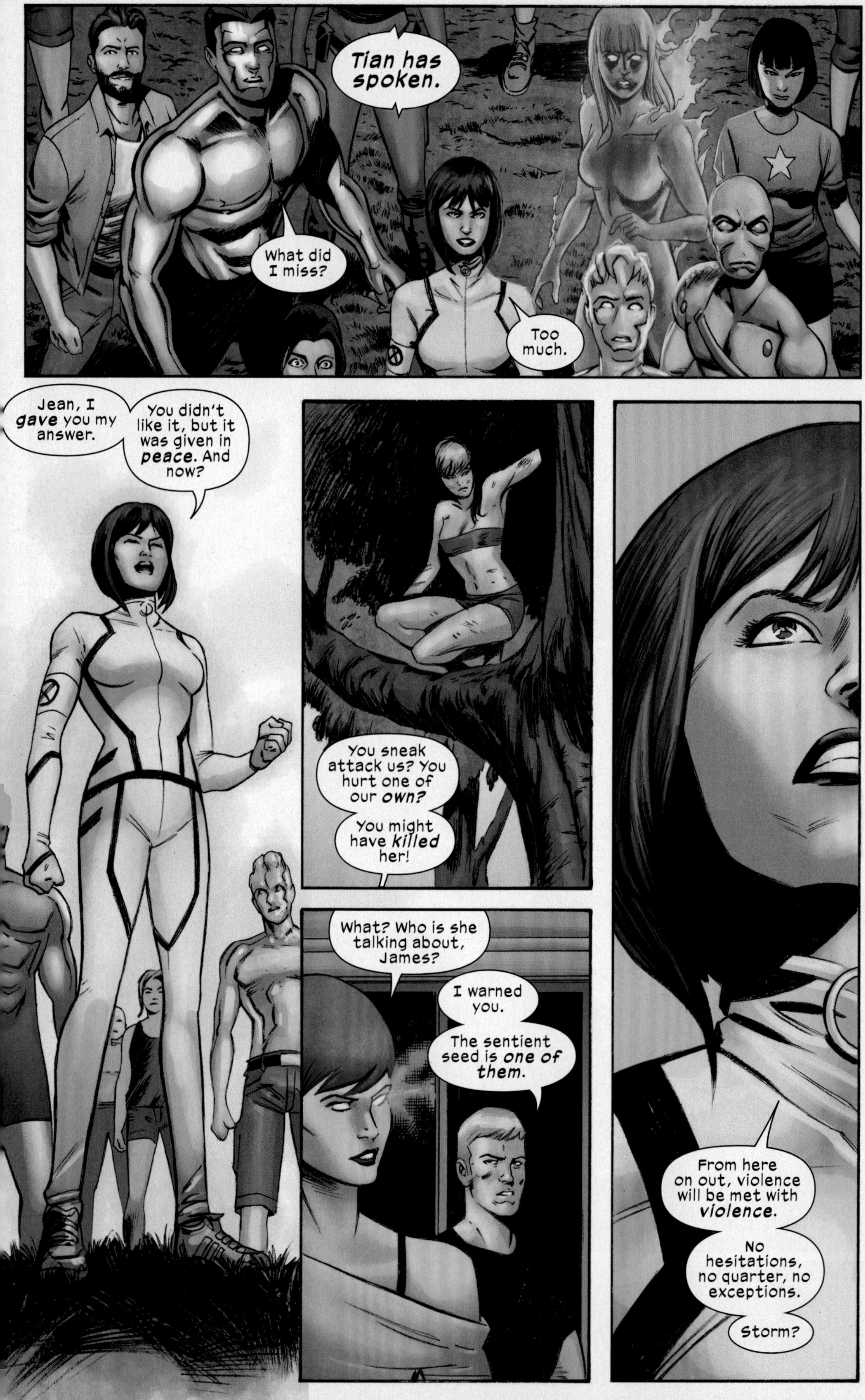
Tian has spoken.
What did I miss?
Too much.
Jean, I gave you my answer.
You didn't like it, but it was given in peace. And now?
You sneak attack us? You hurt one of our own?
You might have killed her!
What? Who is she talking about, James?
I warned you.
The sentient seed is one of them.
From here on out, violence will be met with violence.
No hesitations, no quarter, no exceptions.
Storm?

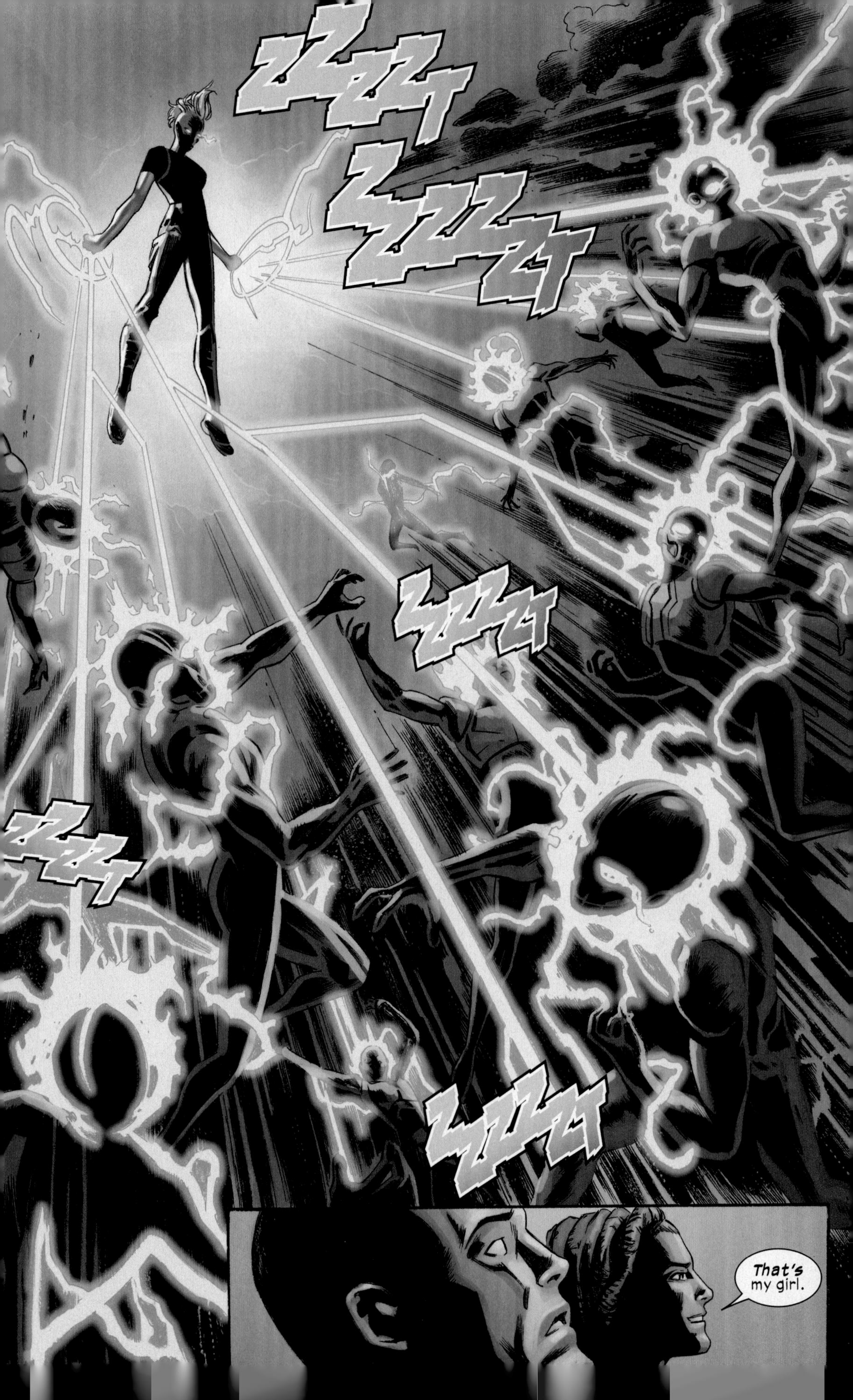
ZZZZZT
ZZZZZZT
ZZZZZT
ZZZZT
ZZZZZT
That's my girl.

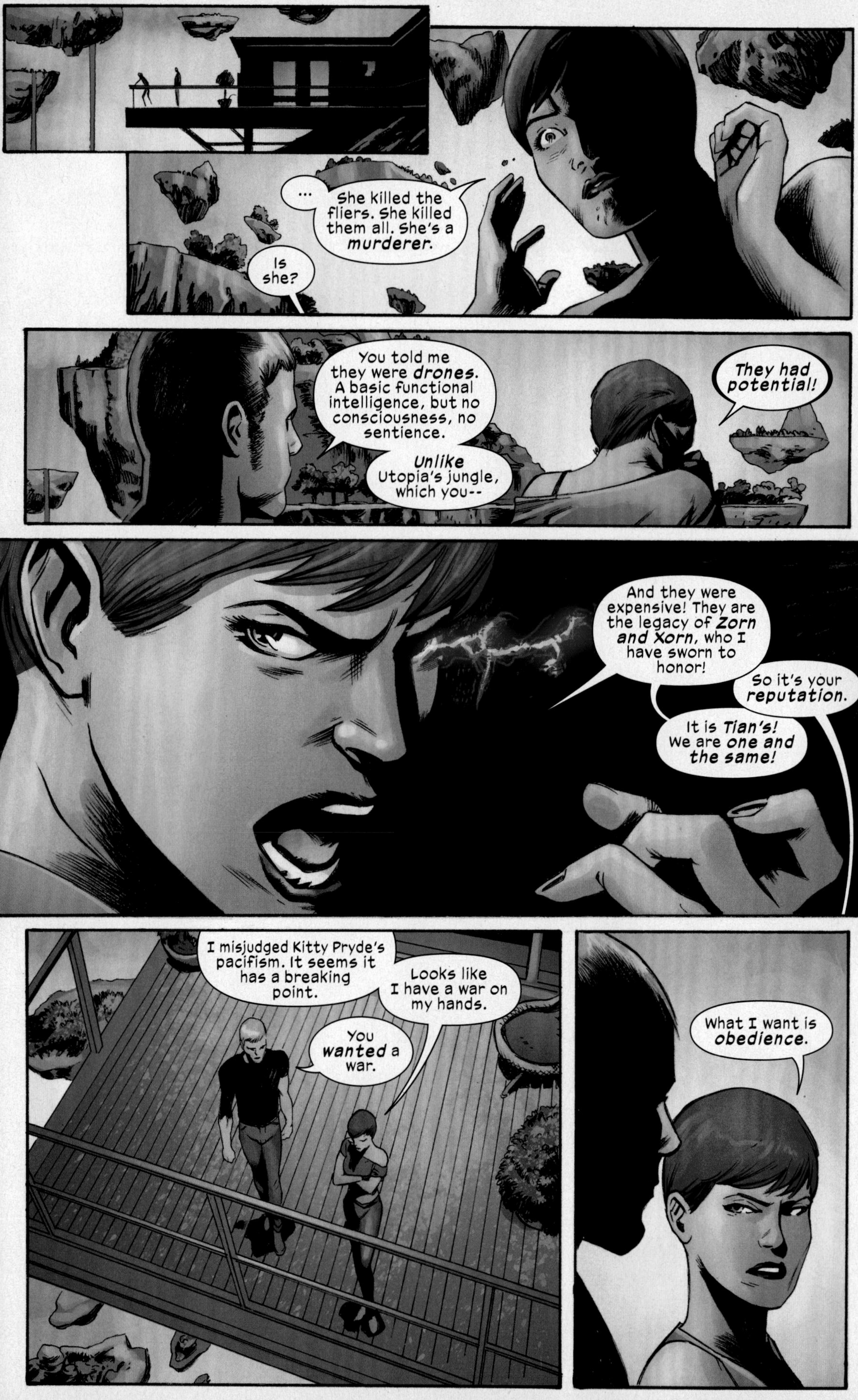
...
She killed the fliers. She killed them all. She's a murderer.
Is she?
You told me they were drones. A basic functional intelligence, but no consciousness, no sentience.
Unlike Utopia's jungle, which you--
They had potential!
And they were expensive! They are the legacy of Zorn and Xorn, who I have sworn to honor!
So it's your reputation.
It is Tian's! We are one and the same!
I misjudged Kitty Pryde's pacifism. It seems it has a breaking point.
Looks like I have a war on my hands.
You wanted a war.
What I want is obedience.

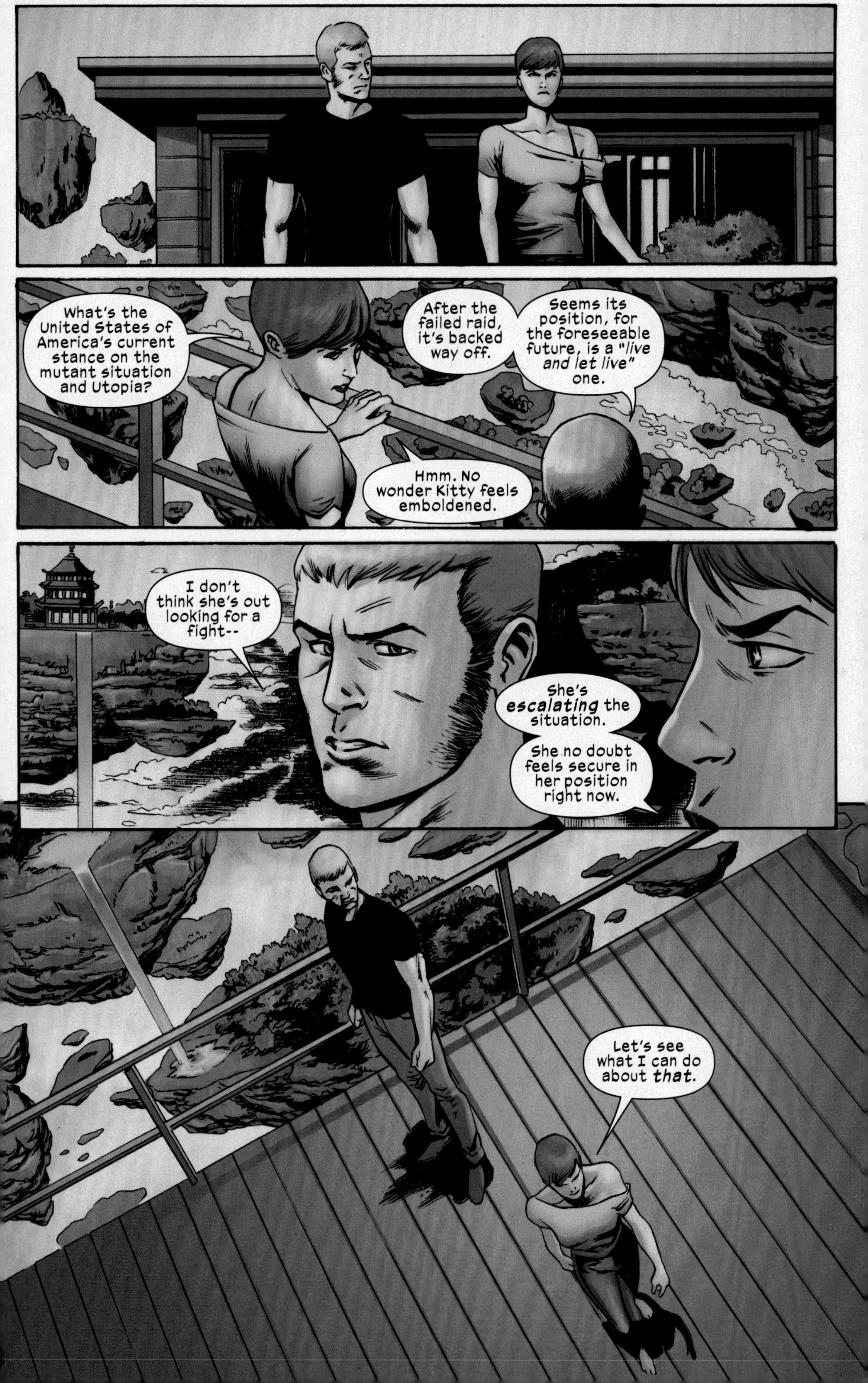
What's the United States of America's current stance on the mutant situation and Utopia?
After the failed raid, it's backed way off.
Seems its position, for the foreseeable future, is a "live and let live" one.
Hmm. No wonder Kitty feels emboldened.
I don't think she's out looking for a fight--
She's escalating the situation.
She no doubt feels secure in her position right now.
Let's see what I can do about that.

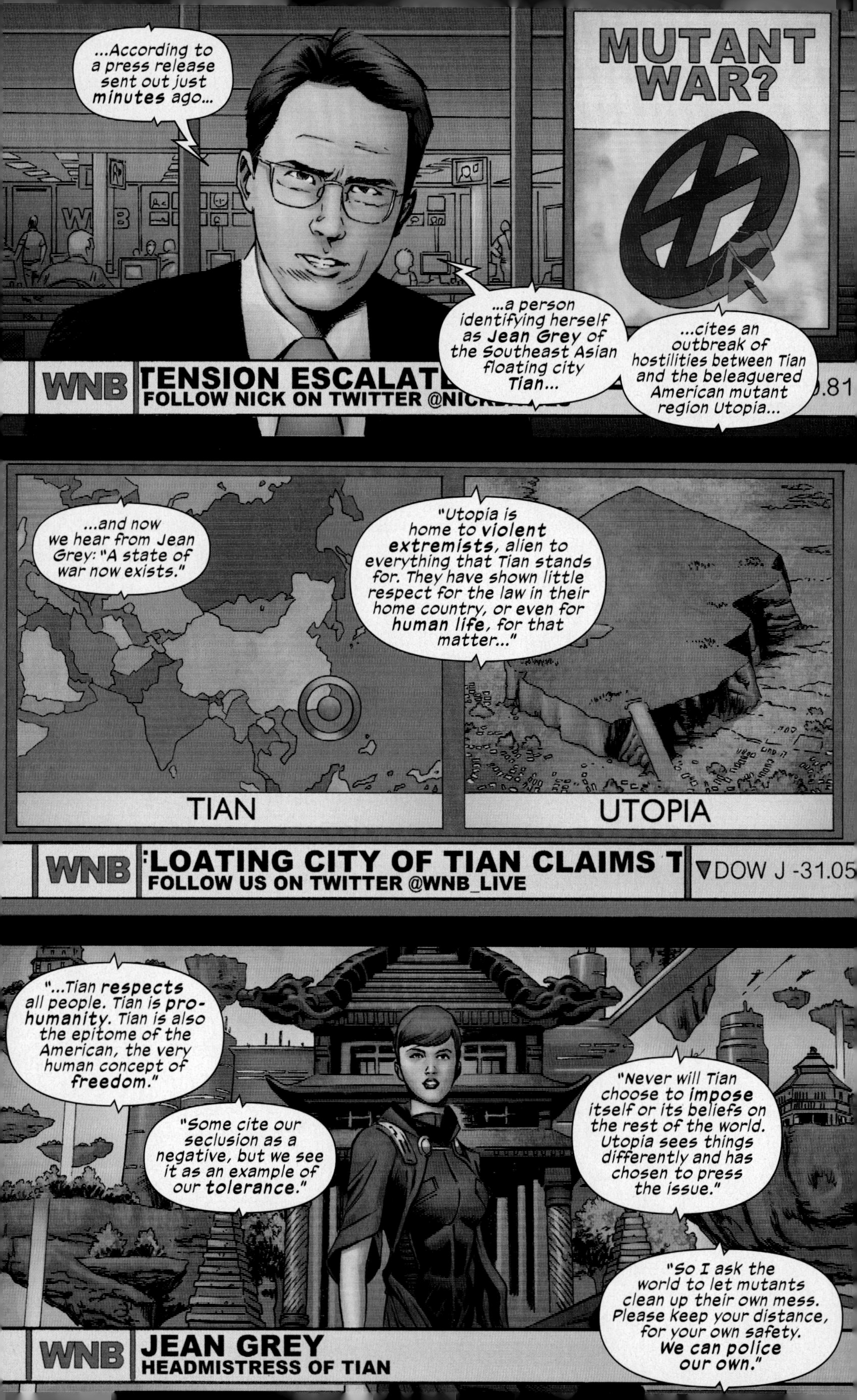
...According to a press release sent out just minutes ago...
MUTANT WAR?
...a person identifying herself as Jean Grey of the Southeast Asian floating city Tian...
...cites an outbreak of hostilities between Tian and the beleaguered American mutant region Utopia...
WNB TENSION ESCALATE
FOLLOW NICK ON TWITTER @NICK
...and now we hear from Jean Grey: "A state of war now exists."
"Utopia is home to violent extremists, alien to everything that Tian stands for. They have shown little respect for the law in their home country, or even for human life, for that matter..."
TIAN
UTOPIA
WNB FLOATING CITY OF TIAN CLAIMS T
FOLLOW US ON TWITTER @WNB_LIVE
▼DOW J -31.05
"...Tian respects all people. Tian is pro-humanity. Tian is also the epitome of the American, the very human concept of freedom."
"Some cite our seclusion as a negative, but we see it as an example of our tolerance."
"Never will Tian choose to impose itself or its beliefs on the rest of the world. Utopia sees things differently and has chosen to press the issue."
"So I ask the world to let mutants clean up their own mess. Please keep your distance, for your own safety. We can police our own."
WNB JEAN GREY
HEADMISTRESS OF TIAN

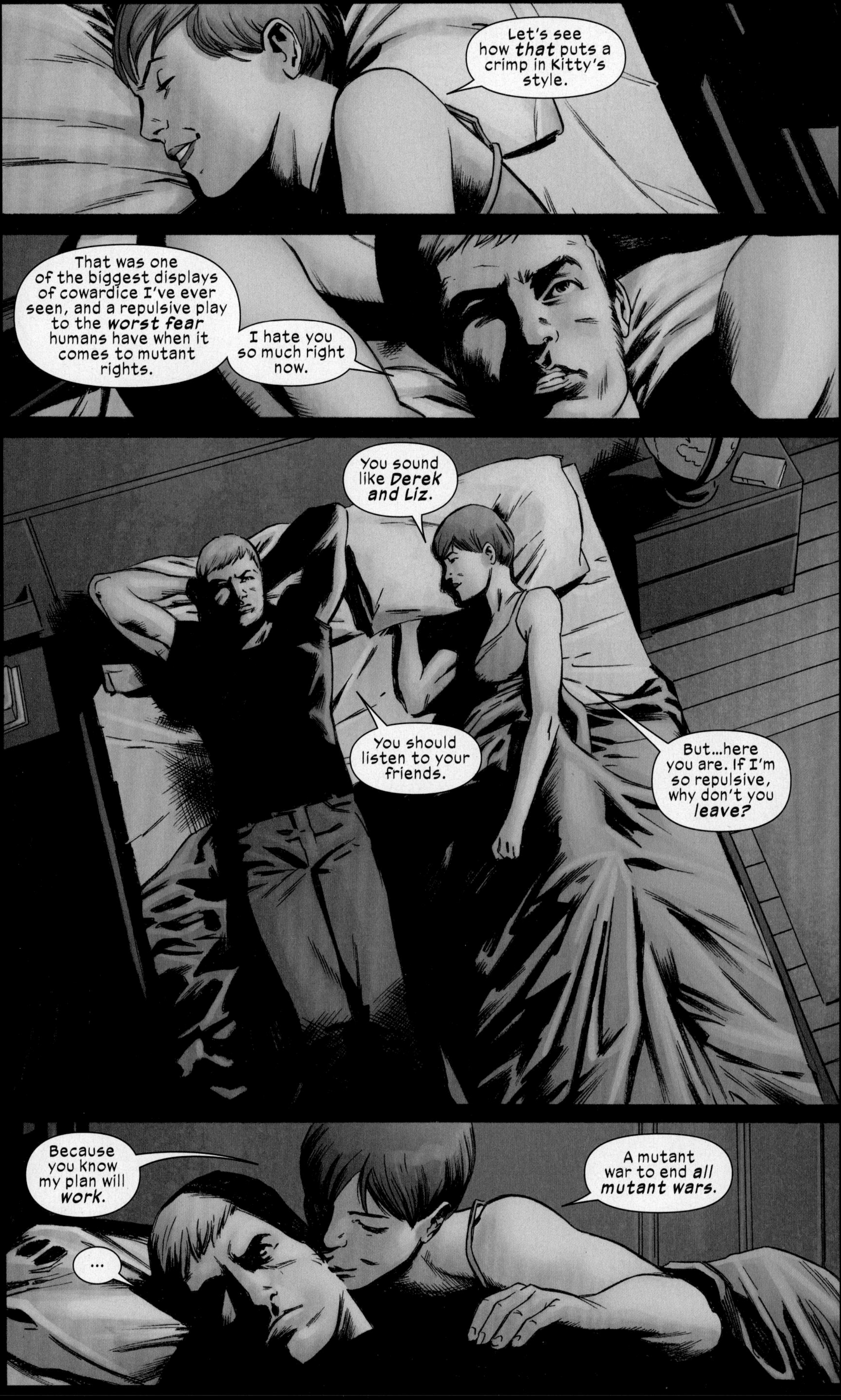
Let's see how that puts a crimp in Kitty's style.
That was one of the biggest displays of cowardice I've ever seen, and a repulsive play to the worst fear humans have when it comes to mutant rights.
I hate you so much right now.
You sound like Derek and Liz.
You should listen to your friends.
But...here you are. If I'm so repulsive, why don't you leave?
Because you know my plan will work.
...
A mutant war to end all mutant wars.

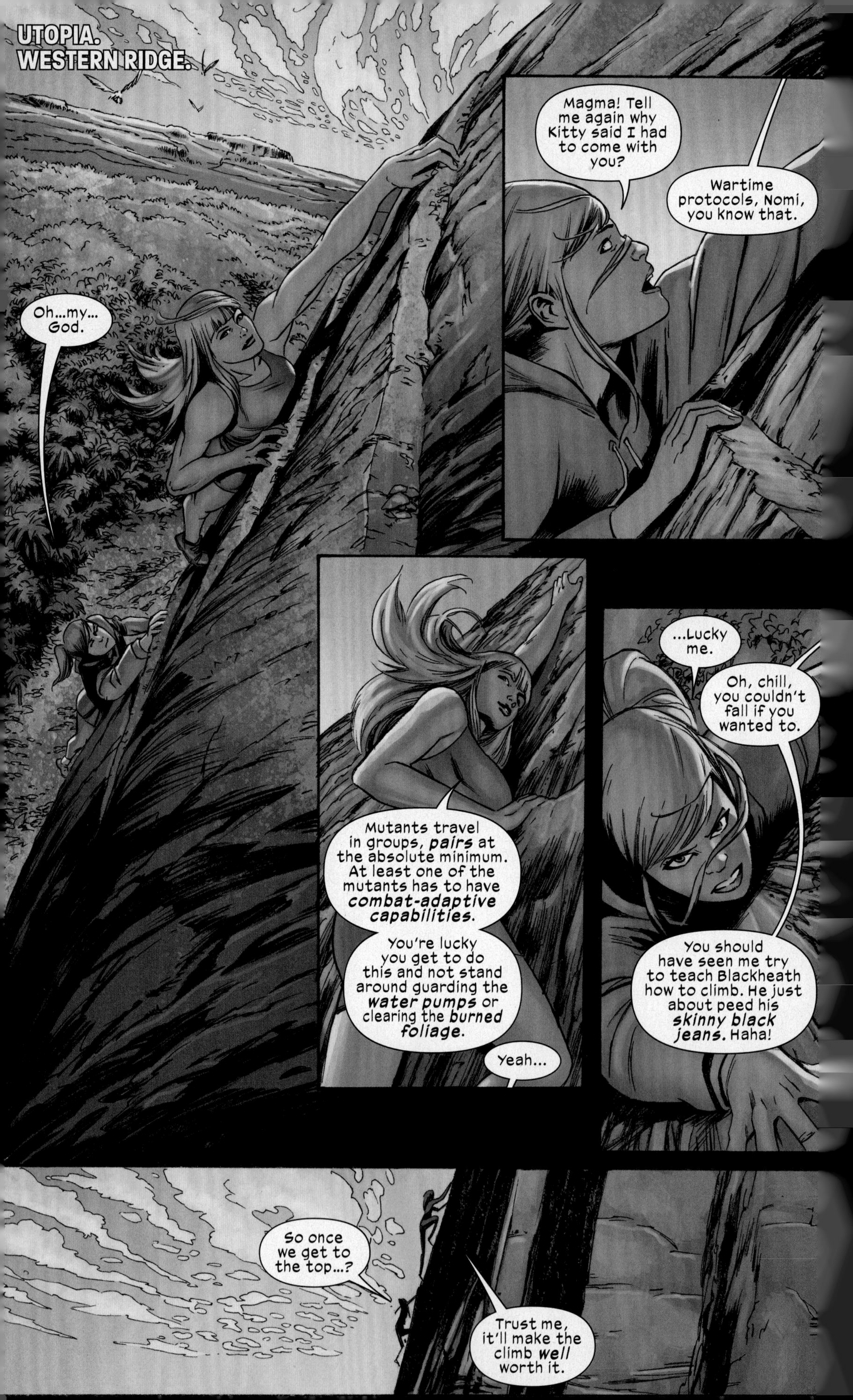
UTOPIA.
WESTERN RIDGE.
Oh...my... God.
Magma! Tell me again why Kitty said I had to come with you?
Wartime protocols, Nomi, you know that.
Mutants travel in groups, *pairs* at the absolute minimum. At least one of the mutants has to have *combat-adaptive capabilities*.
You're lucky you get to do this and not stand around guarding the *water pumps* or clearing the *burned foliage*.
Yeah...
...Lucky me.
Oh, chill, you couldn't fall if you wanted to.
You should have seen me try to teach Blackheath how to climb. He just about peed his *skinny black jeans*. Haha!
So once we get to the top...?
Trust me, it'll make the climb *well* worth it.

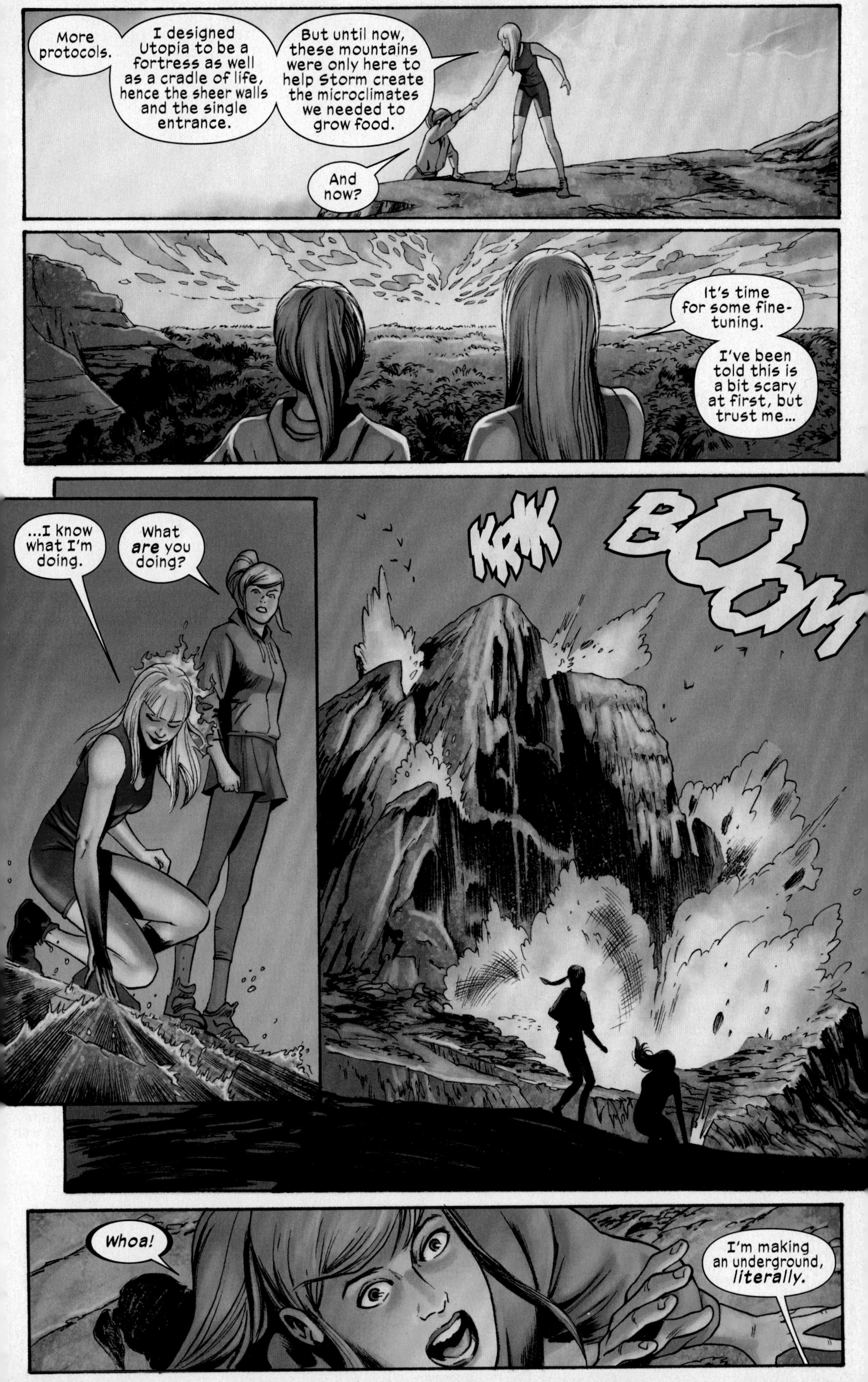
More protocols.
I designed Utopia to be a fortress as well as a cradle of life, hence the sheer walls and the single entrance.
But until now, these mountains were only here to help Storm create the microclimates we needed to grow food.
And now?
It's time for some fine-tuning.
I've been told this is a bit scary at first, but trust me...
...I know what I'm doing.
What *are* you doing?
KRAK
BOOM
Whoa!
I'm making an underground, *literally*.

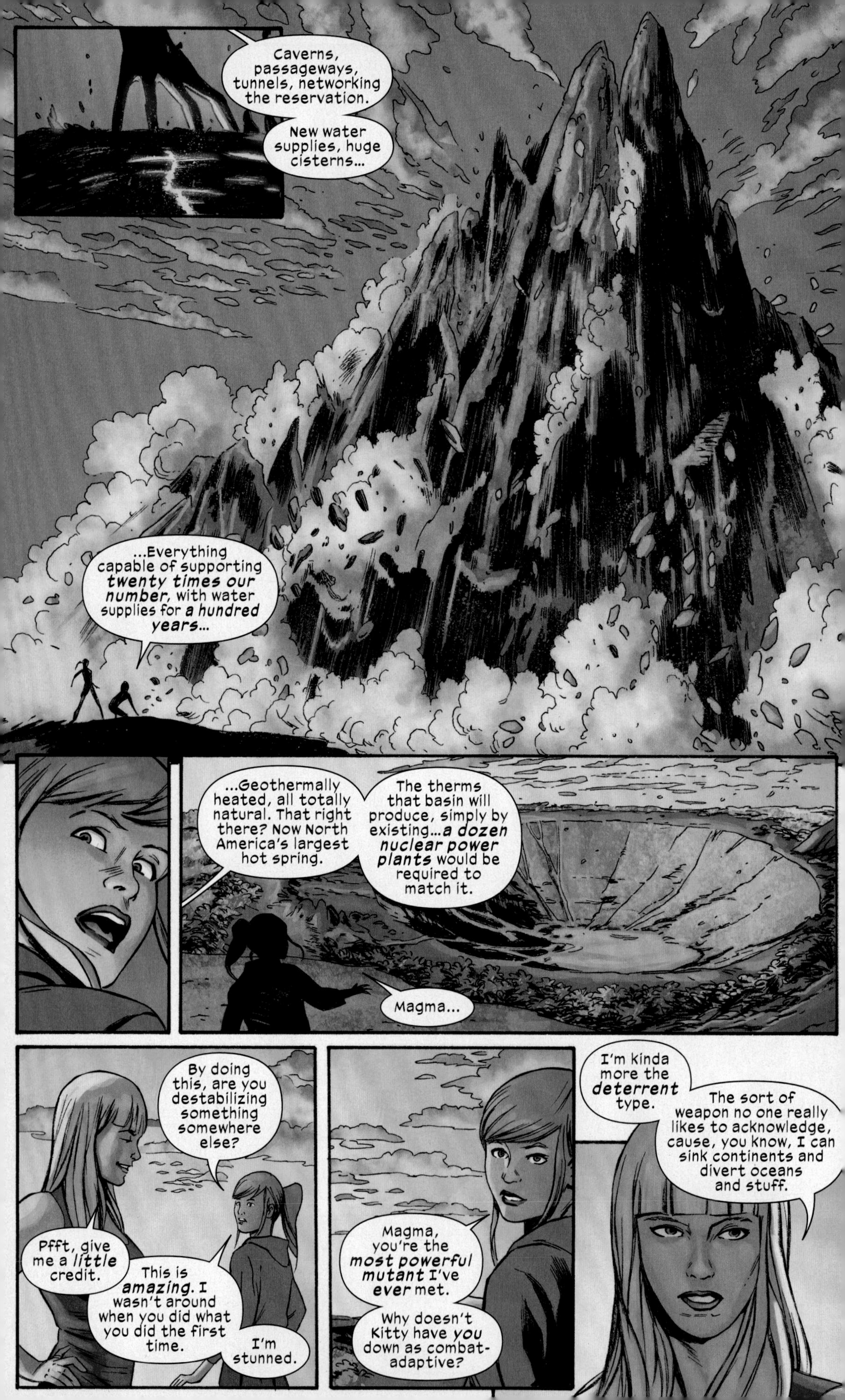
Caverns, passageways, tunnels, networking the reservation.
New water supplies, huge cisterns...
...Everything capable of supporting *twenty times our number*, with water supplies for *a hundred years*...
...Geothermally heated, all totally natural. That right there? Now North America's largest hot spring.
The therms that basin will produce, simply by existing...*a dozen nuclear power plants* would be required to match it.
Magma...
By doing this, are you destabilizing something somewhere else?
Pfft, give me a *little* credit.
This is *amazing*. I wasn't around when you did what you did the first time.
I'm stunned.
Magma, you're the *most powerful mutant* I've *ever* met.
Why doesn't Kitty have *you* down as combat-adaptive?
I'm kinda more the *deterrent* type.
The sort of weapon no one really likes to acknowledge, cause, you know, I can sink continents and divert oceans and stuff.

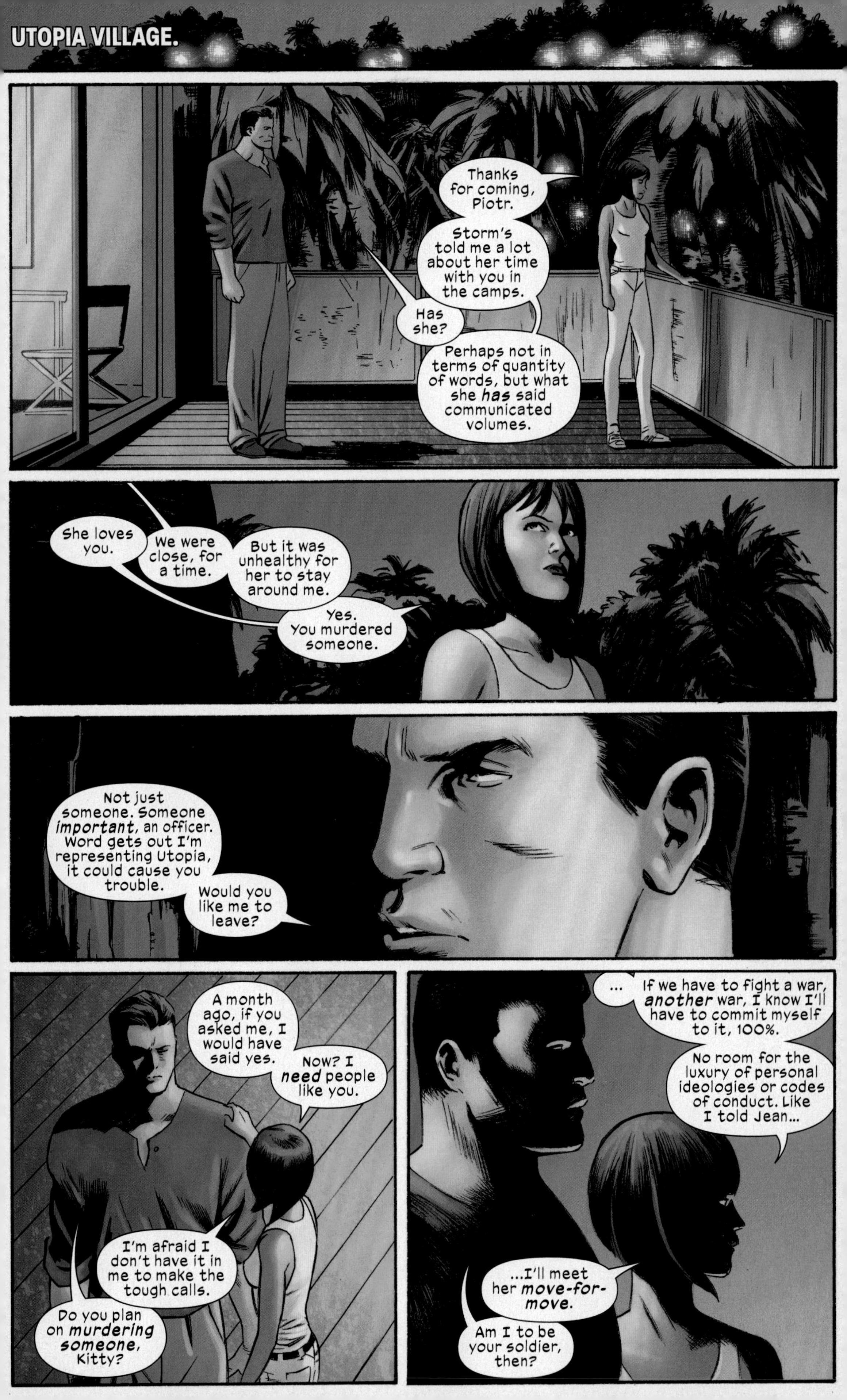

UTOPIA VILLAGE.
Thanks for coming, Piotr.
Storm's told me a lot about her time with you in the camps.
Has she?
Perhaps not in terms of quantity of words, but what she *has* said communicated volumes.
She loves you.
We were close, for a time.
But it was unhealthy for her to stay around me.
Yes. You murdered someone.
Not just someone. Someone *important*, an officer. Word gets out I'm representing Utopia, it could cause you trouble.
Would you like me to leave?
A month ago, if you asked me, I would have said yes.
Now? I *need* people like you.
I'm afraid I don't have it in me to make the tough calls.
Do you plan on *murdering someone*, Kitty?
...
If we have to fight a war, *another* war, I know I'll have to commit myself to it, 100%.
No room for the luxury of personal ideologies or codes of conduct. Like I told Jean...
...I'll meet her *move-for-move*.
Am I to be your soldier, then?

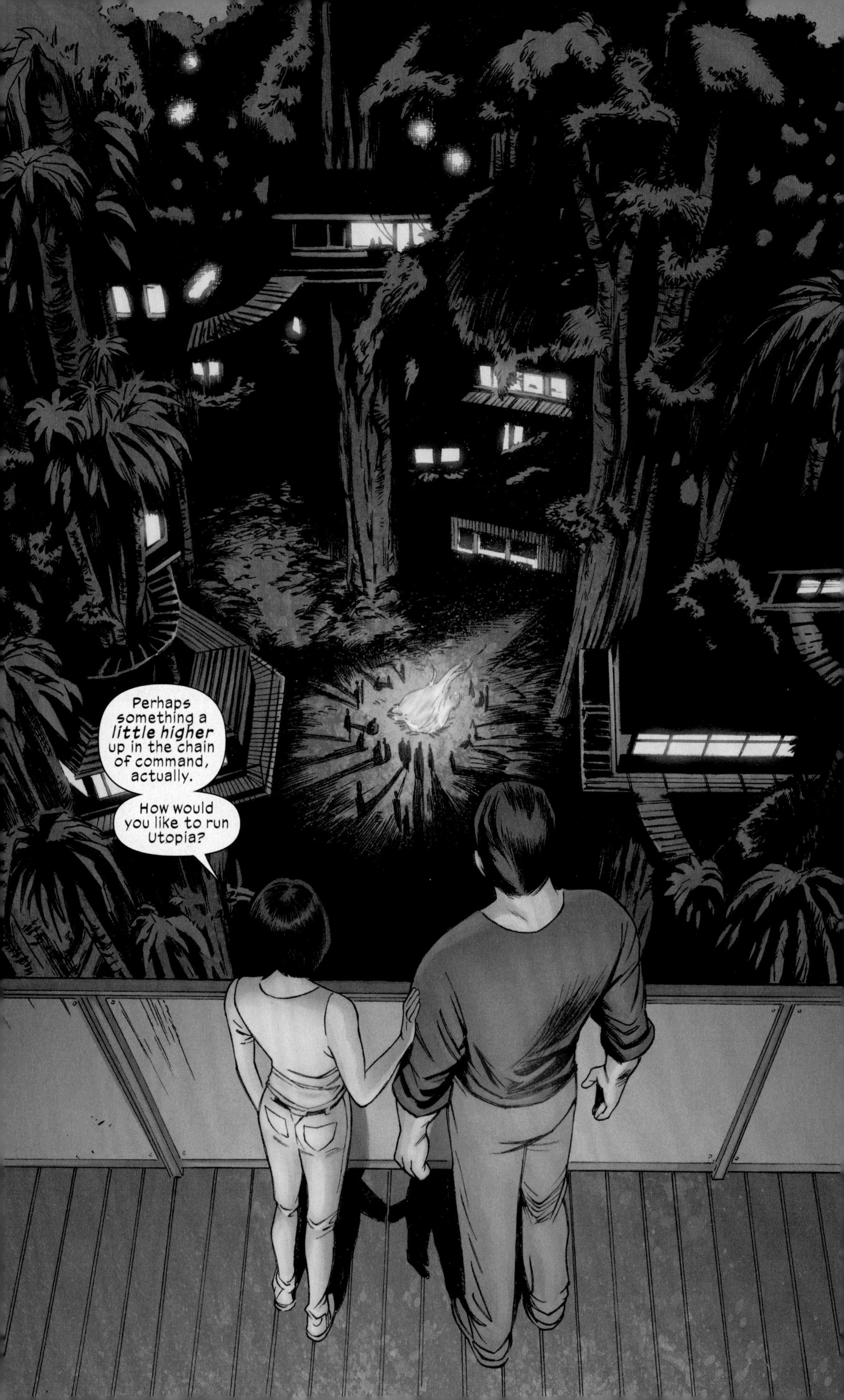
Perhaps something a *little higher* up in the chain of command, actually.
How would you like to run Utopia?

WORLD WAR X

31

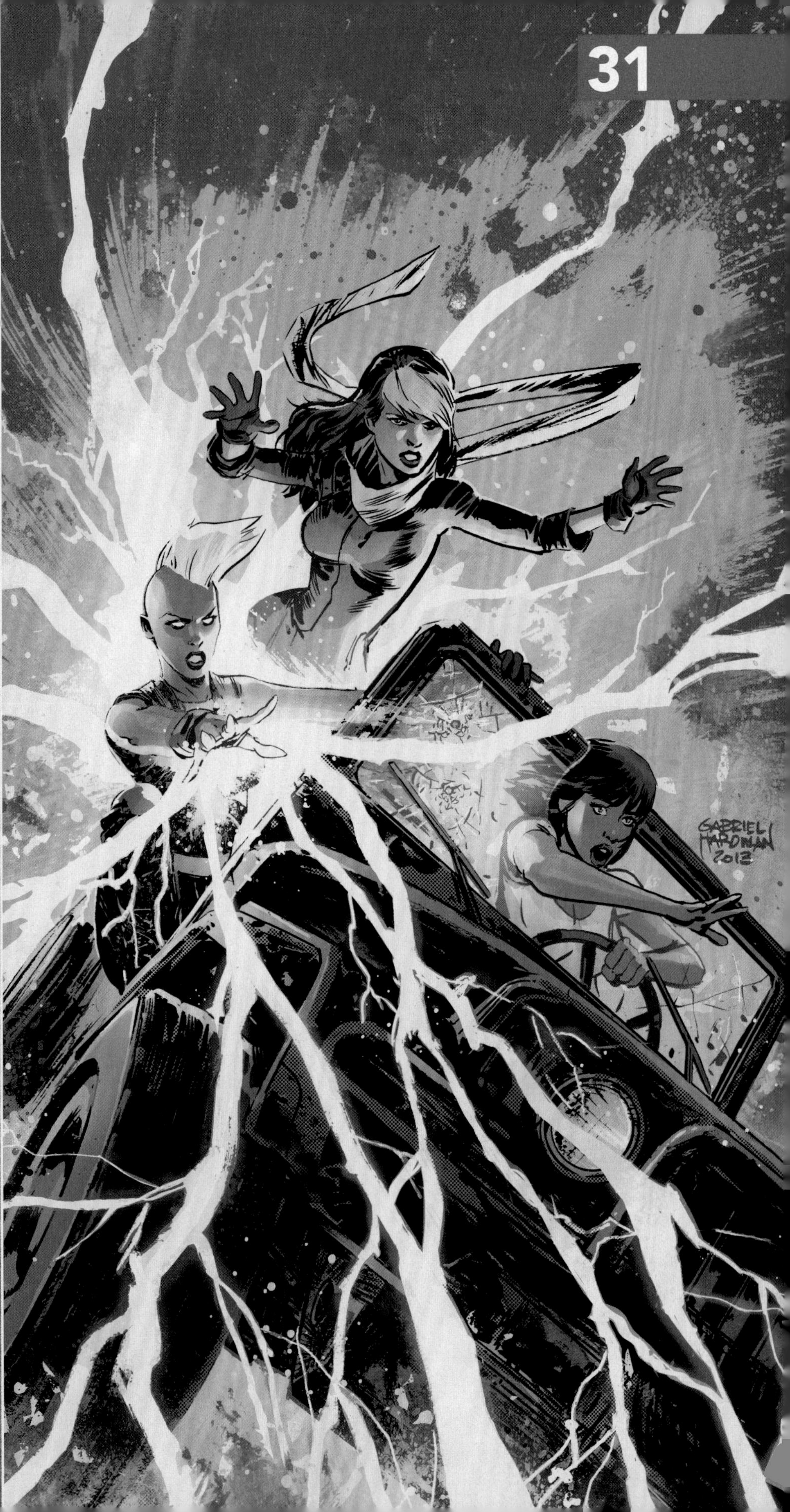

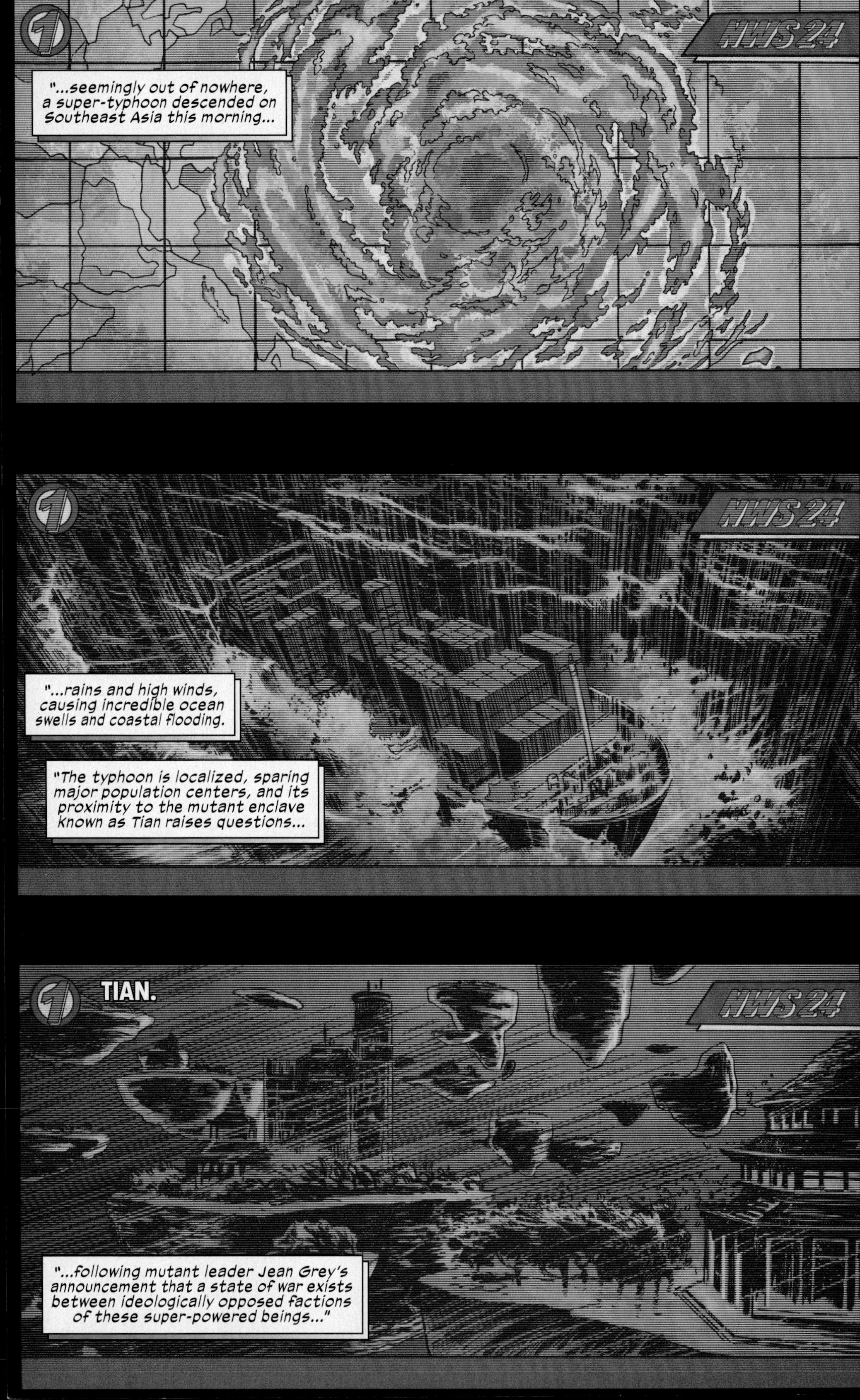
NWS 24
"...seemingly out of nowhere, a super-typhoon descended on Southeast Asia this morning...
NWS 24
"...rains and high winds, causing incredible ocean swells and coastal flooding.
"The typhoon is localized, sparing major population centers, and its proximity to the mutant enclave known as Tian raises questions...
TIAN.
NWS 24
"...following mutant leader Jean Grey's announcement that a state of war exists between ideologically opposed factions of these super-powered beings..."

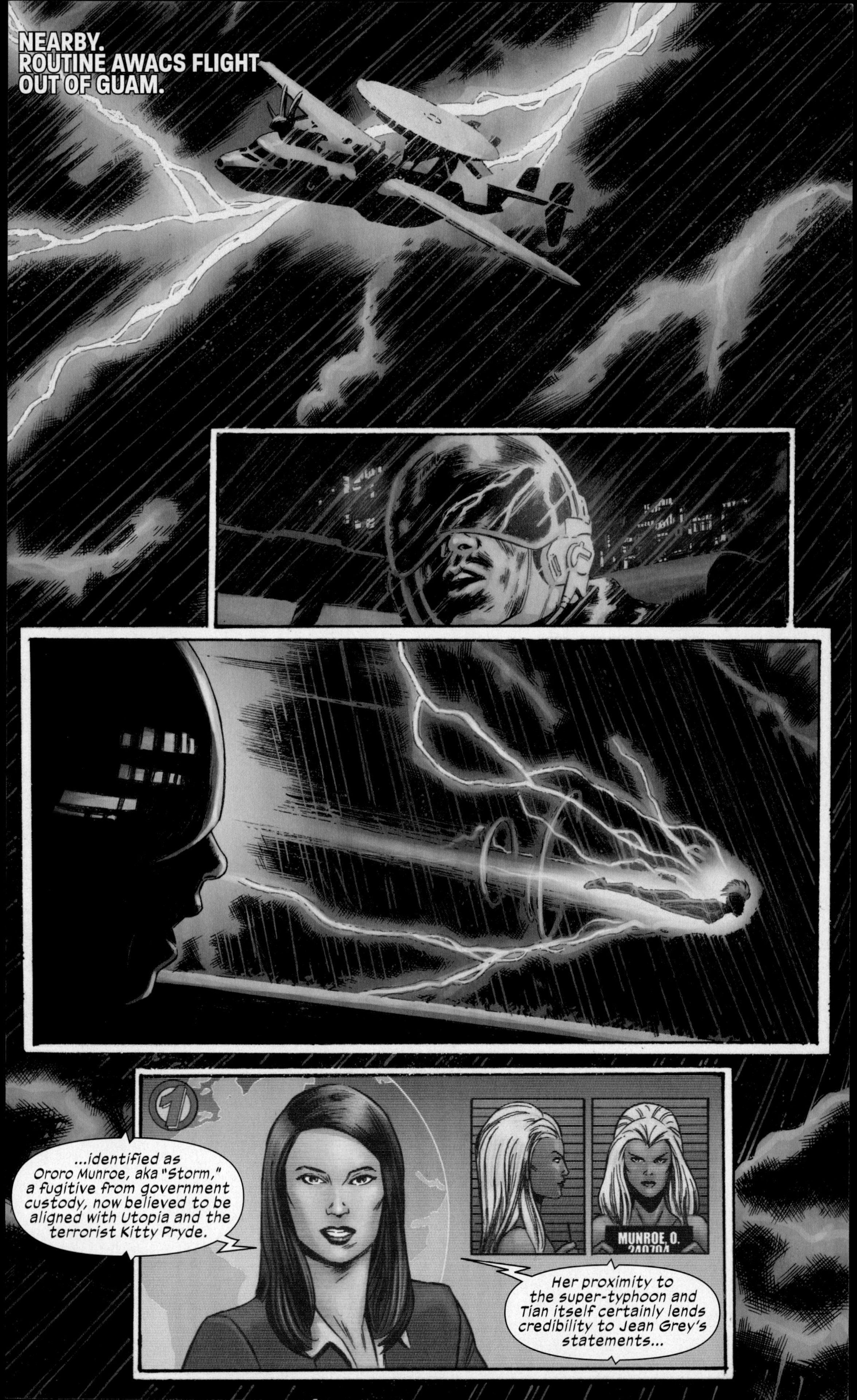
NEARBY.
ROUTINE AWACS FLIGHT OUT OF GUAM.
MUNROE, O.
...identified as Ororo Munroe, aka "Storm," a fugitive from government custody, now believed to be aligned with Utopia and the terrorist Kitty Pryde.
Her proximity to the super-typhoon and Tian itself certainly lends credibility to Jean Grey's statements...

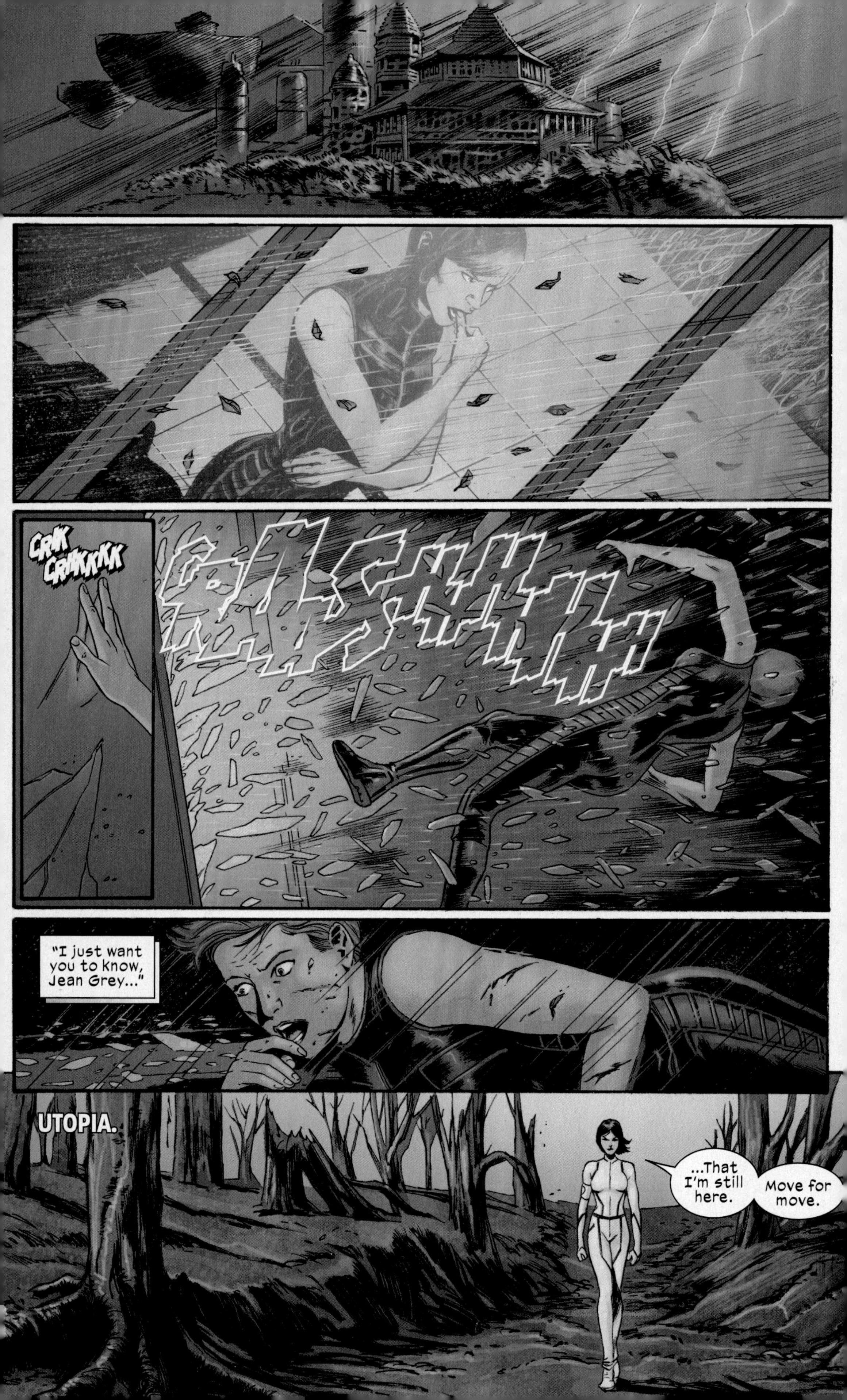
"I just want you to know, Jean Grey..."
UTOPIA.
...That I'm still here.
Move for move.

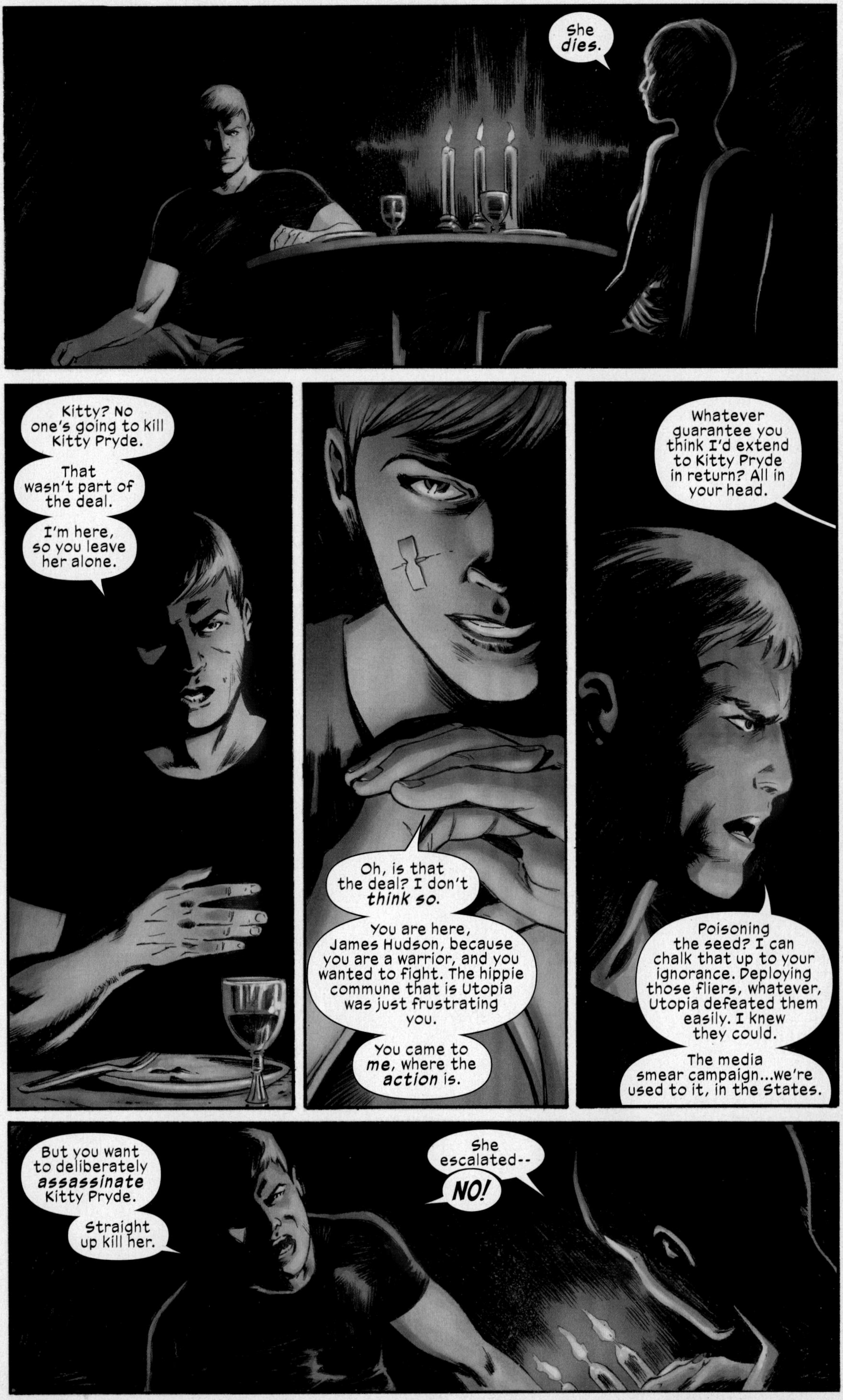
She dies.
Kitty? No one's going to kill Kitty Pryde.
That wasn't part of the deal.
I'm here, so you leave her alone.
Oh, is that the deal? I don't think so.
You are here, James Hudson, because you are a warrior, and you wanted to fight. The hippie commune that is Utopia was just frustrating you.
You came to me, where the action is.
Whatever guarantee you think I'd extend to Kitty Pryde in return? All in your head.
Poisoning the seed? I can chalk that up to your ignorance. Deploying those fliers, whatever, Utopia defeated them easily. I knew they could.
The media smear campaign...we're used to it, in the States.
But you want to deliberately assassinate Kitty Pryde.
Straight up kill her.
She escalated--
NO!

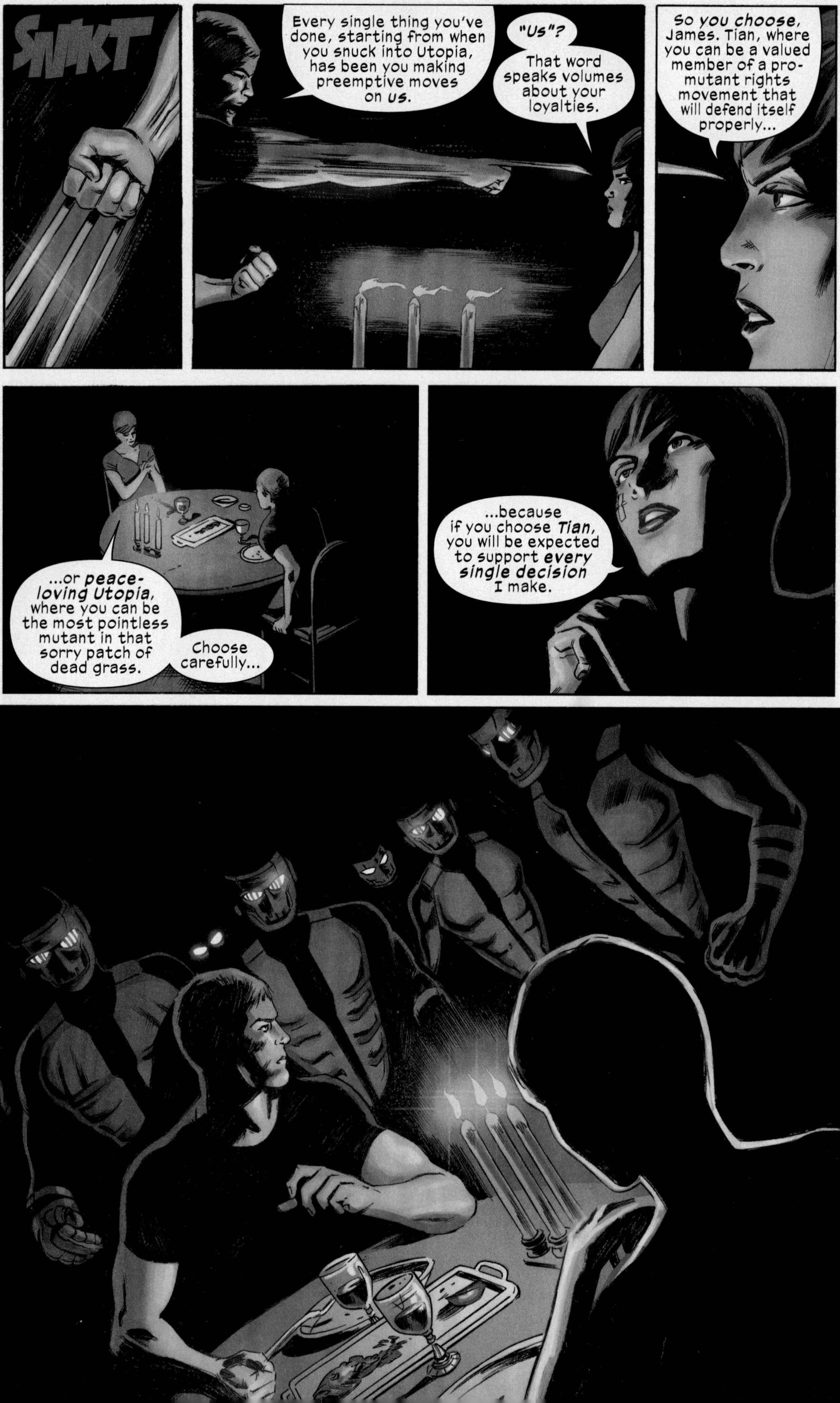
SNIKT
Every single thing you've done, starting from when you snuck into Utopia, has been you making preemptive moves on *us*.
"*Us*"?
That word speaks volumes about your loyalties.
So *you choose*, James. Tian, where you can be a valued member of a pro-mutant rights movement that will defend itself properly...
...or ***peace-loving Utopia***, where you can be the most pointless mutant in that sorry patch of dead grass.
Choose carefully...
...because if you choose *Tian*, you will be expected to support ***every single decision*** I make.

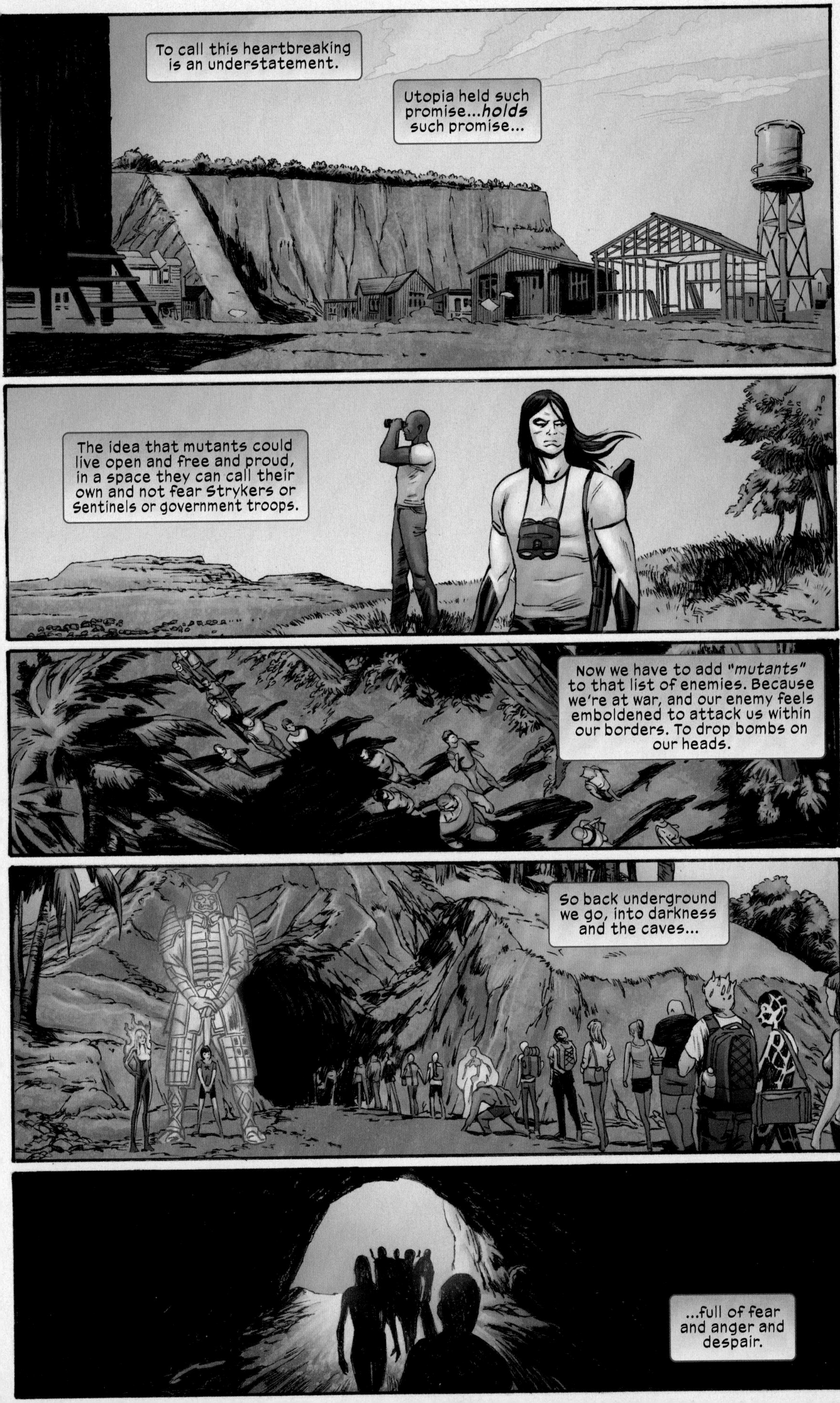
To call this heartbreaking is an understatement.
Utopia held such promise...*holds* such promise...
The idea that mutants could live open and free and proud, in a space they can call their own and not fear Strykers or Sentinels or government troops.
Now we have to add "*mutants*" to that list of enemies. Because we're at war, and our enemy feels emboldened to attack us within our borders. To drop bombs on our heads.
So back underground we go, into darkness and the caves...
...full of fear and anger and despair.

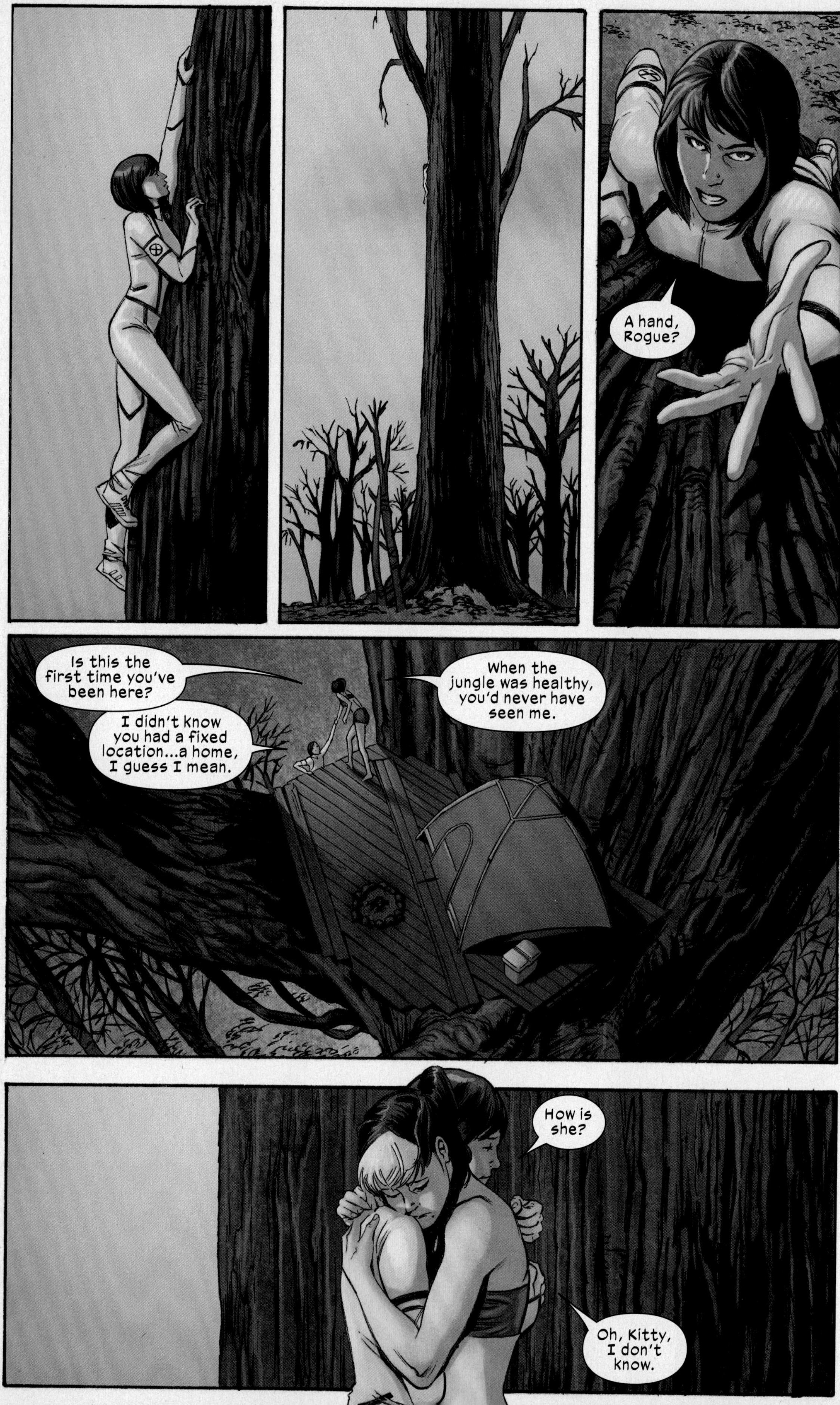
A hand, Rogue?
Is this the first time you've been here?
I didn't know you had a fixed location...a home, I guess I mean.
When the jungle was healthy, you'd never have seen me.
How is she?
Oh, Kitty, I don't know.

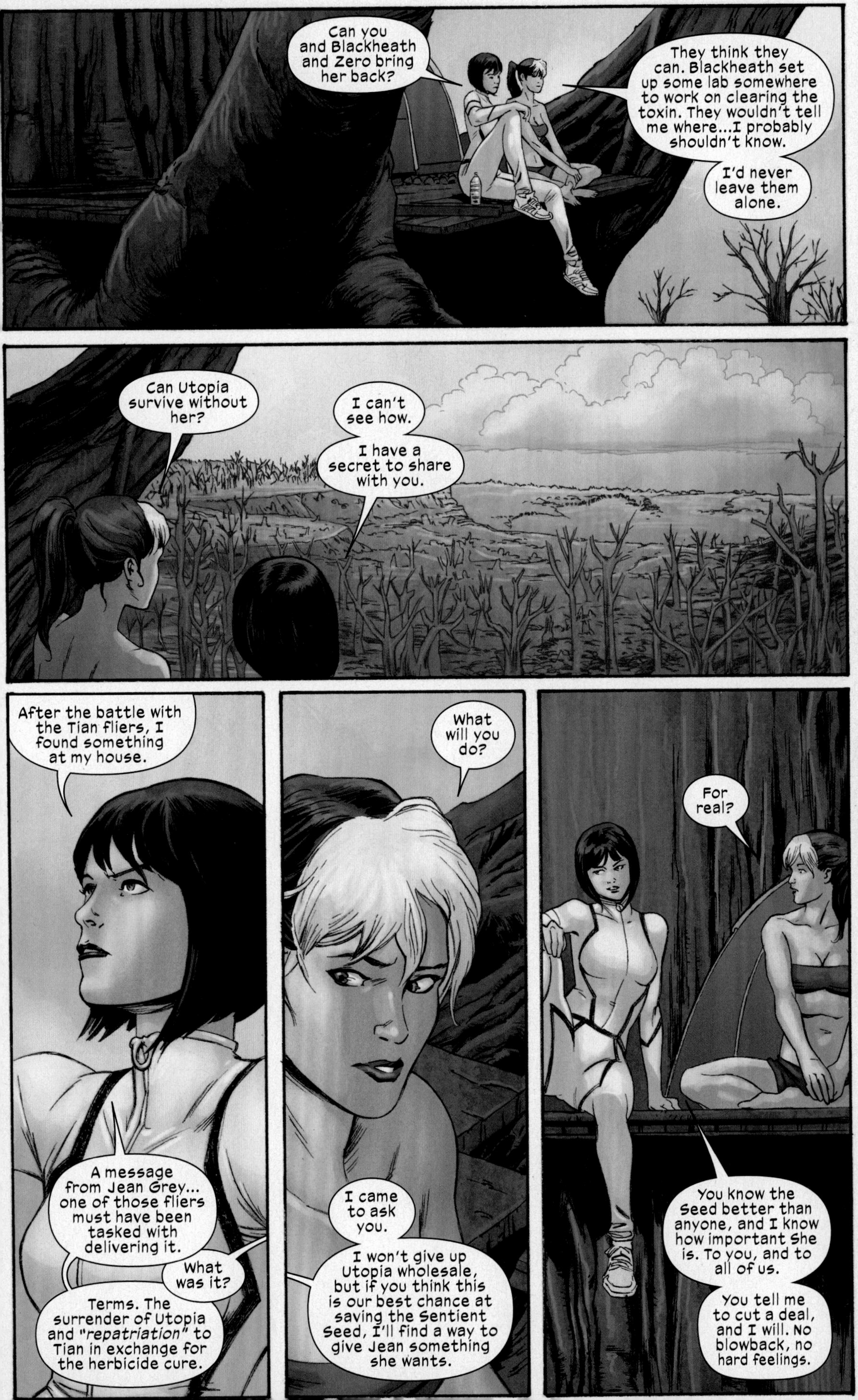
Can you and Blackheath and Zero bring her back?
They think they can. Blackheath set up some lab somewhere to work on clearing the toxin. They wouldn't tell me where...I probably shouldn't know.
I'd never leave them alone.
Can Utopia survive without her?
I can't see how.
I have a secret to share with you.
After the battle with the Tian fliers, I found something at my house.
A message from Jean Grey... one of those fliers must have been tasked with delivering it.
What was it?
Terms. The surrender of Utopia and "*repatriation*" to Tian in exchange for the herbicide cure.
What will you do?
I came to ask you.
I won't give up Utopia wholesale, but if you think this is our best chance at saving the Sentient Seed, I'll find a way to give Jean something she wants.
For real?
You know the Seed better than anyone, and I know how important She is. To you, and to all of us.
You tell me to cut a deal, and I will. No blowback, no hard feelings.

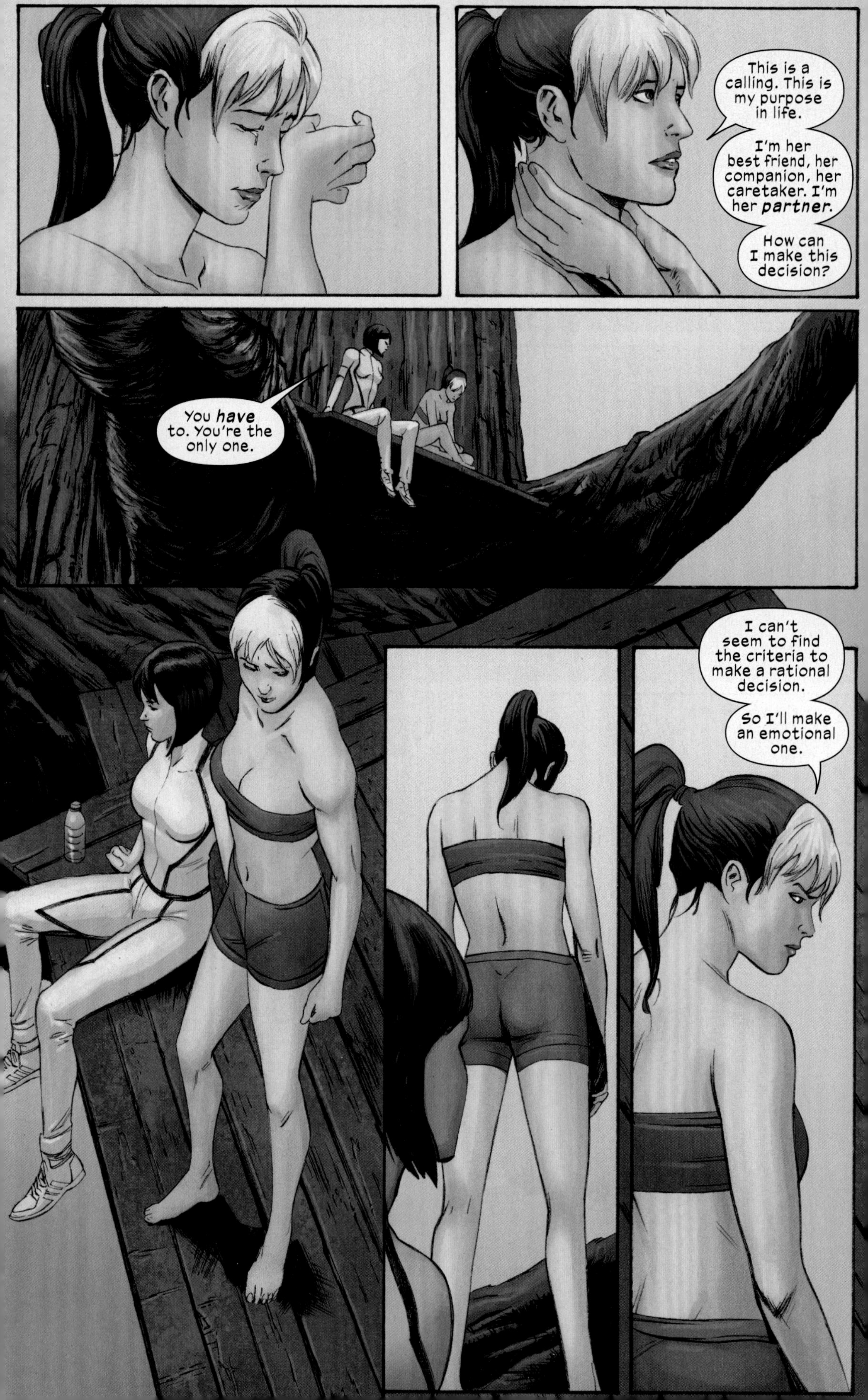
This is a calling. This is my purpose in life.
I'm her best friend, her companion, her caretaker. I'm her *partner*.
How can I make this decision?
You *have* to. You're the only one.
I can't seem to find the criteria to make a rational decision.
So I'll make an emotional one.

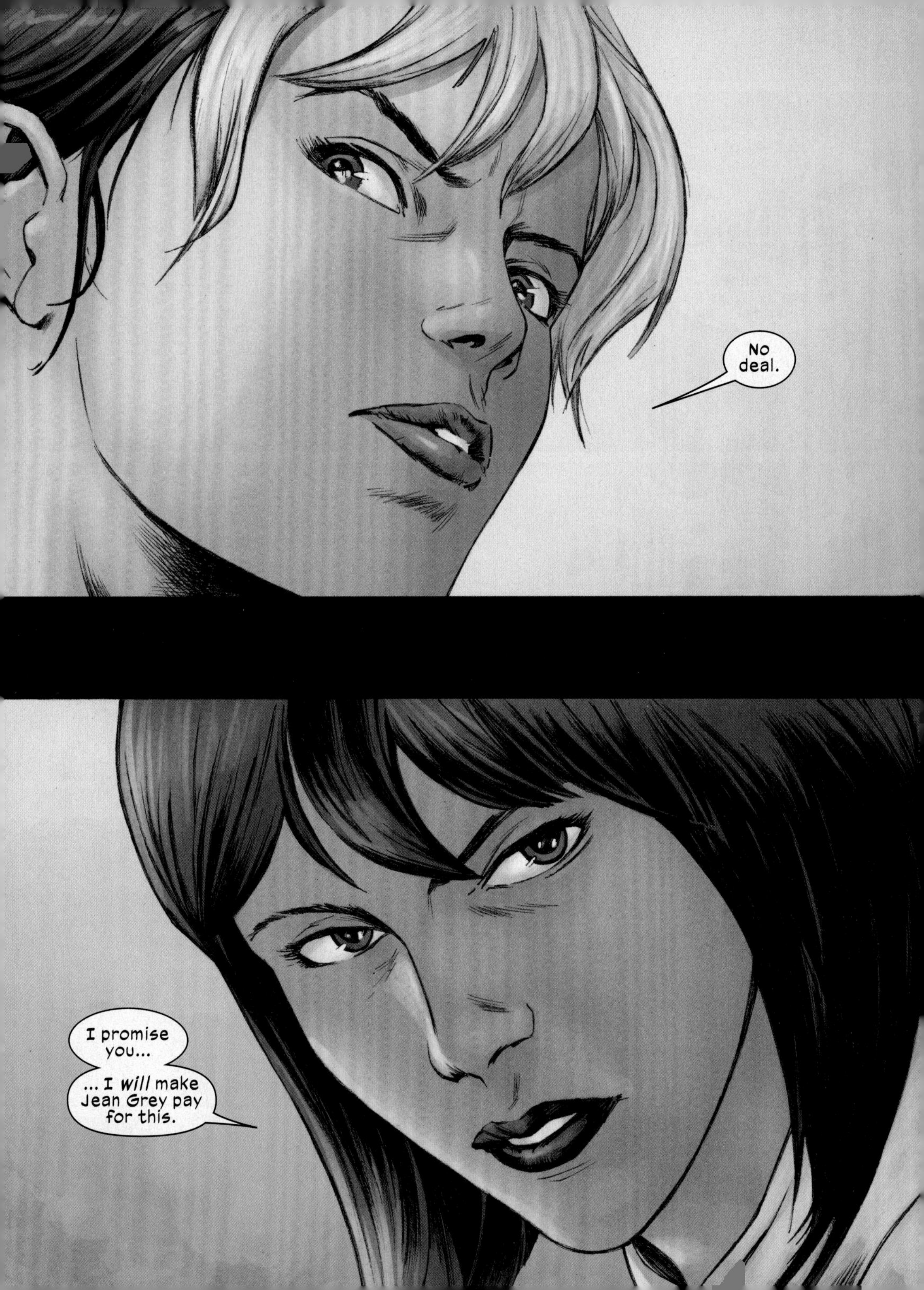
No deal.
I promise you...
...I will make Jean Grey pay for this.

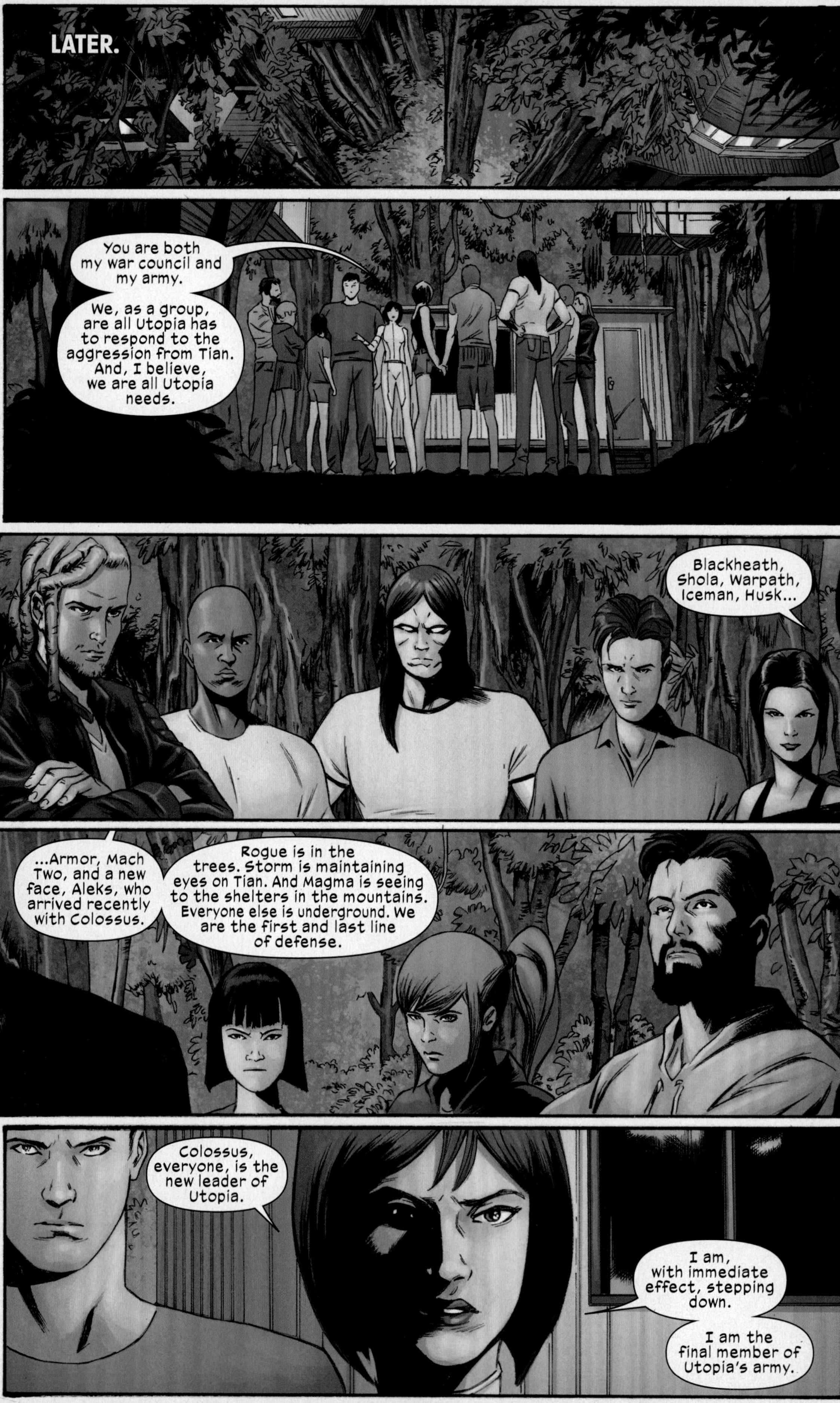
LATER.
You are both my war council and my army.
We, as a group, are all Utopia has to respond to the aggression from Tian. And, I believe, we are all Utopia needs.
Blackheath, Shola, Warpath, Iceman, Husk...
...Armor, Mach Two, and a new face, Aleks, who arrived recently with Colossus.
Rogue is in the trees. Storm is maintaining eyes on Tian. And Magma is seeing to the shelters in the mountains. Everyone else is underground. We are the first and last line of defense.
Colossus, everyone, is the new leader of Utopia.
I am, with immediate effect, stepping down.
I am the final member of Utopia's army.

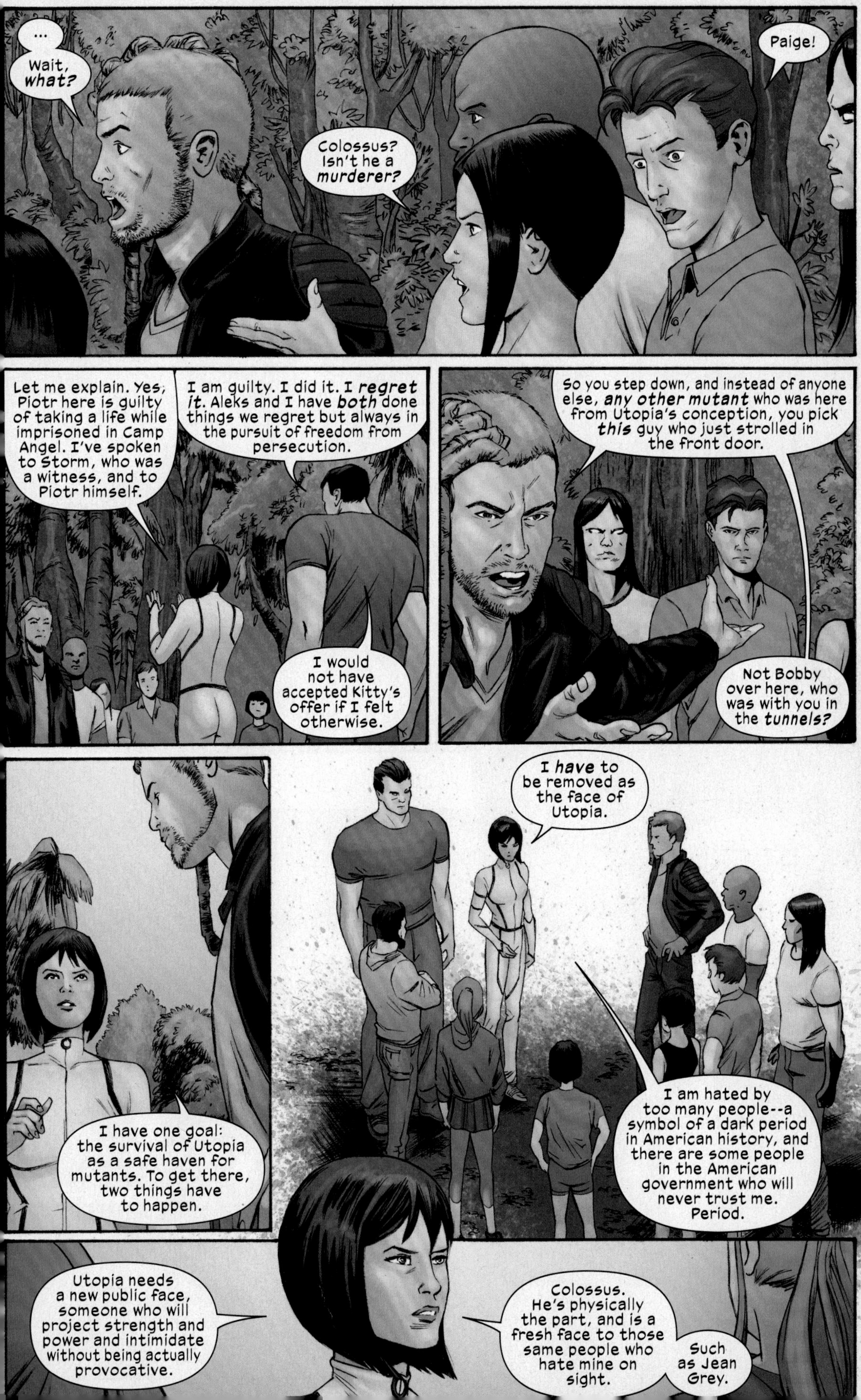
...
Wait, *what?*
Colossus? Isn't he a *murderer?*
Paige!
Let me explain. Yes, Piotr here is guilty of taking a life while imprisoned in Camp Angel. I've spoken to Storm, who was a witness, and to Piotr himself.
I am guilty. I did it. I *regret it.* Aleks and I have *both* done things we regret but always in the pursuit of freedom from persecution.
I would not have accepted Kitty's offer if I felt otherwise.
So you step down, and instead of anyone else, *any other mutant* who was here from Utopia's conception, you pick *this* guy who just strolled in the front door.
Not Bobby over here, who was with you in the *tunnels?*
I have one goal: the survival of Utopia as a safe haven for mutants. To get there, two things have to happen.
I *have* to be removed as the face of Utopia.
I am hated by too many people--a symbol of a dark period in American history, and there are some people in the American government who will never trust me. Period.
Utopia needs a new public face, someone who will project strength and power and intimidate without being actually provocative.
Colossus. He's physically the part, and is a fresh face to those same people who hate mine on sight.
Such as Jean Grey.

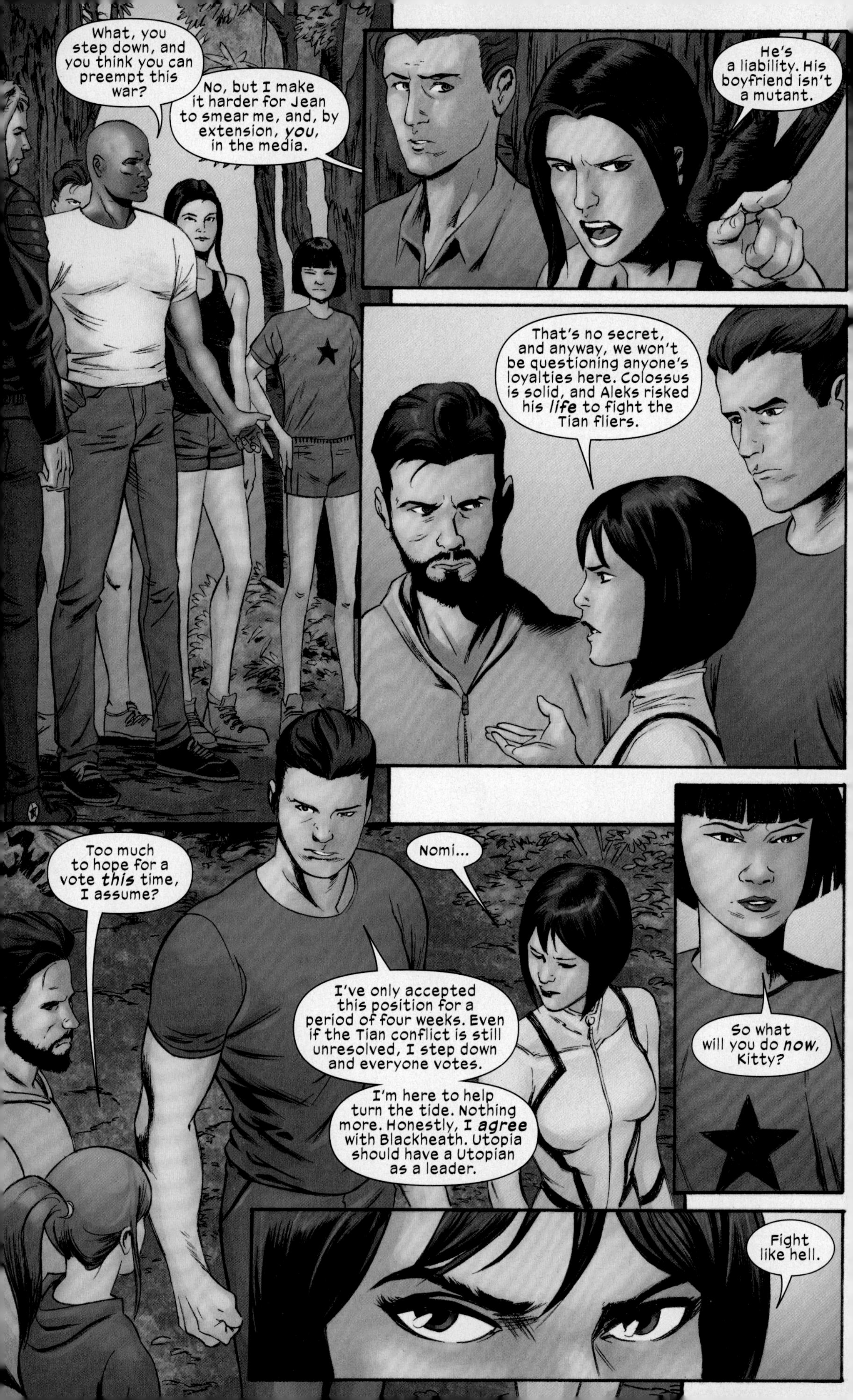
What, you step down, and you think you can preempt this war?
No, but I make it harder for Jean to smear me, and, by extension, *you*, in the media.
He's a liability. His boyfriend isn't a mutant.
That's no secret, and anyway, we won't be questioning anyone's loyalties here. Colossus is solid, and Aleks risked his *life* to fight the Tian fliers.
Too much to hope for a vote *this* time, I assume?
Nomi...
I've only accepted this position for a period of four weeks. Even if the Tian conflict is still unresolved, I step down and everyone votes.
I'm here to help turn the tide. Nothing more. Honestly, I *agree* with Blackheath. Utopia should have a Utopian as a leader.
So what will you do *now*, Kitty?
Fight like hell.

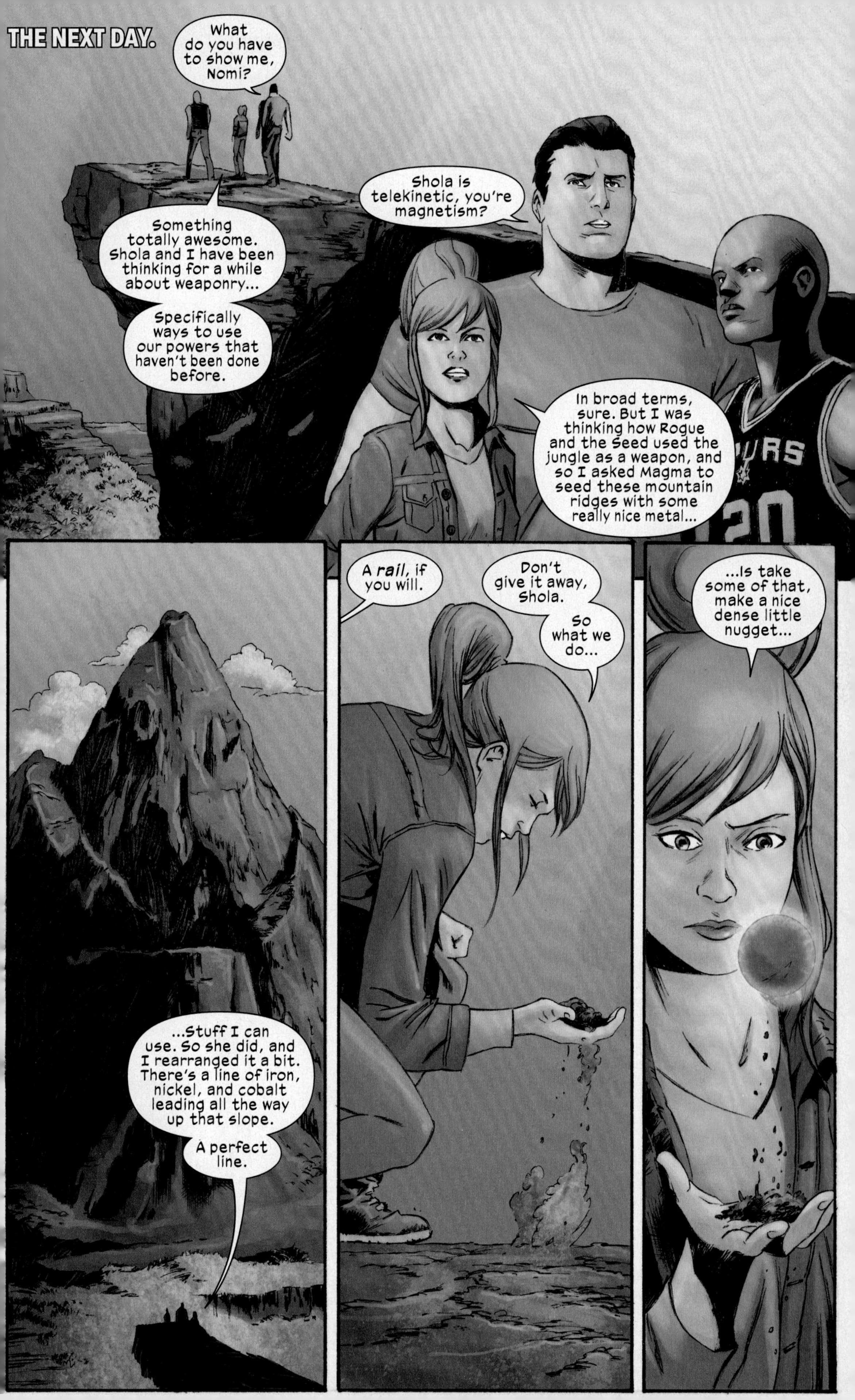
THE NEXT DAY.
What do you have to show me, Nomi?
Something totally awesome. Shola and I have been thinking for a while about weaponry...
Specifically ways to use our powers that haven't been done before.
Shola is telekinetic, you're magnetism?
In broad terms, sure. But I was thinking how Rogue and the Seed used the jungle as a weapon, and so I asked Magma to seed these mountain ridges with some really nice metal...
...Stuff I can use. So she did, and I rearranged it a bit. There's a line of iron, nickel, and cobalt leading all the way up that slope.
A perfect line.
A *rail*, if you will.
Don't give it away, Shola.
So what we do...
...Is take some of that, make a nice dense little nugget...

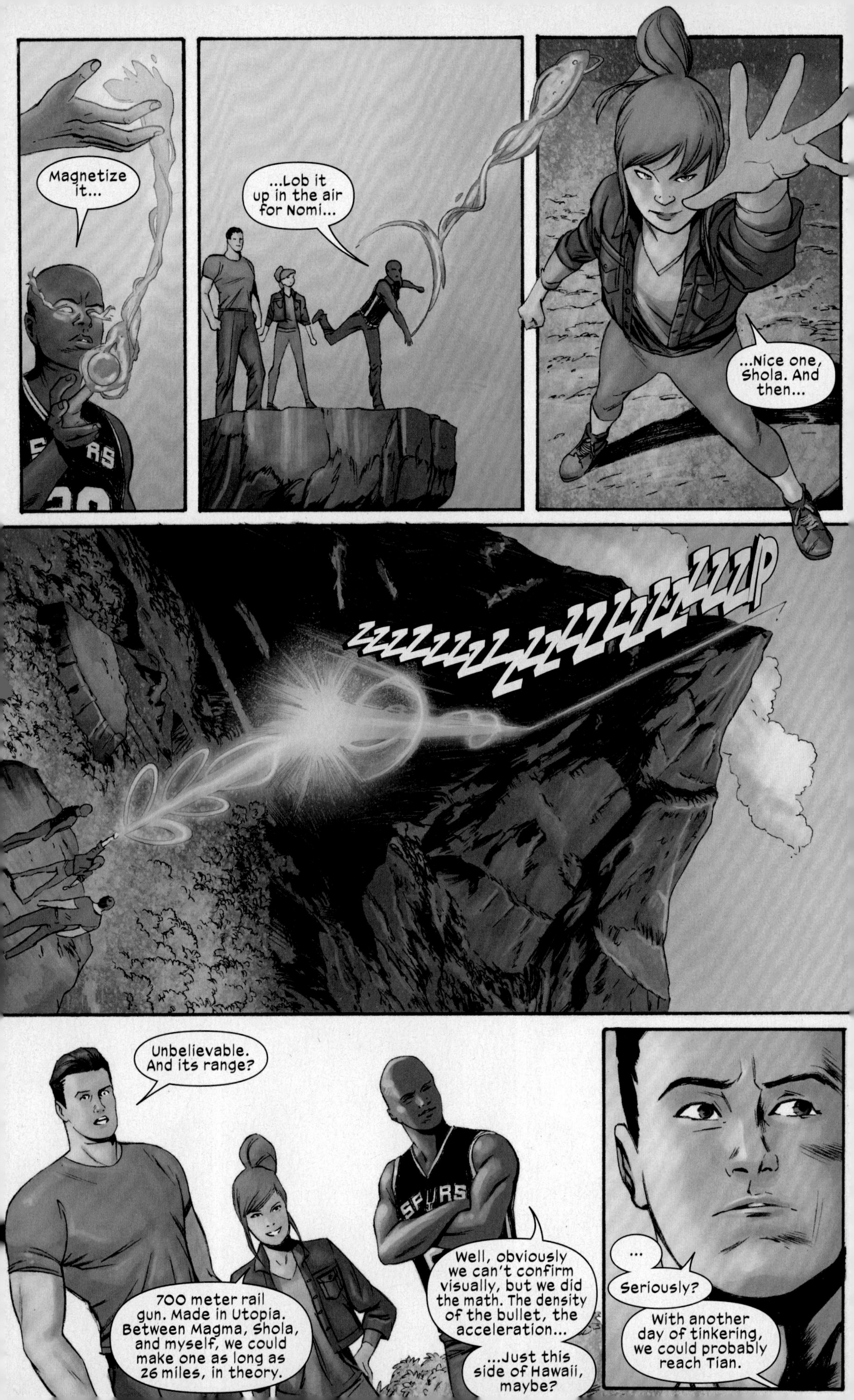
Magnetize it...
...Lob it up in the air for Nomi...
...Nice one, Shola. And then...
ZZZZZZZZZZZZZZZZZZZZZZZZP
Unbelievable. And its range?
700 meter rail gun. Made in Utopia. Between Magma, Shola, and myself, we could make one as long as 26 miles, in theory.
Well, obviously we can't confirm visually, but we did the math. The density of the bullet, the acceleration...
...Just this side of Hawaii, maybe?
...
Seriously?
With another day of tinkering, we could probably reach Tian.

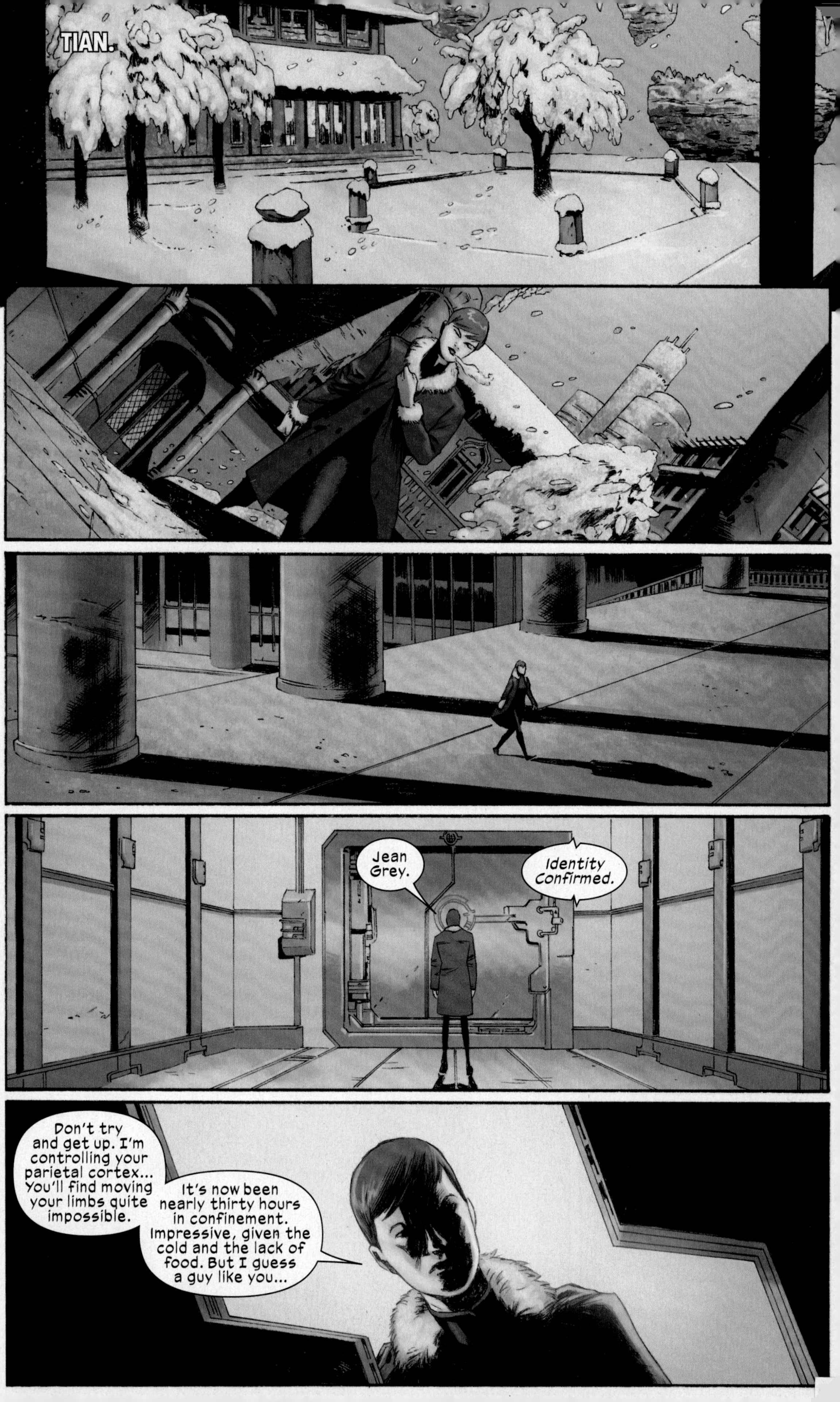
TIAN.
Jean Grey.
Identity Confirmed.
Don't try and get up. I'm controlling your parietal cortex... You'll find moving your limbs quite impossible.
It's now been nearly thirty hours in confinement. Impressive, given the cold and the lack of food. But I guess a guy like you...

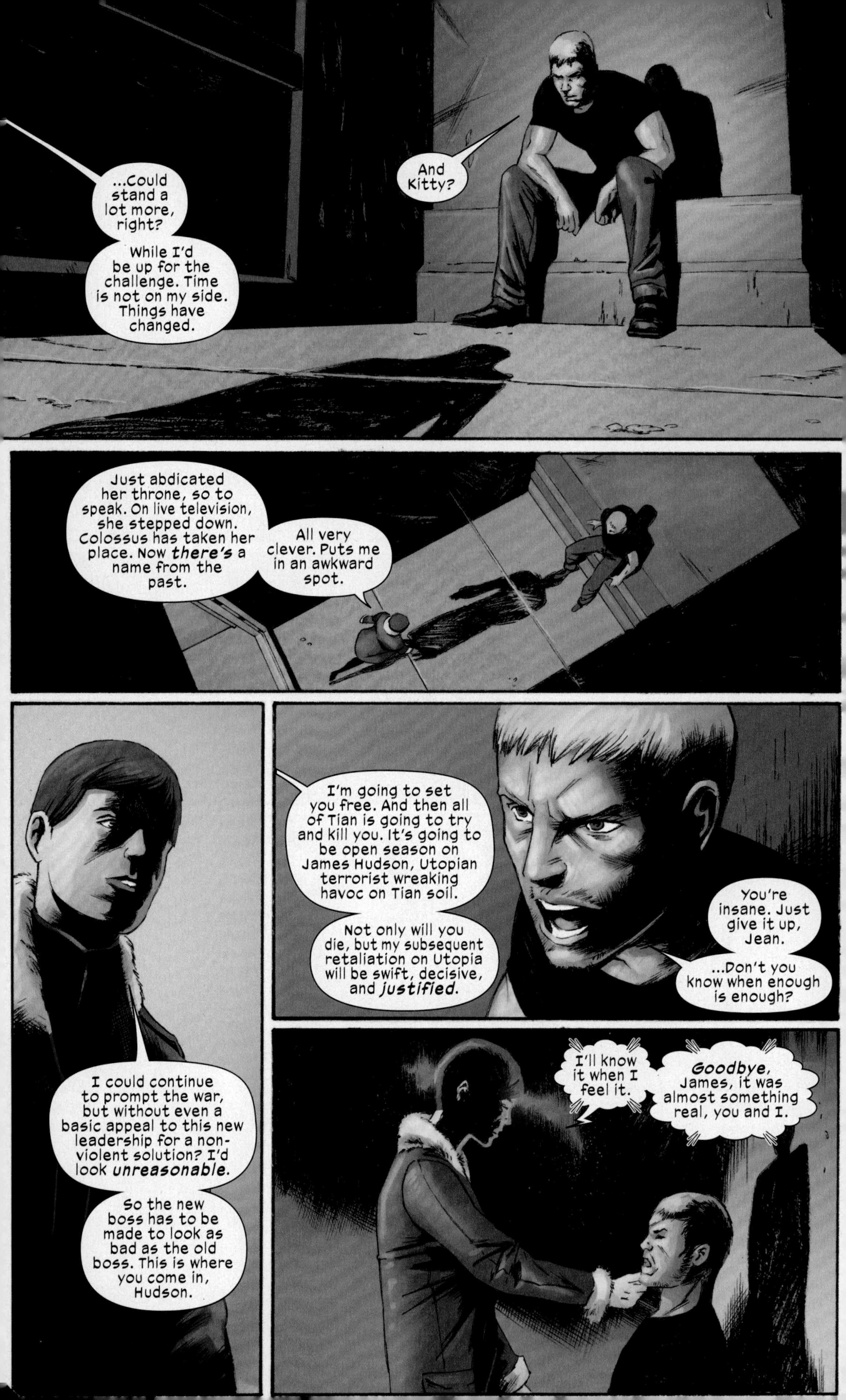

...Could stand a lot more, right?
While I'd be up for the challenge. Time is not on my side. Things have changed.
And Kitty?
Just abdicated her throne, so to speak. On live television, she stepped down. Colossus has taken her place. Now *there's* a name from the past.
All very clever. Puts me in an awkward spot.
I could continue to prompt the war, but without even a basic appeal to this new leadership for a non-violent solution? I'd look *unreasonable*.
So the new boss has to be made to look as bad as the old boss. This is where you come in, Hudson.
I'm going to set you free. And then all of Tian is going to try and kill you. It's going to be open season on James Hudson, Utopian terrorist wreaking havoc on Tian soil.
Not only will you die, but my subsequent retaliation on Utopia will be swift, decisive, and *justified*.
You're insane. Just give it up, Jean.
...Don't you know when enough is enough?
I'll know it when I feel it.
Goodbye, James, it was almost something real, you and I.

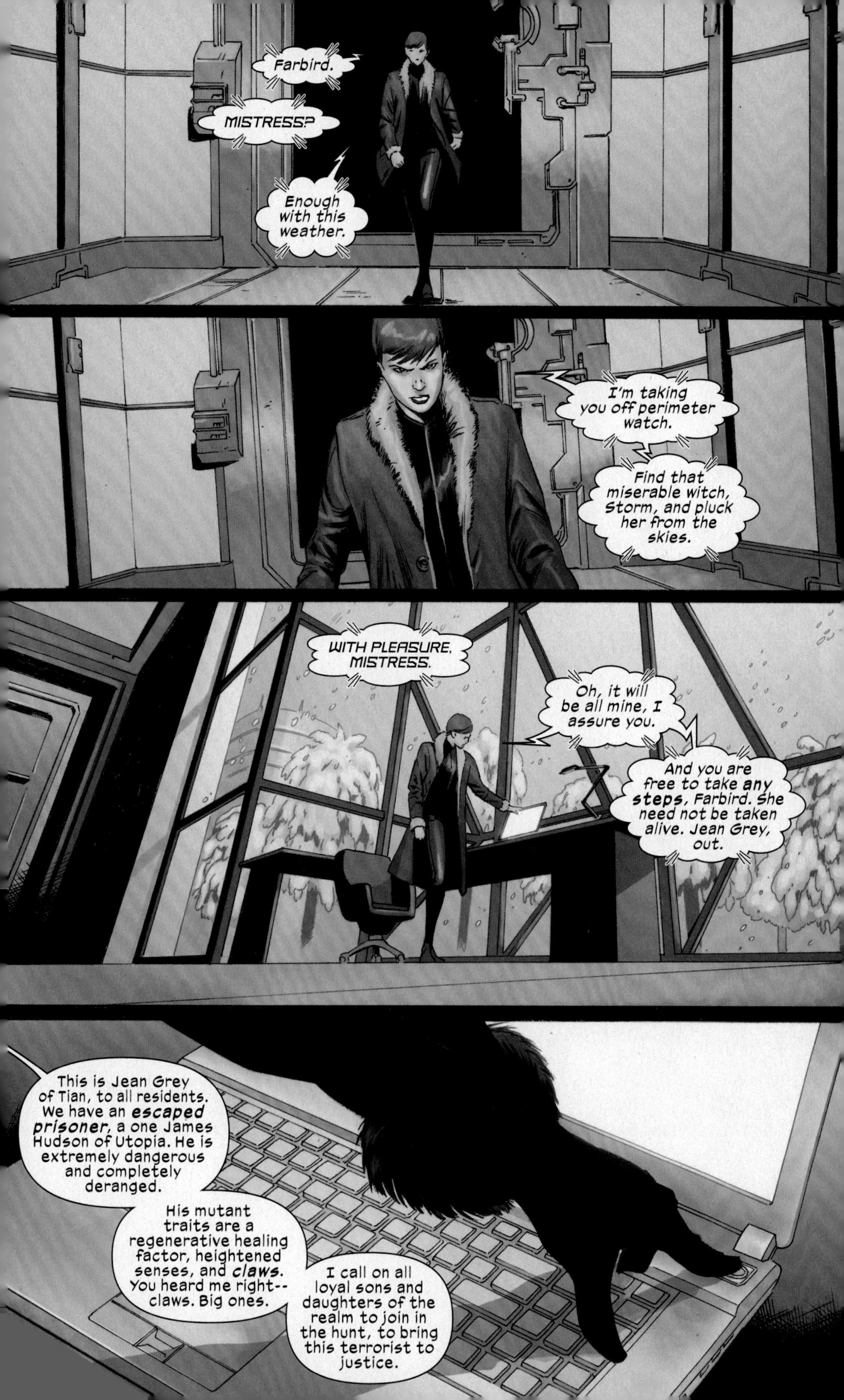

Farbird.
MISTRESS?
Enough with this weather.
I'm taking you off perimeter watch.
Find that miserable witch, Storm, and pluck her from the skies.
WITH PLEASURE, MISTRESS.
Oh, it will be all mine, I assure you.
And you are free to take any steps, Farbird. She need not be taken alive. Jean Grey, out.
This is Jean Grey of Tian, to all residents. We have an escaped prisoner, a one James Hudson of Utopia. He is extremely dangerous and completely deranged.
His mutant traits are a regenerative healing factor, heightened senses, and claws. You heard me right--claws. Big ones.
I call on all loyal sons and daughters of the realm to join in the hunt, to bring this terrorist to justice.

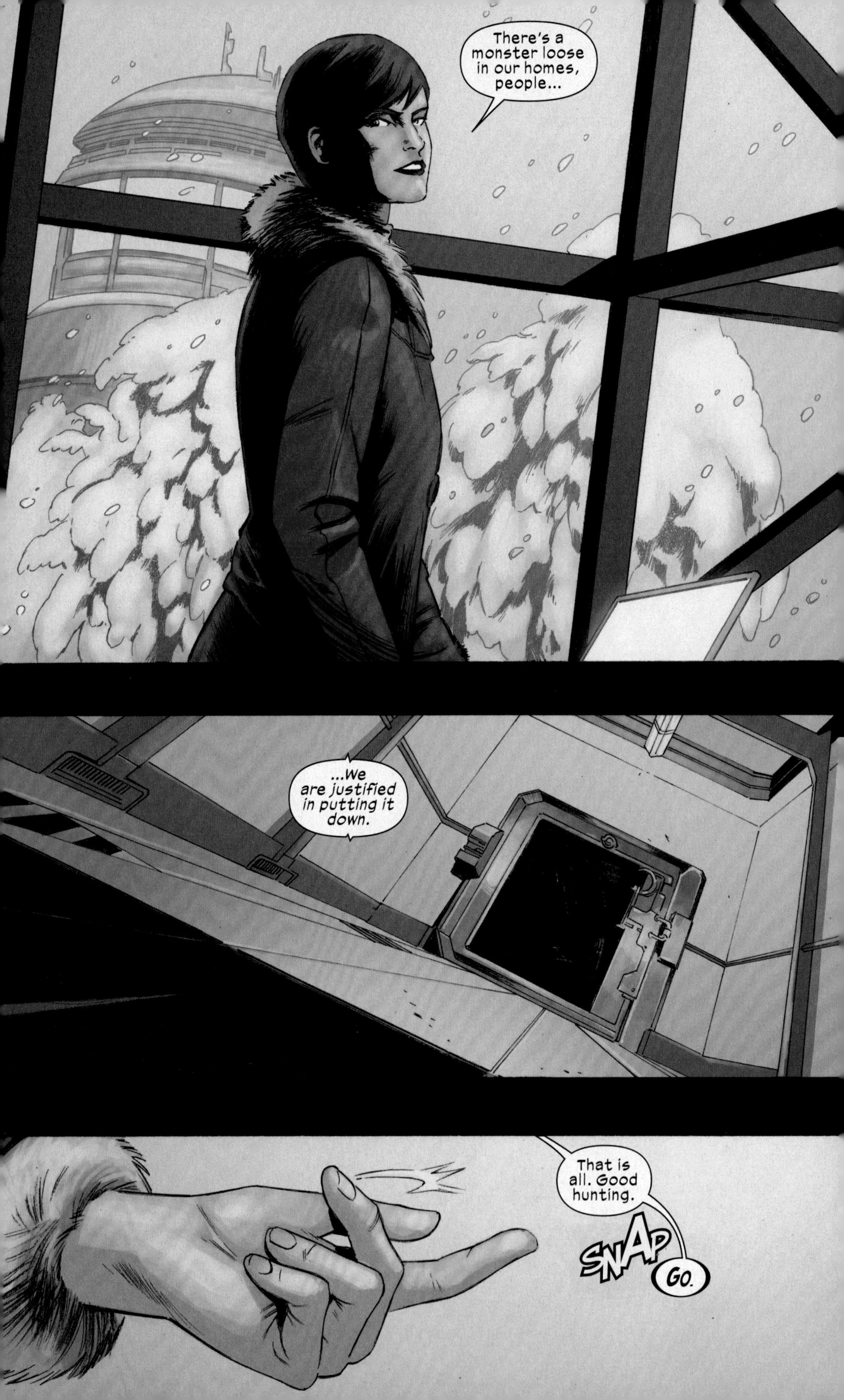
There's a monster loose in our homes, people...
...We are justified in putting it down.
That is all. Good hunting.
SNAP
GO.

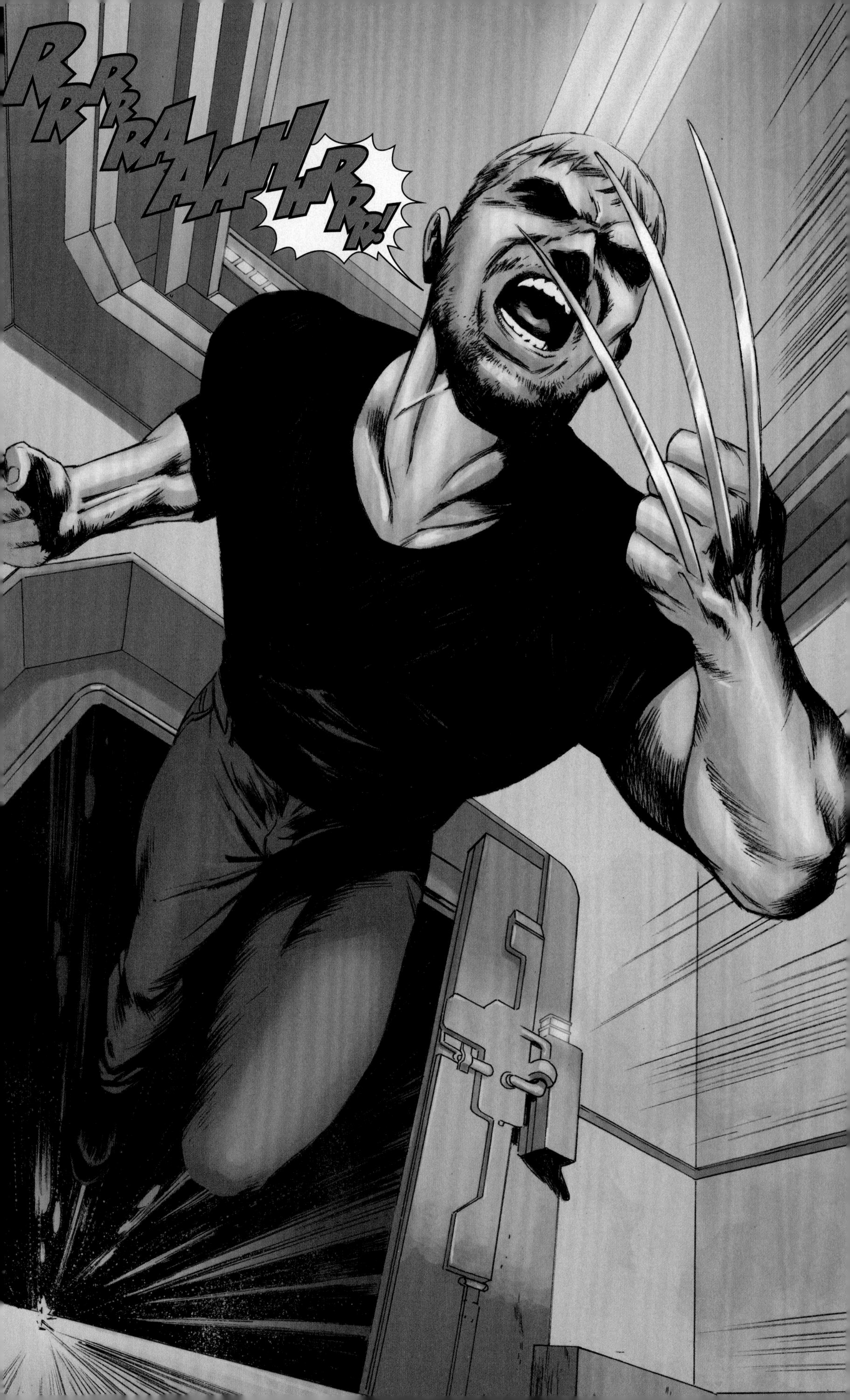
RRRRRAAAHRRR!

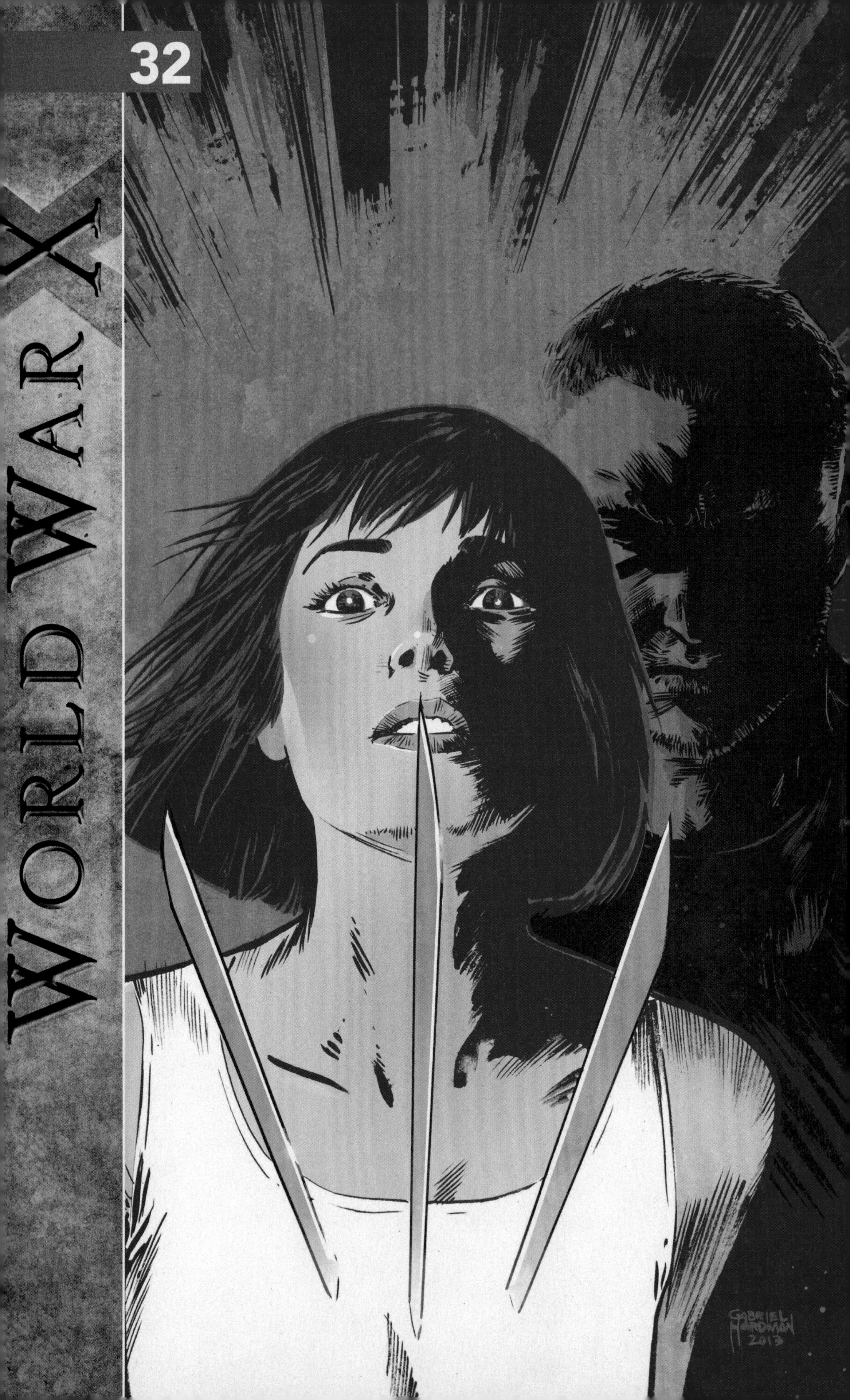
32
WORLD WAR X
GABRIEL HARDMAN 2013

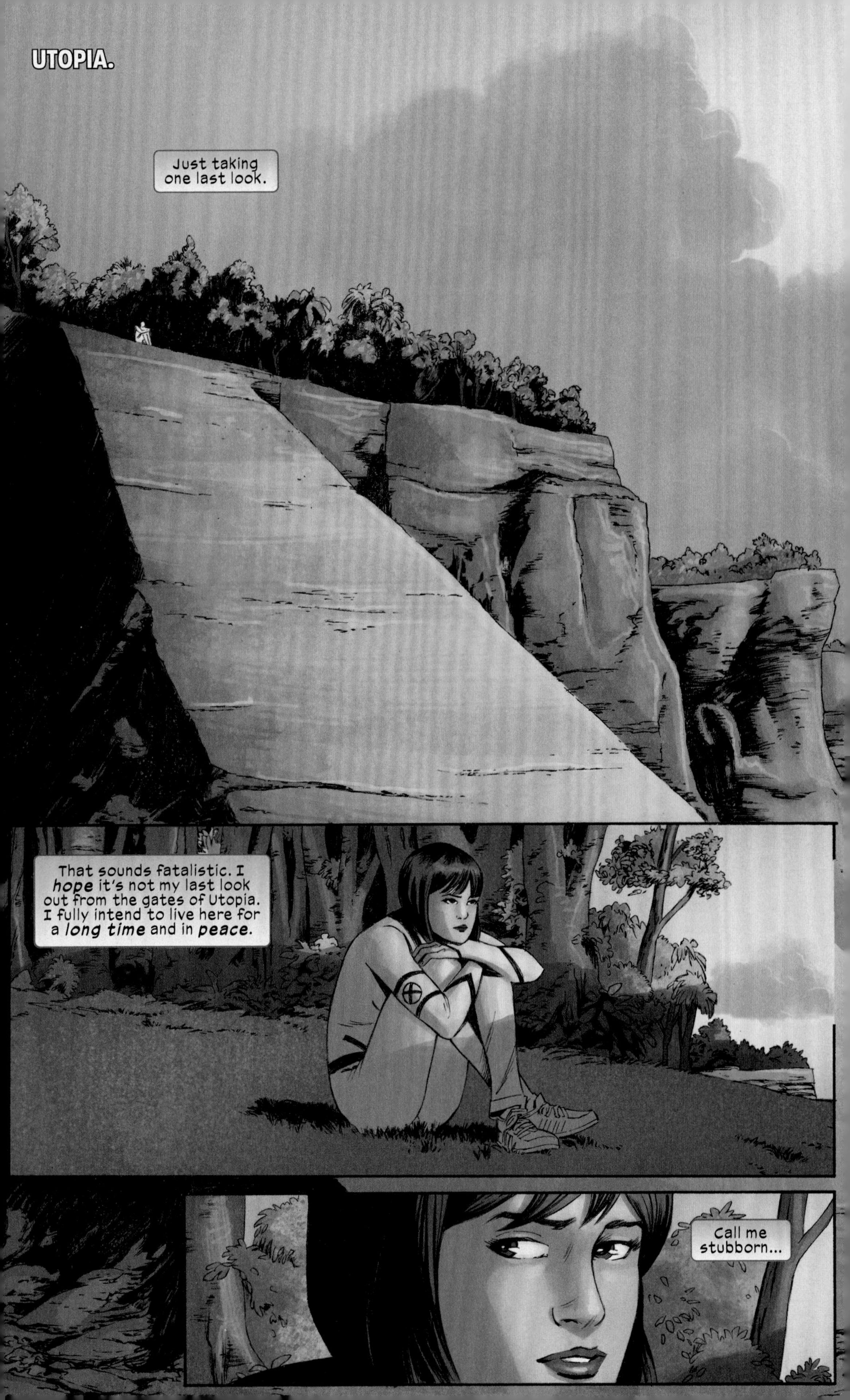
UTOPIA.
Just taking one last look.
That sounds fatalistic. I *hope* it's not my last look out from the gates of Utopia. I fully intend to live here for a *long time* and in *peace*.
Call me stubborn...

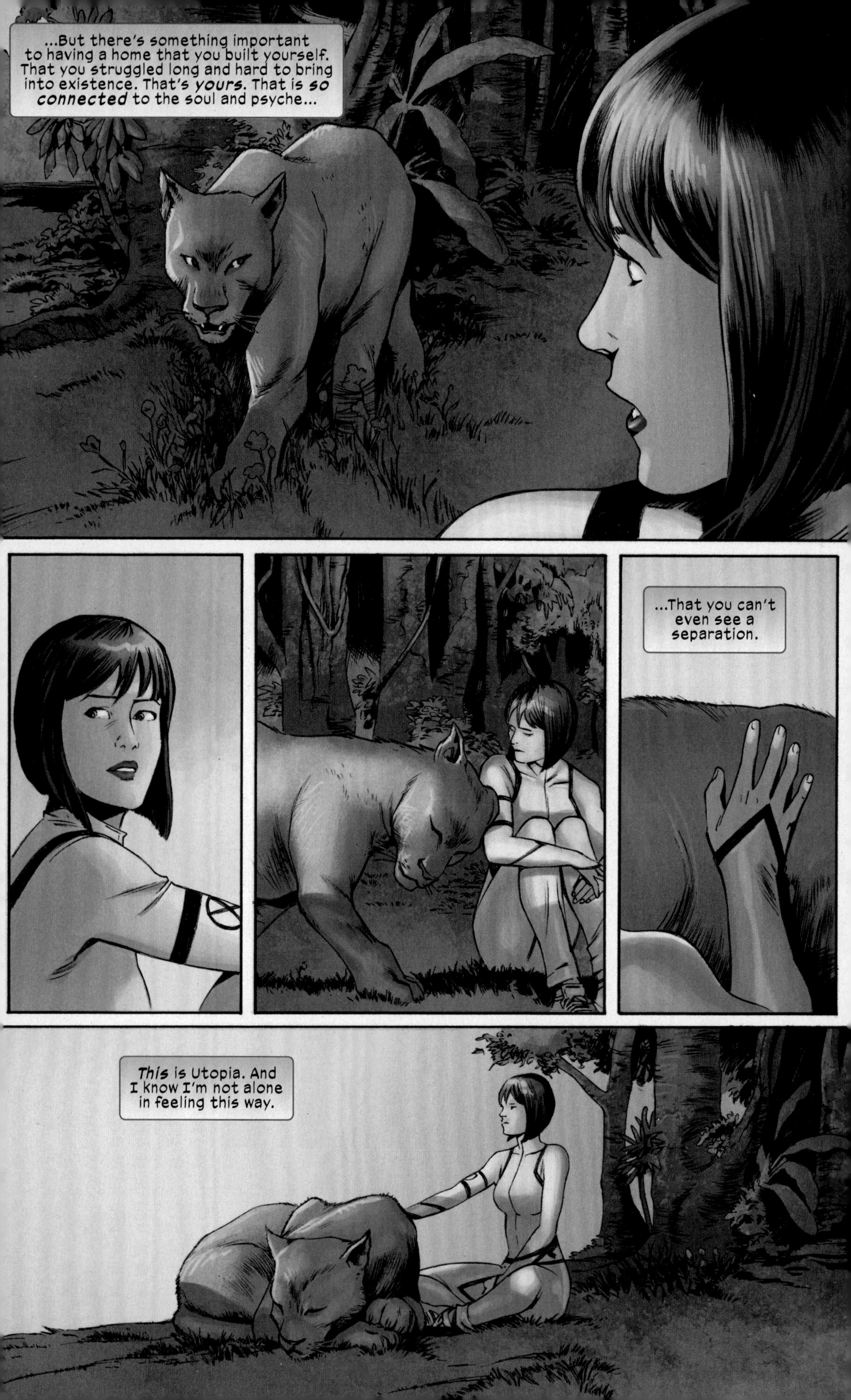
...But there's something important to having a home that you built yourself. That you struggled long and hard to bring into existence. That's *yours*. That is *so connected* to the soul and psyche...
...That you can't even see a separation.
This is Utopia. And I know I'm not alone in feeling this way.

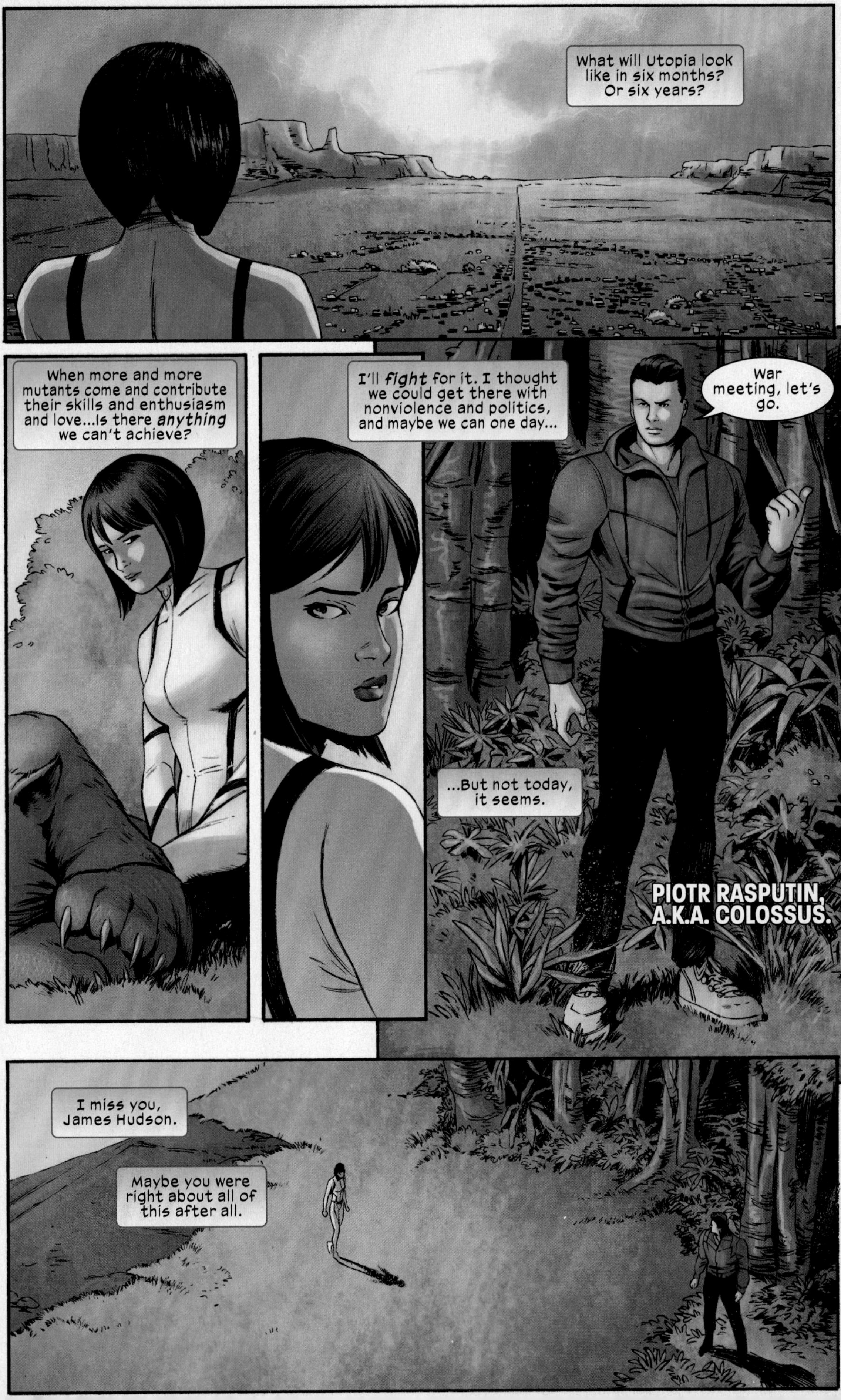
What will Utopia look like in six months? Or six years?
When more and more mutants come and contribute their skills and enthusiasm and love...is there *anything* we can't achieve?
I'll *fight* for it. I thought we could get there with nonviolence and politics, and maybe we can one day...
War meeting, let's go.
...But not today, it seems.
PIOTR RASPUTIN, A.K.A. COLOSSUS.
I miss you, James Hudson.
Maybe you were right about all of this after all.

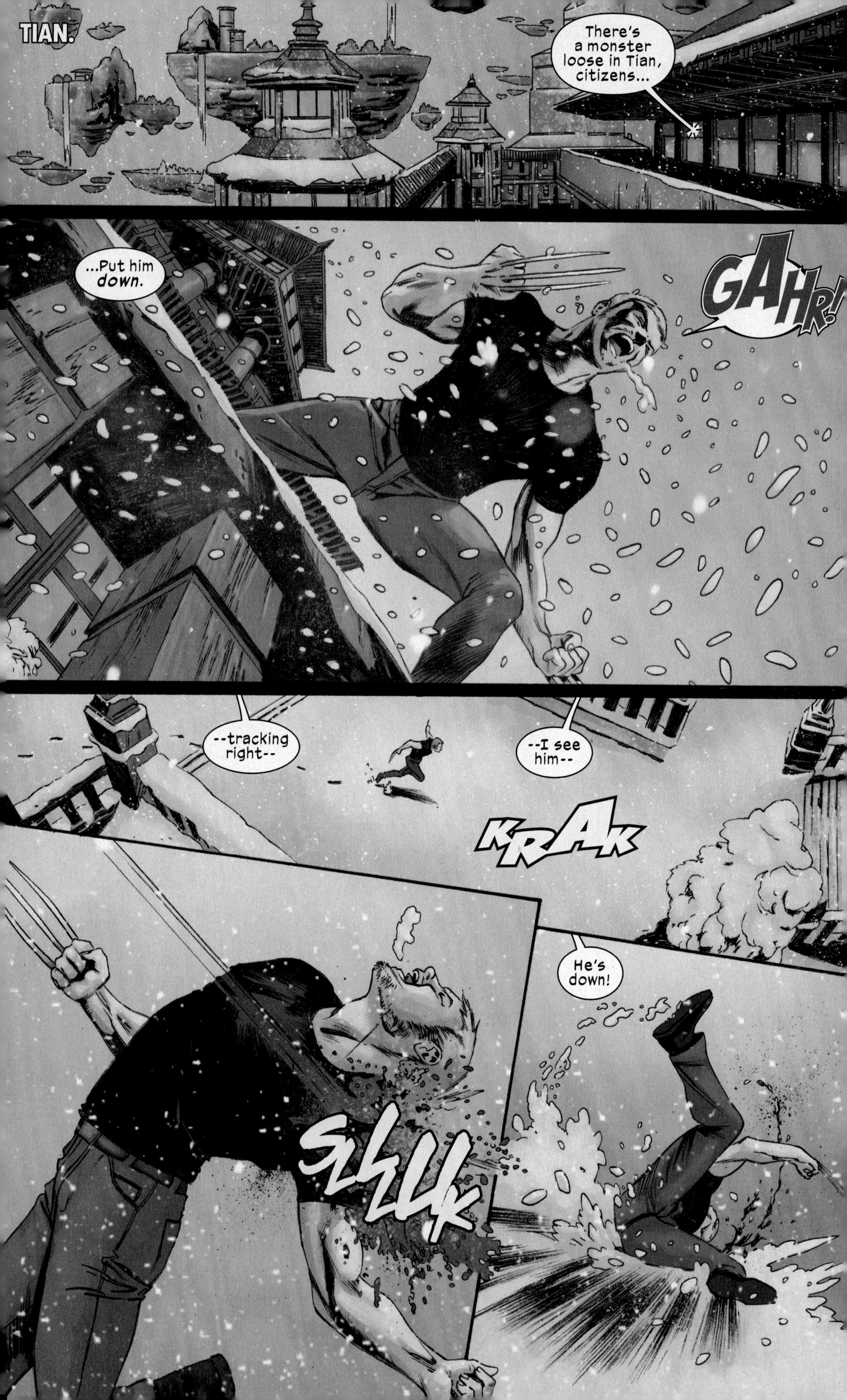
TIAN.
There's a monster loose in Tian, citizens...
...Put him down.
GAHR!
--tracking right--
--I see him--
KRAK
He's down!
SHLUK

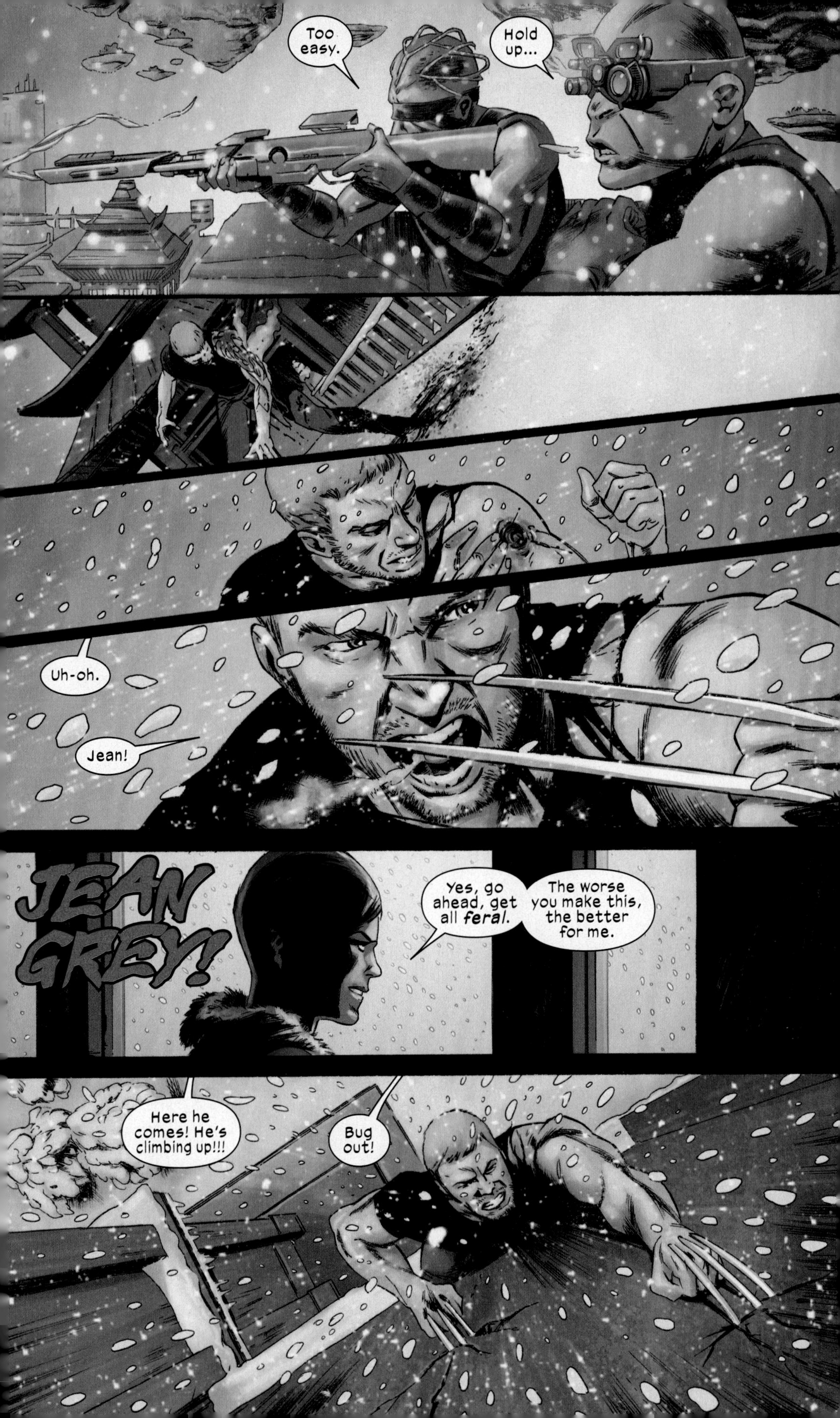
Too easy.
Hold up...
Uh-oh.
Jean!
JEAN GREY!
Yes, go ahead, get all *feral*.
The worse you make this, the better for me.
Here he comes! He's climbing up!!!
Bug out!

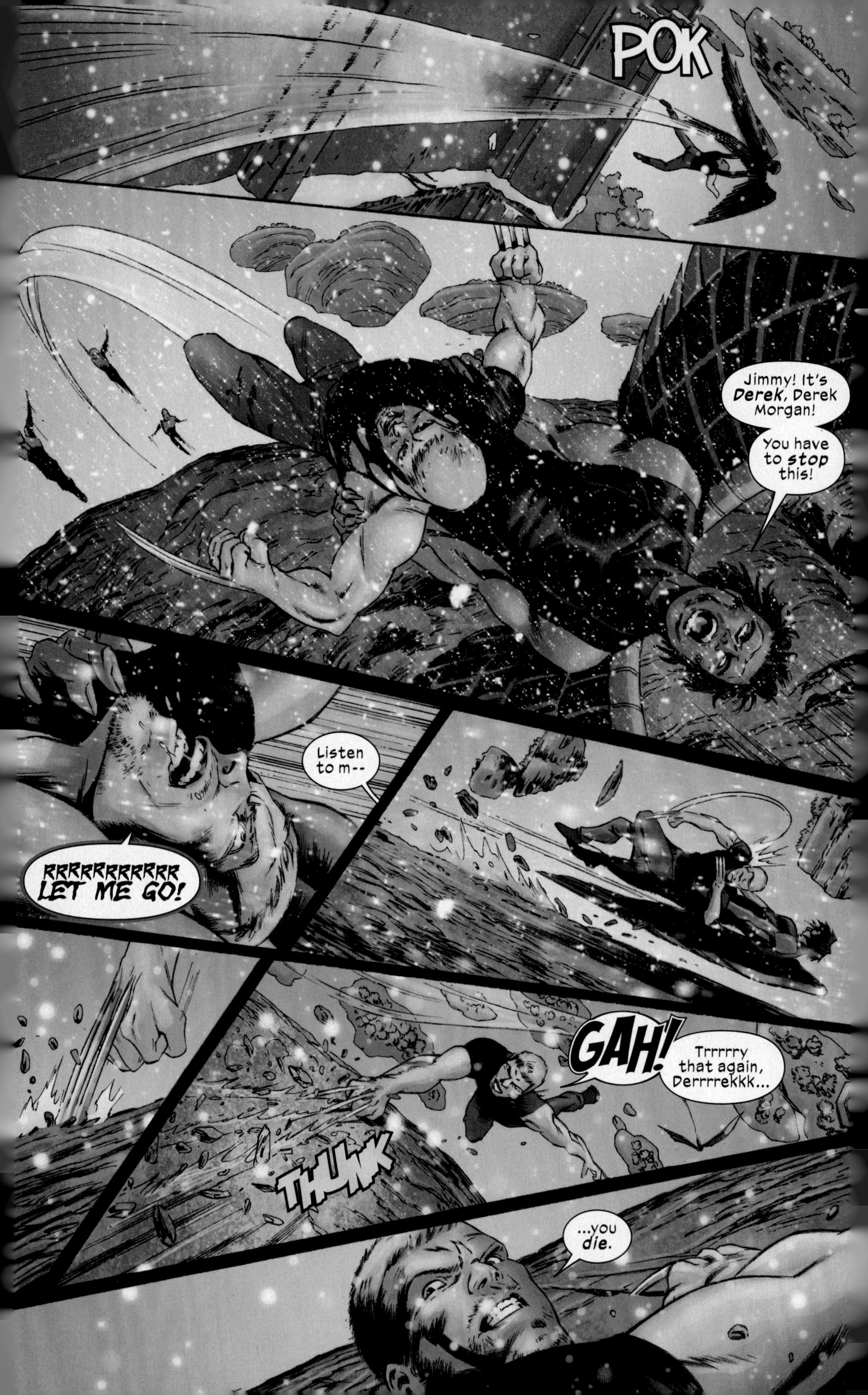
POK
Jimmy! It's Derek, Derek Morgan!
You have to stop this!
Listen to m--
RRRRRRRRRRR LET ME GO!
GAH!
Trrrrry that again, Derrrrekkk...
THUNK
...you die.

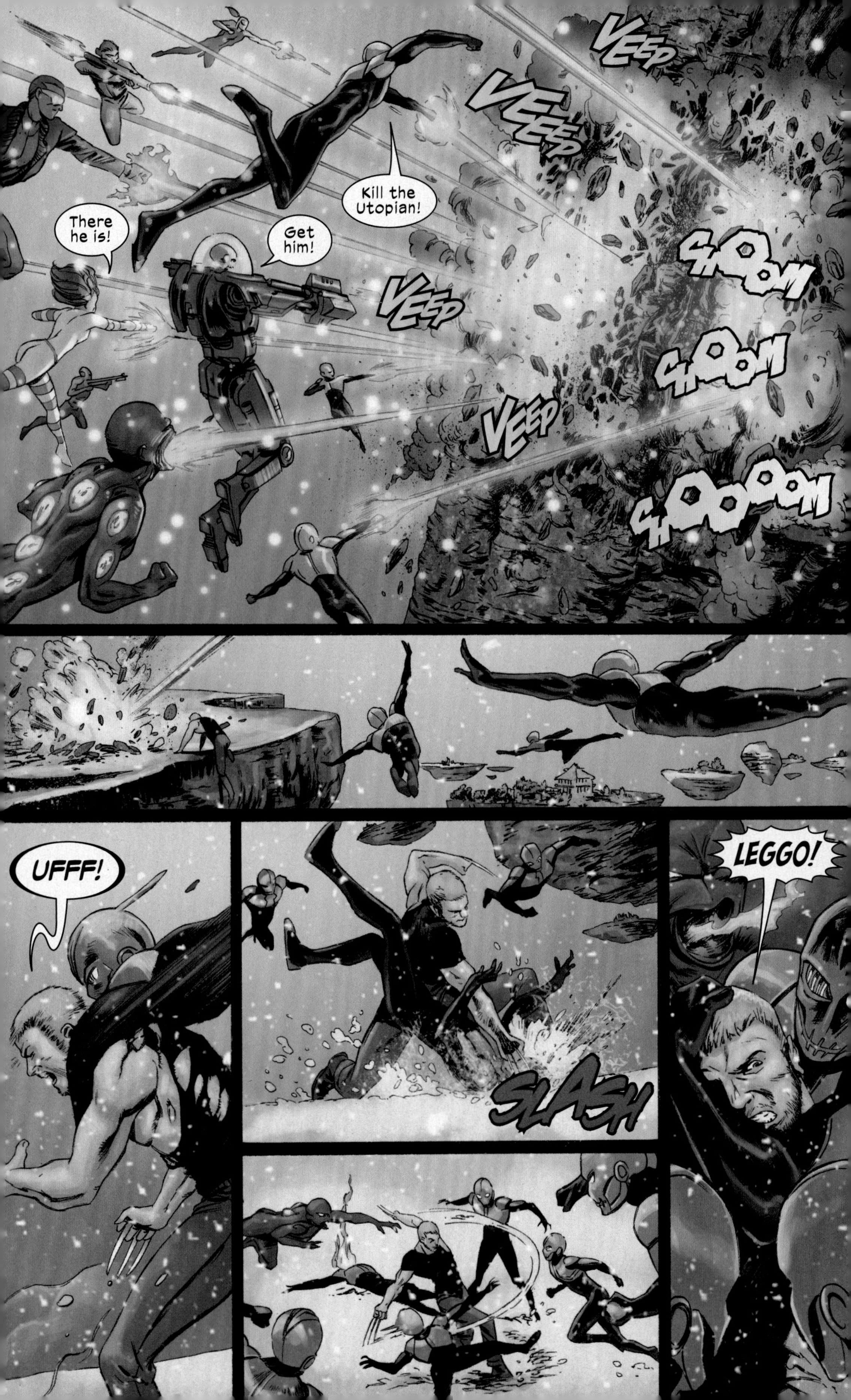
VEEP
VEEEP
Kill the Utopian!
There he is!
Get him!
VEEP
CHOOOM
CHOOM
VEEP
CHOOOOOM
UFFF!
SLASH
LEGGO!

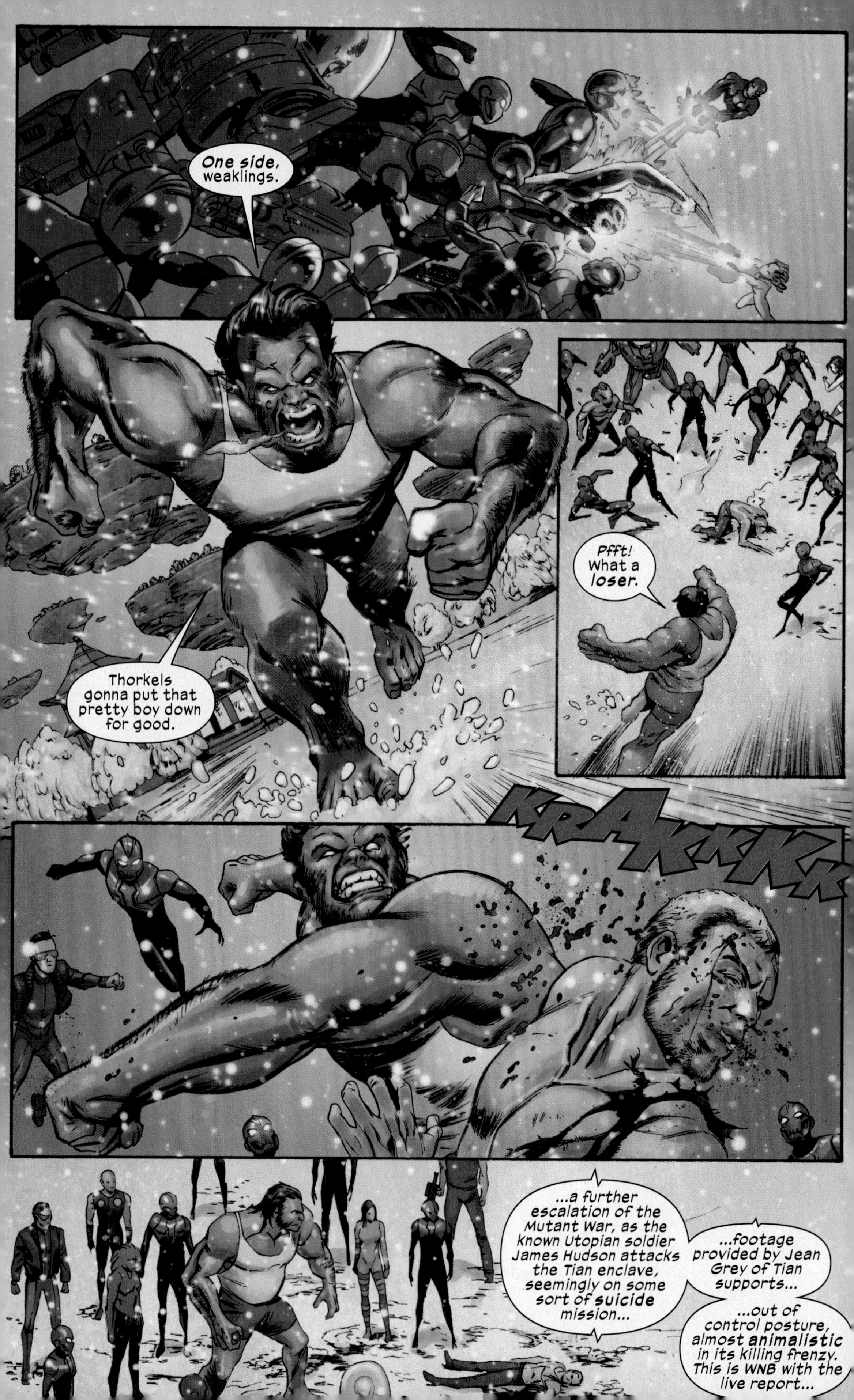
One side, weaklings.
Thorkels gonna put that pretty boy down for good.
Pfft! What a loser.
KRAKKKK
...a further escalation of the Mutant War, as the known Utopian soldier James Hudson attacks the Tian enclave, seemingly on some sort of suicide mission...
...footage provided by Jean Grey of Tian supports...
...out of control posture, almost animalistic in its killing frenzy. This is WNB with the live report...

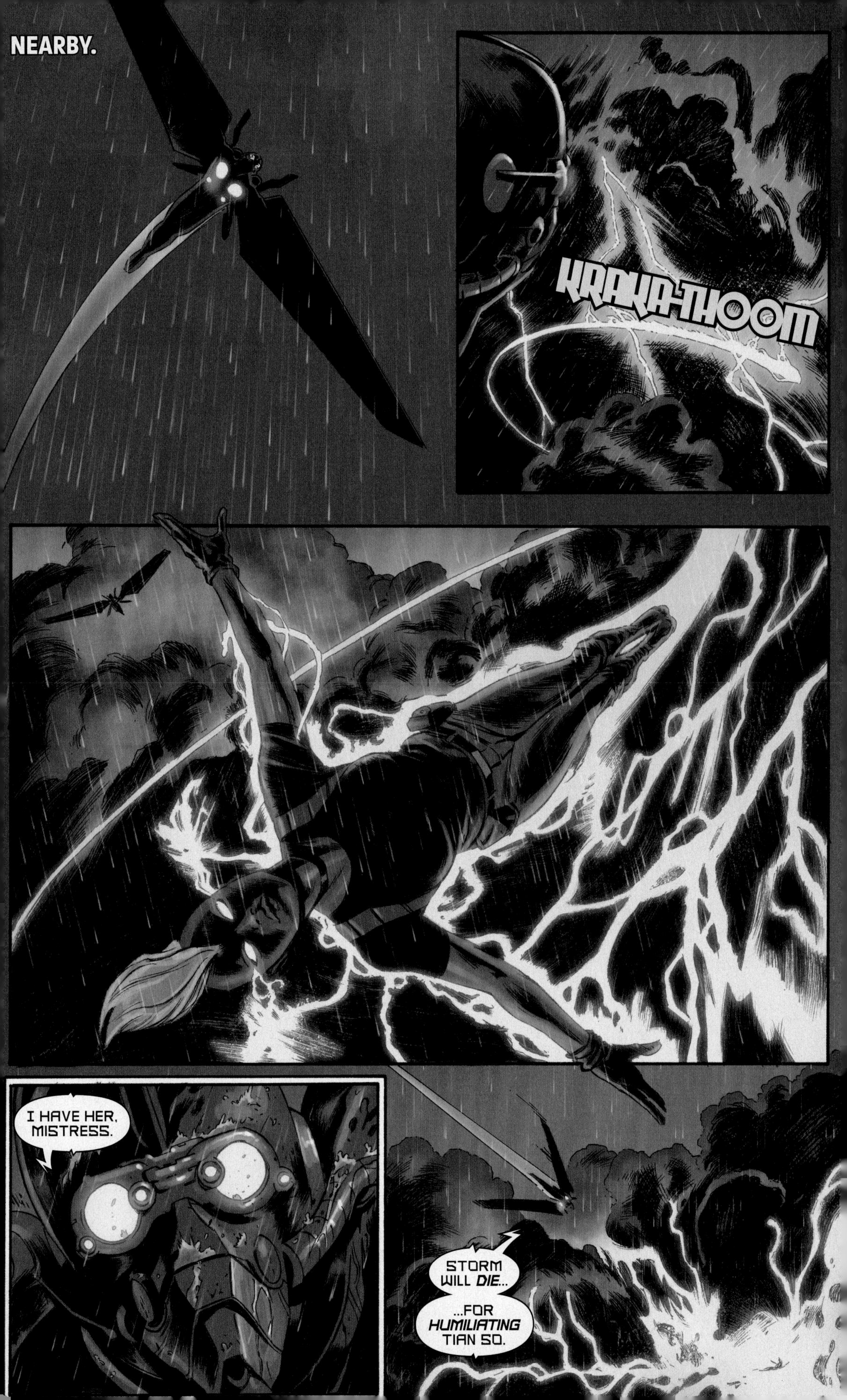
NEARBY.
KRAKA-THOOM
I HAVE HER, MISTRESS.
STORM WILL DIE...
...FOR HUMILIATING TIAN SO.

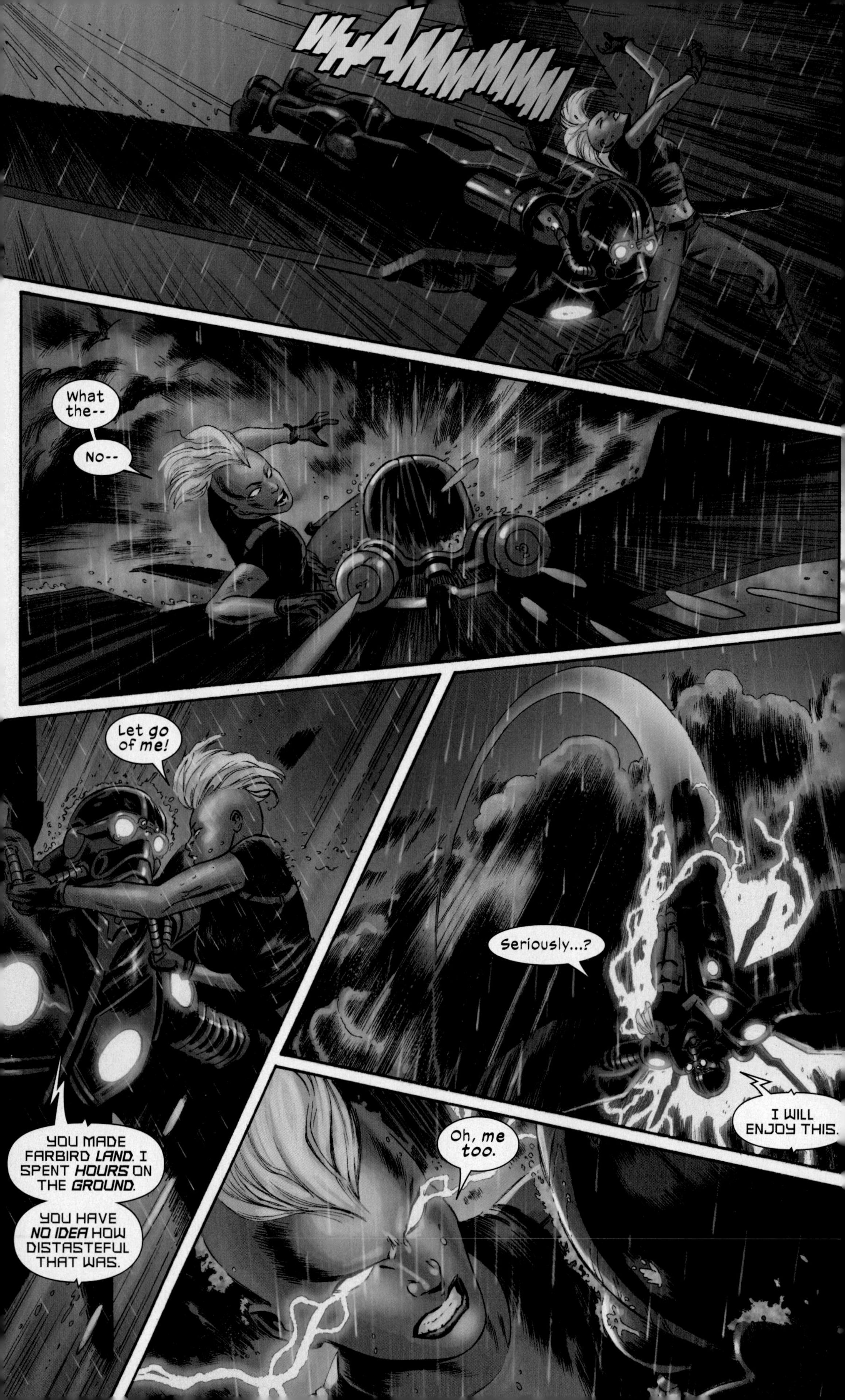
WHAMMMMM
What the--
No--
Let go of me!
YOU MADE FARBIRD LAND. I SPENT HOURS ON THE GROUND.
YOU HAVE NO IDEA HOW DISTASTEFUL THAT WAS.
Seriously...?
I WILL ENJOY THIS.
Oh, me too.

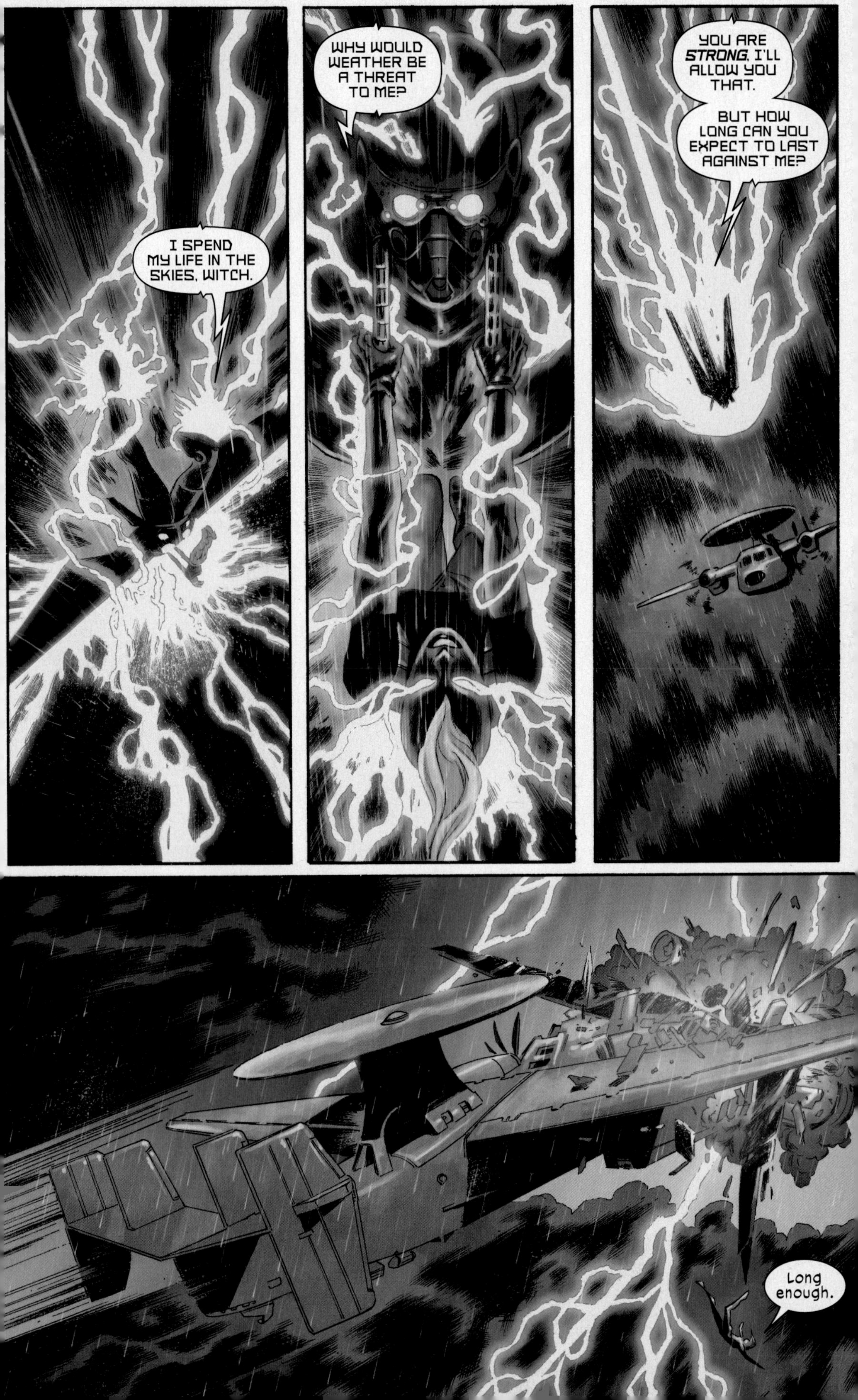
I SPEND MY LIFE IN THE SKIES, WITCH.
WHY WOULD WEATHER BE A THREAT TO ME?
YOU ARE STRONG, I'LL ALLOW YOU THAT.
BUT HOW LONG CAN YOU EXPECT TO LAST AGAINST ME?
Long enough.

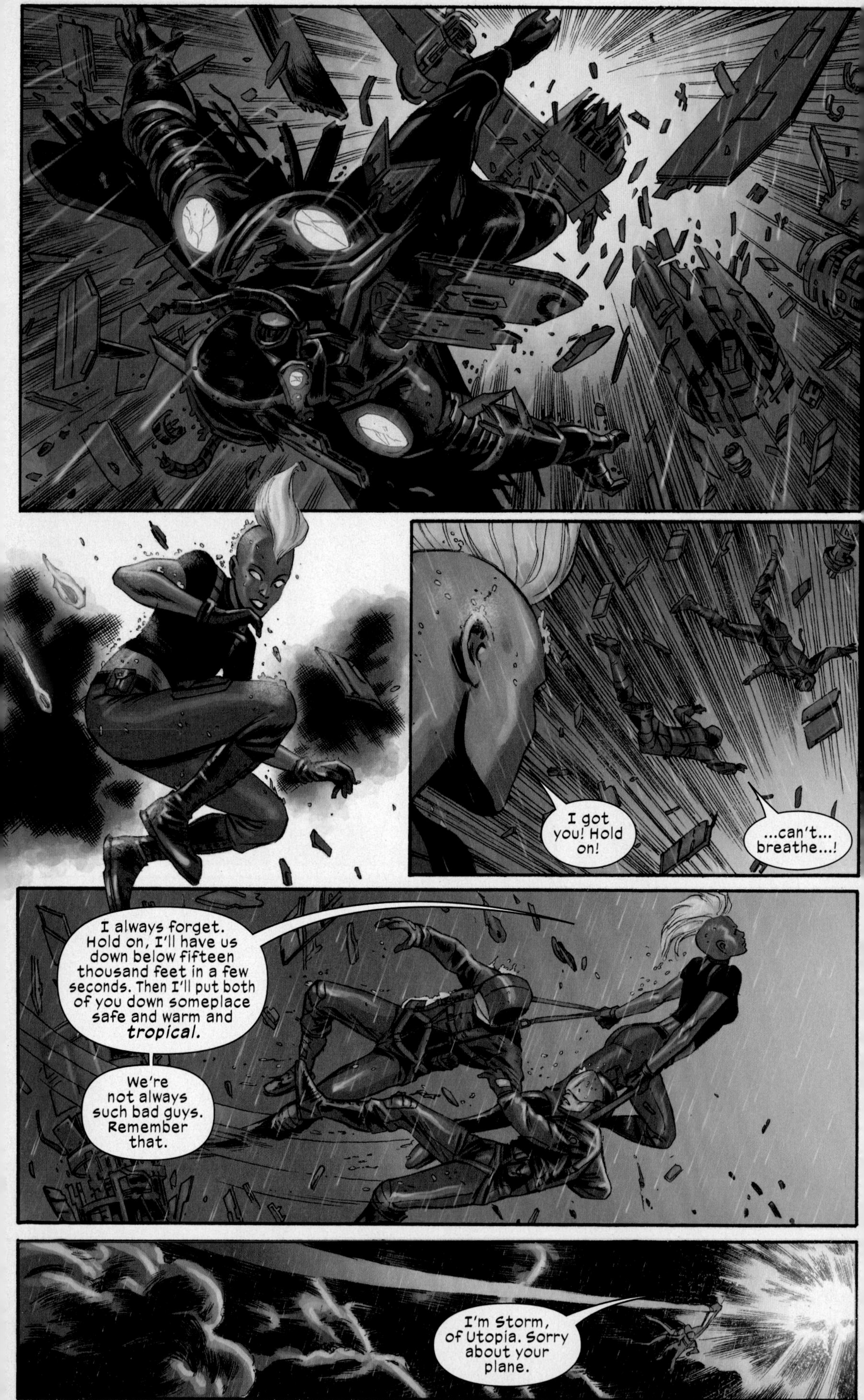
I got you! Hold on!
...can't... breathe...!
I always forget. Hold on, I'll have us down below fifteen thousand feet in a few seconds. Then I'll put both of you down someplace safe and warm and *tropical.*
We're not always such bad guys. Remember that.
I'm Storm, of Utopia. Sorry about your plane.

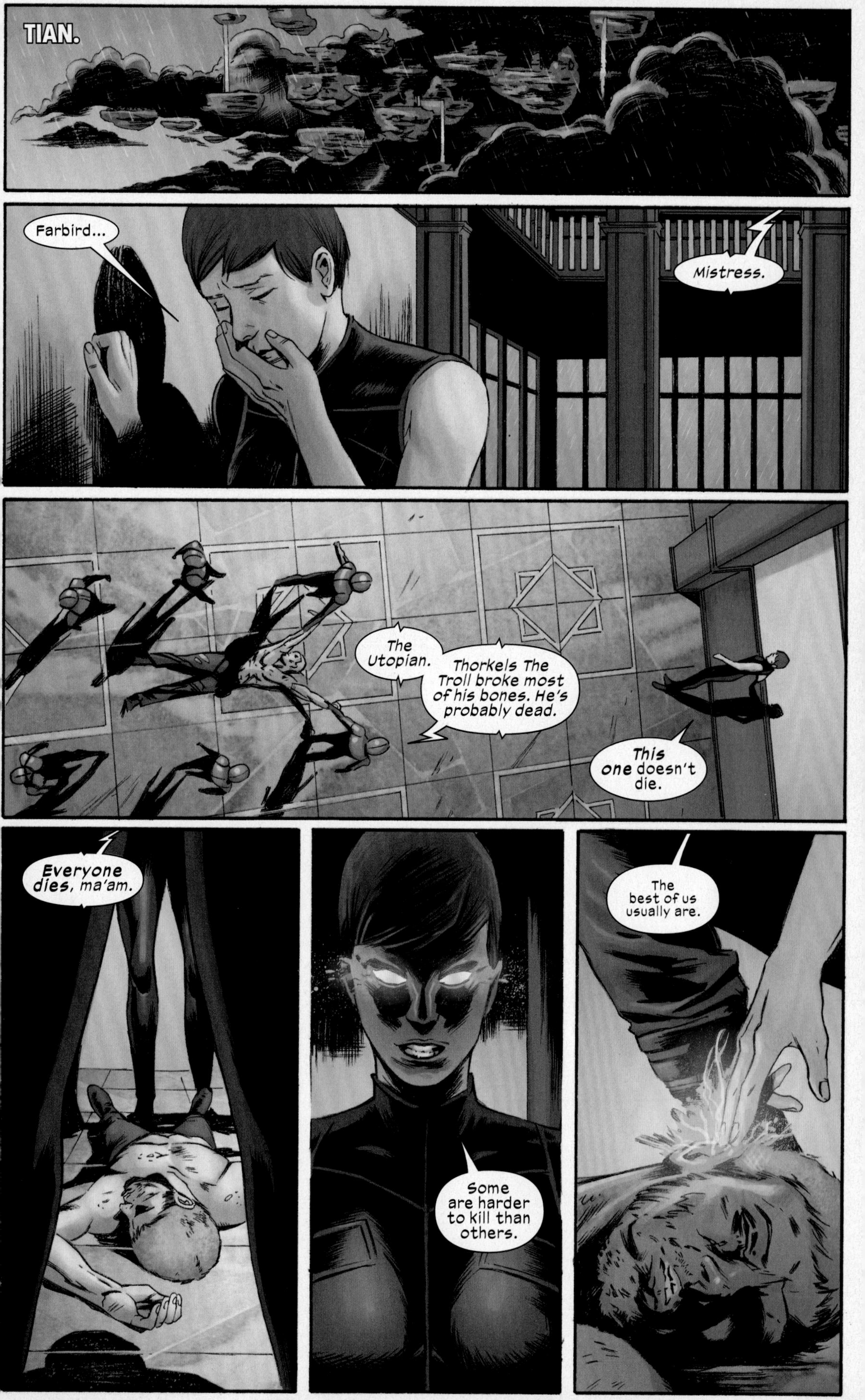
TIAN.
Farbird...
Mistress.
The Utopian.
Thorkels The Troll broke most of his bones. He's probably dead.
This one doesn't die.
Everyone dies, ma'am.
Some are harder to kill than others.
The best of us usually are.

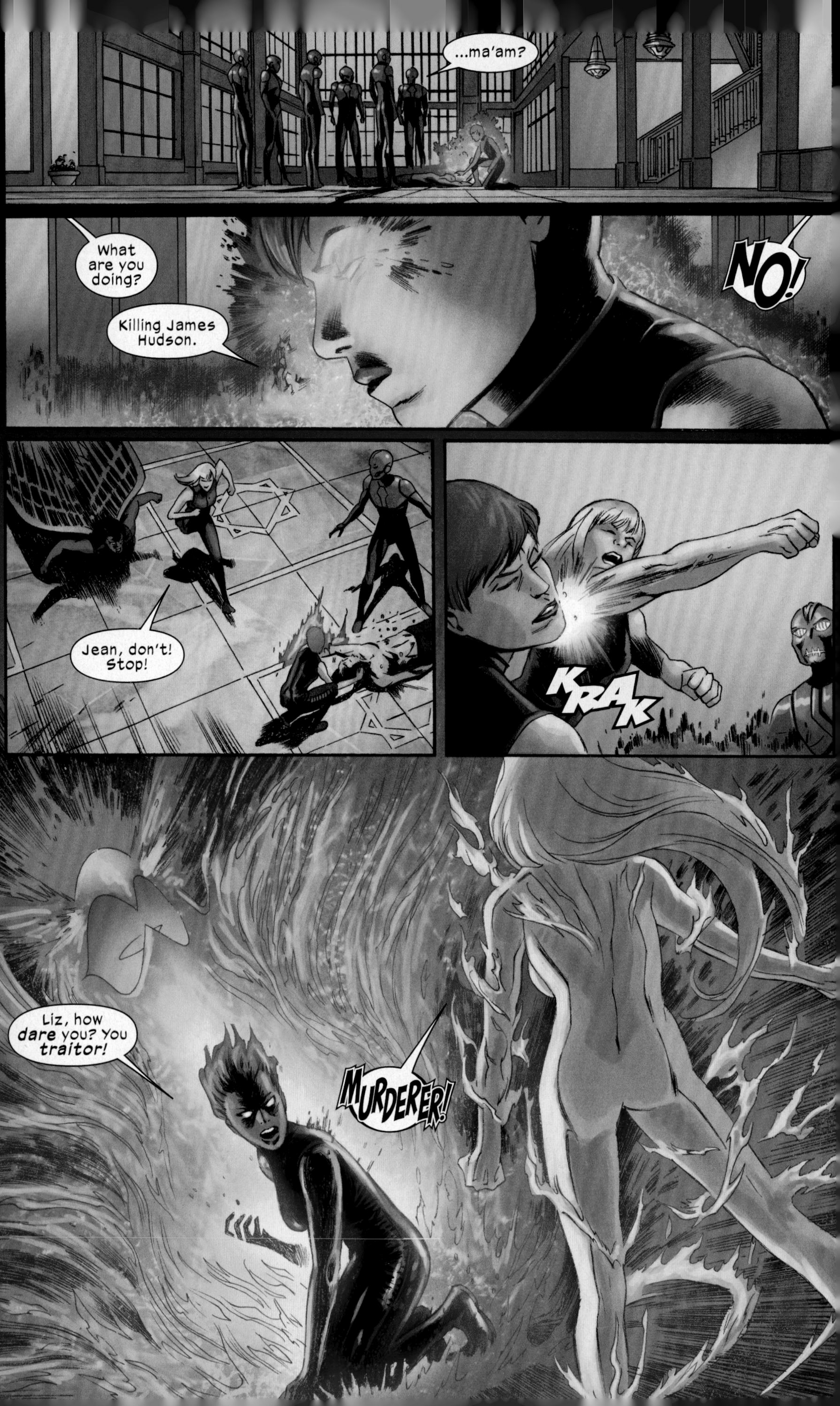
...ma'am?
What are you doing?
Killing James Hudson.
NO!
Jean, don't! Stop!
KRAK
Liz, how dare you? You traitor!
MURDERER!

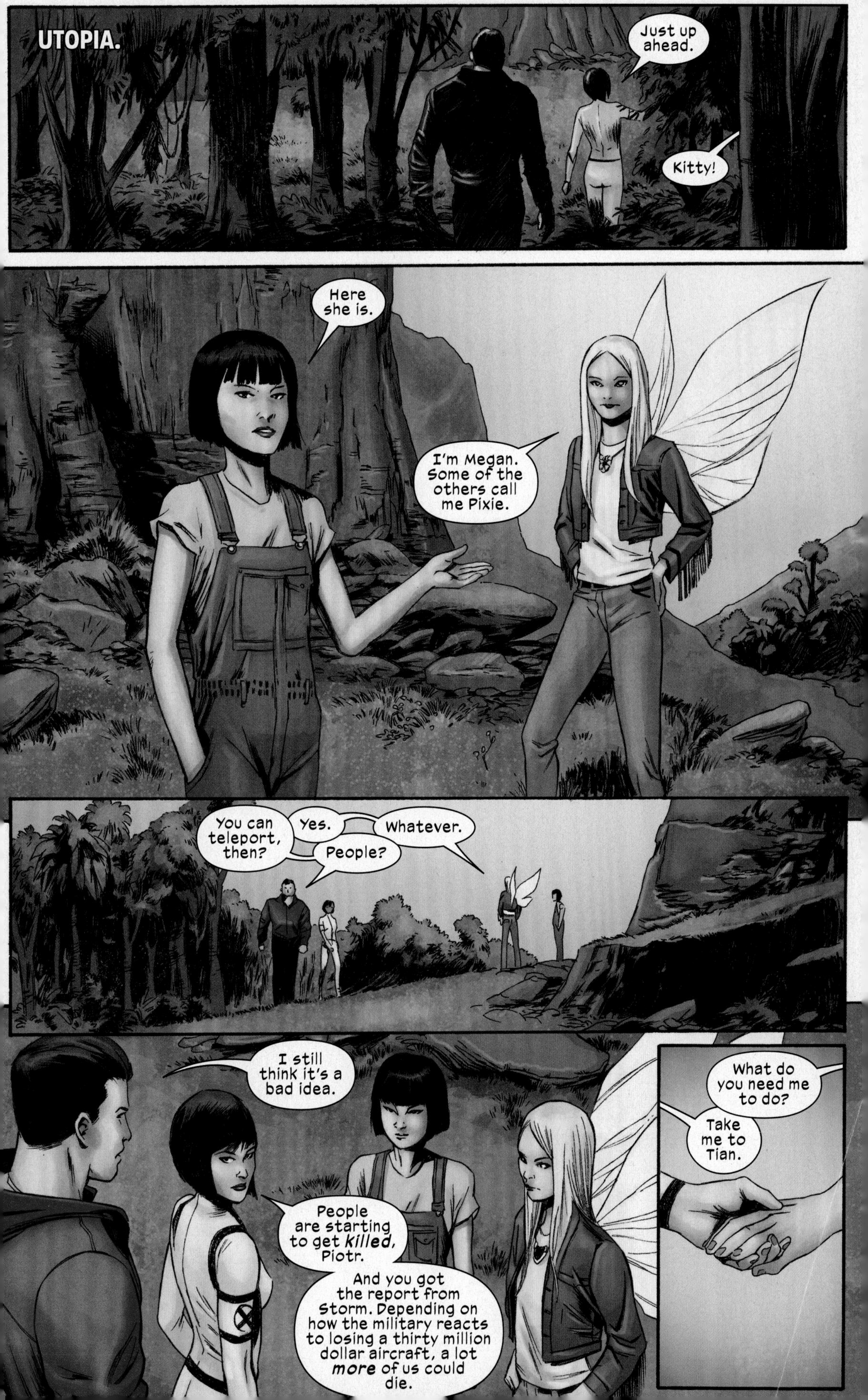
UTOPIA.
Just up ahead.
Kitty!
Here she is.
I'm Megan. Some of the others call me Pixie.
You can teleport, then?
Yes.
People?
Whatever.
I still think it's a bad idea.
People are starting to get *killed*, Piotr.
And you got the report from Storm. Depending on how the military reacts to losing a thirty million dollar aircraft, a lot *more* of us could die.
What do you need me to do?
Take me to Tian.

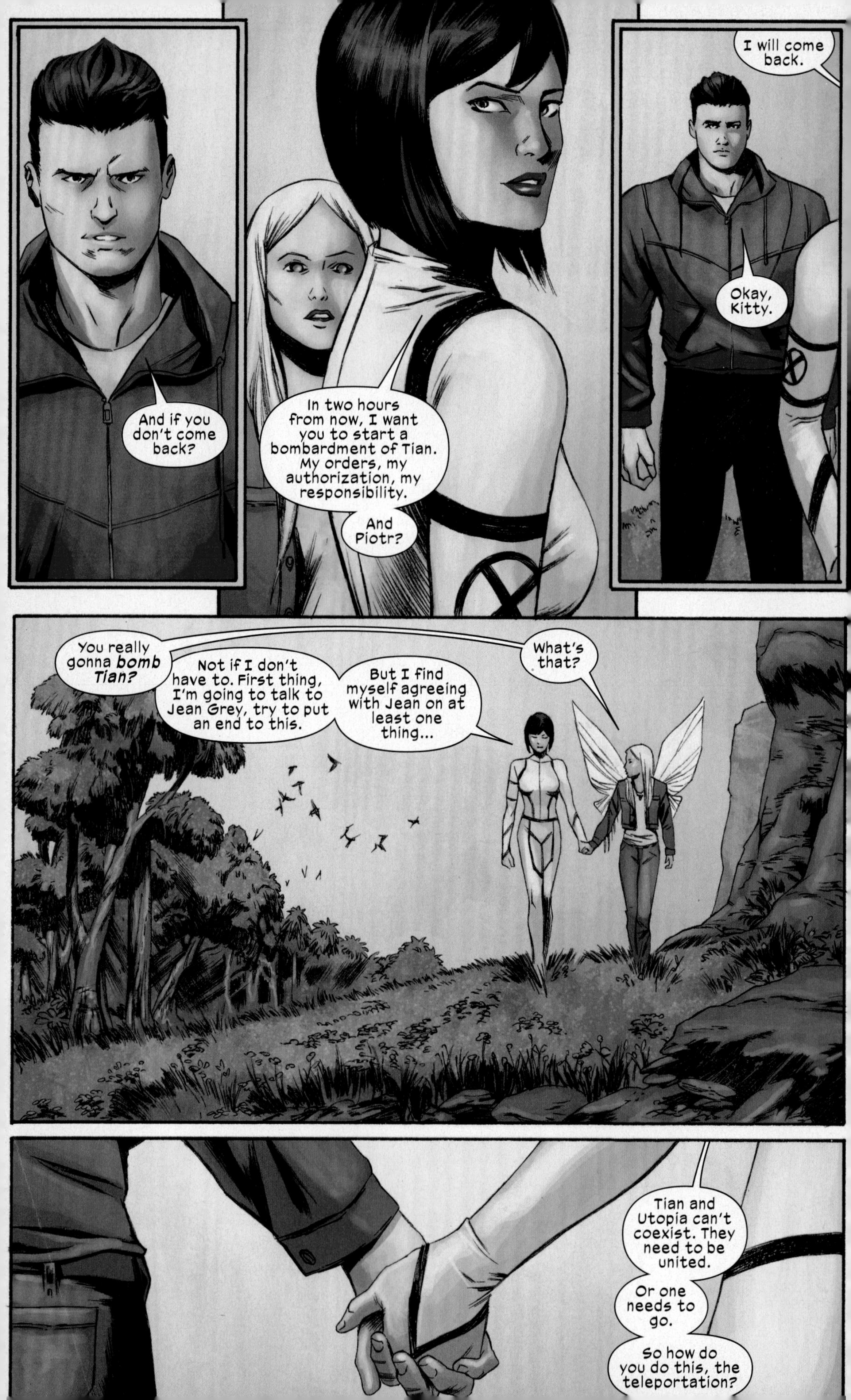

And if you don't come back?
In two hours from now, I want you to start a bombardment of Tian. My orders, my authorization, my responsibility.
And Piotr?
I will come back.
Okay, Kitty.
You really gonna *bomb Tian?*
Not if I don't have to. First thing, I'm going to talk to Jean Grey, try to put an end to this.
But I find myself agreeing with Jean on at least one thing...
What's that?
Tian and Utopia can't coexist. They need to be united.
Or one needs to go.
So how do you do this, the teleportation?

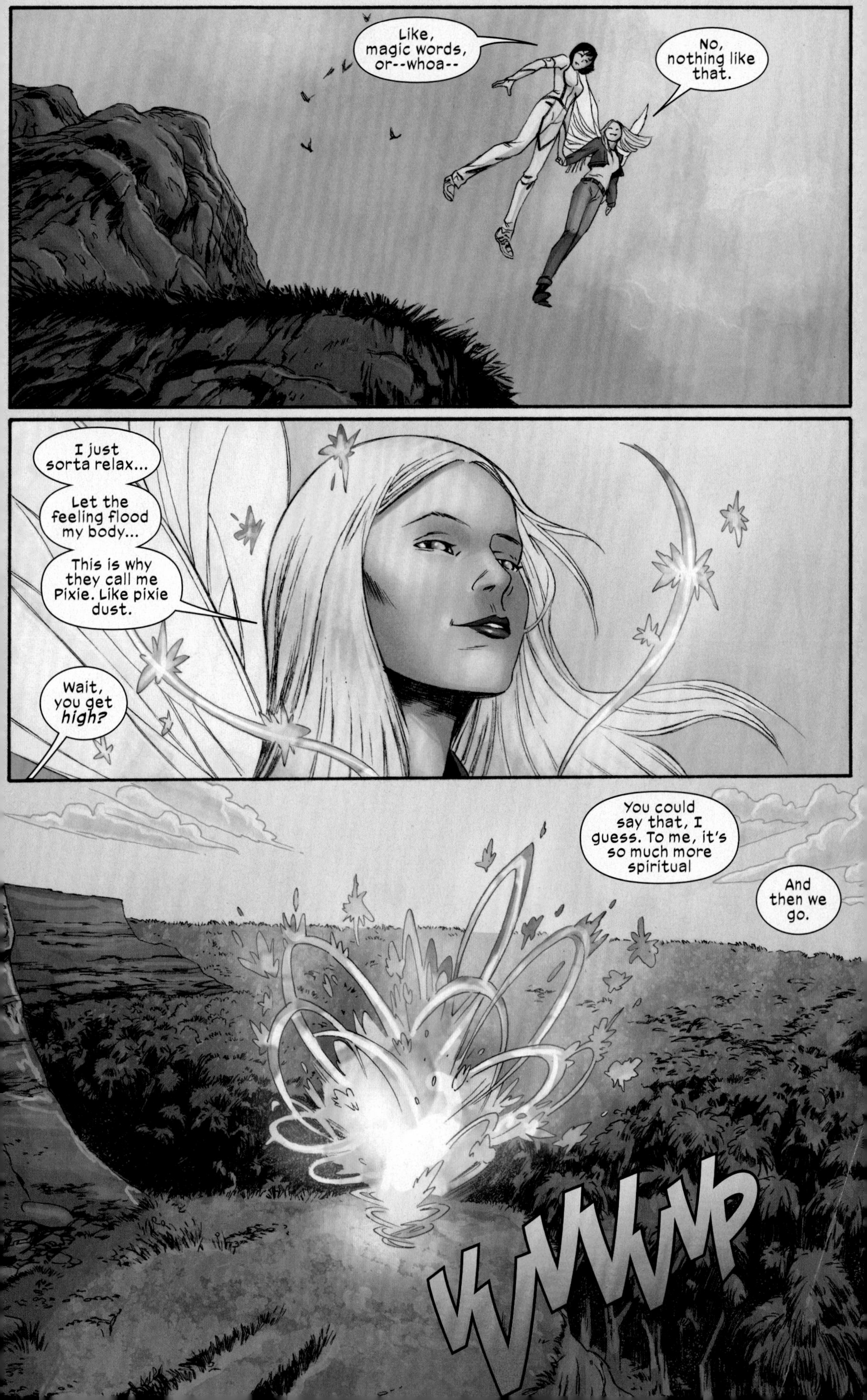

Like, magic words, or--whoa--
No, nothing like that.
I just sorta relax...
Let the feeling flood my body...
This is why they call me Pixie. Like pixie dust.
Wait, you get *high?*
You could say that, I guess. To me, it's so much more spiritual
And then we go.
WWWWP

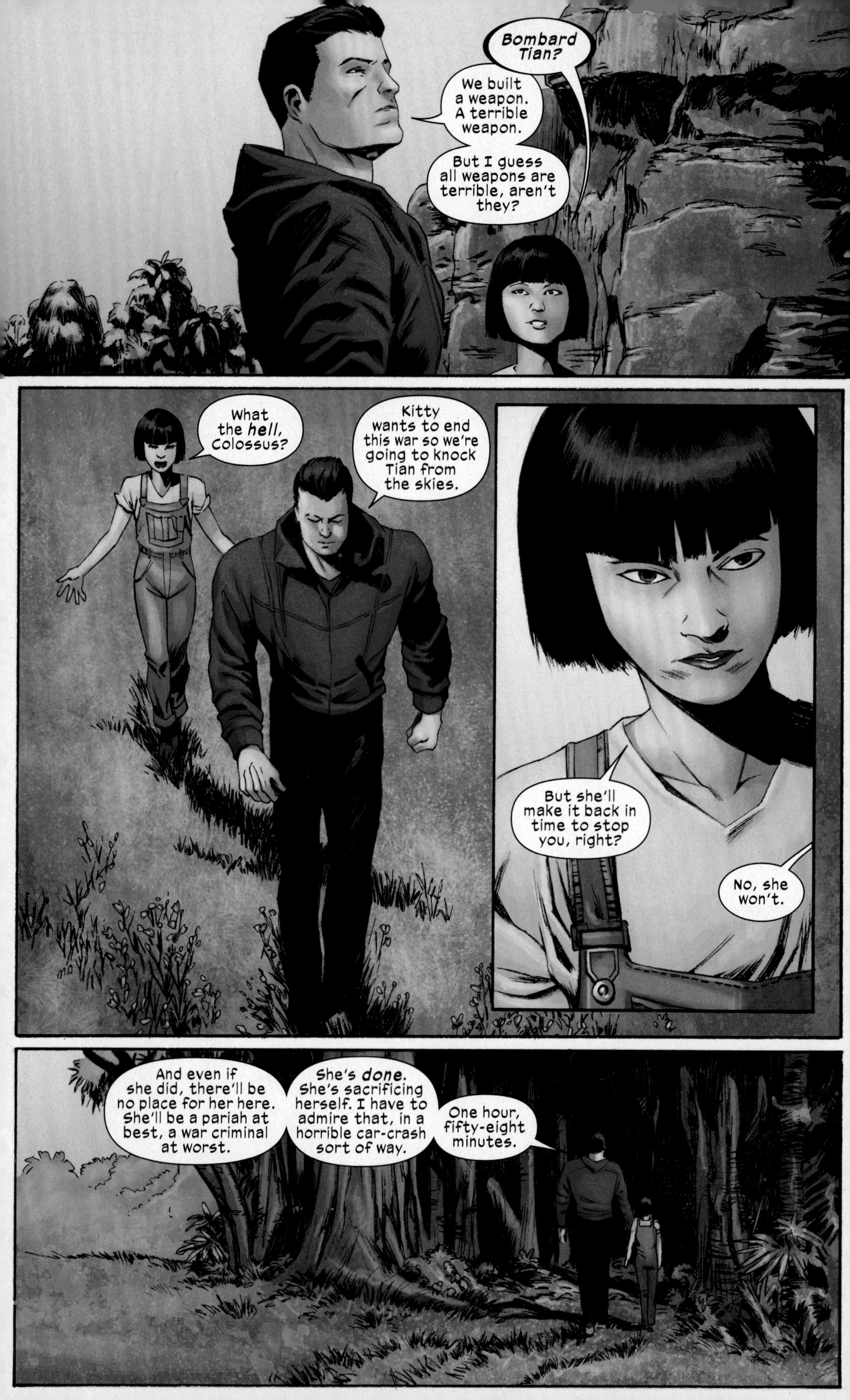
Bombard Tian?
We built a weapon. A terrible weapon.
But I guess all weapons are terrible, aren't they?
What the *hell*, Colossus?
Kitty wants to end this war so we're going to knock Tian from the skies.
But she'll make it back in time to stop you, right?
No, she won't.
And even if she did, there'll be no place for her here. She'll be a pariah at best, a war criminal at worst.
She's *done*. She's sacrificing herself. I have to admire that, in a horrible car-crash sort of way.
One hour, fifty-eight minutes.

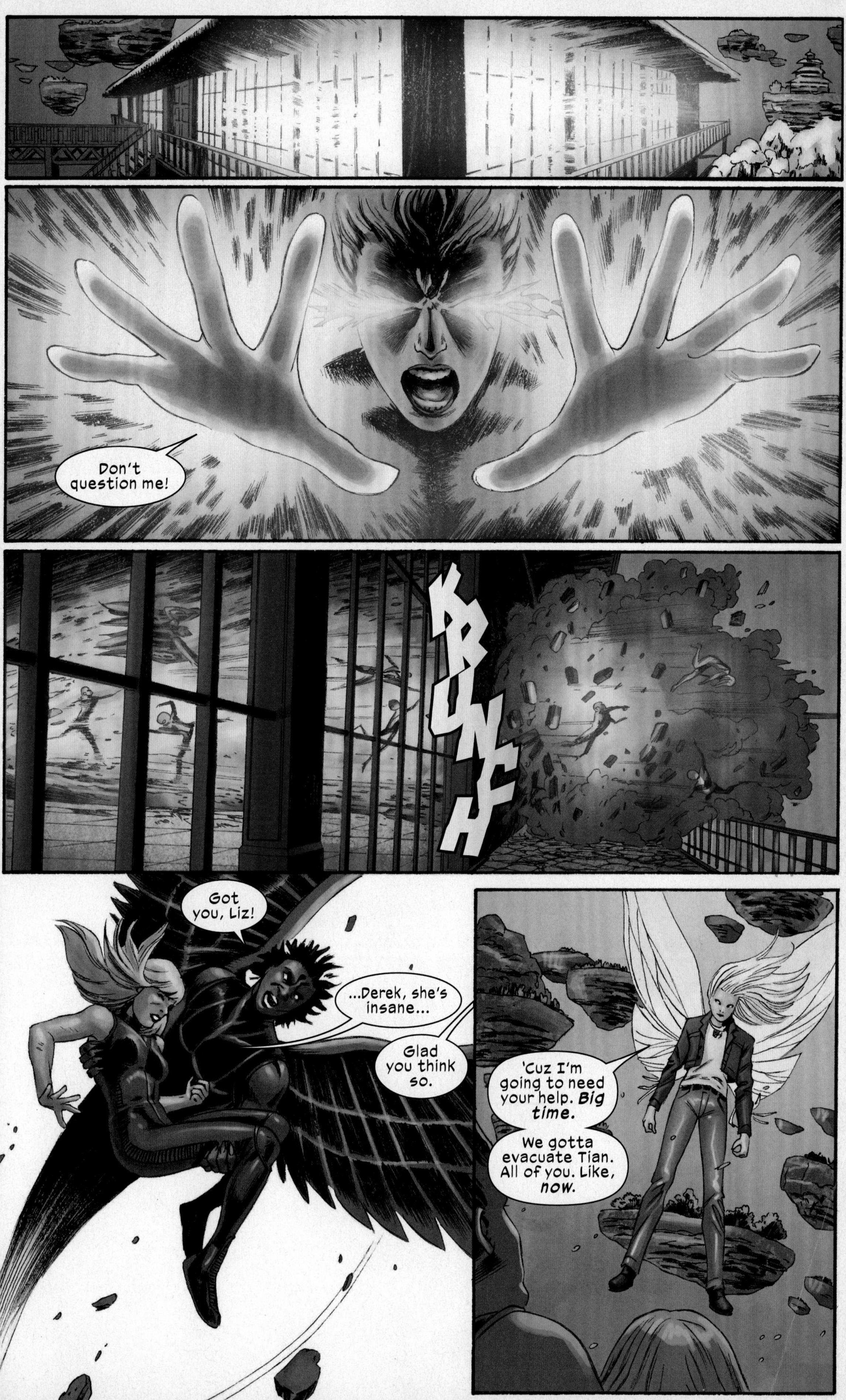
Don't question me!
KRUNCH
Got you, Liz!
...Derek, she's insane...
Glad you think so.
'Cuz I'm going to need your help. *Big time.*
We gotta evacuate Tian. All of you. Like, *now.*

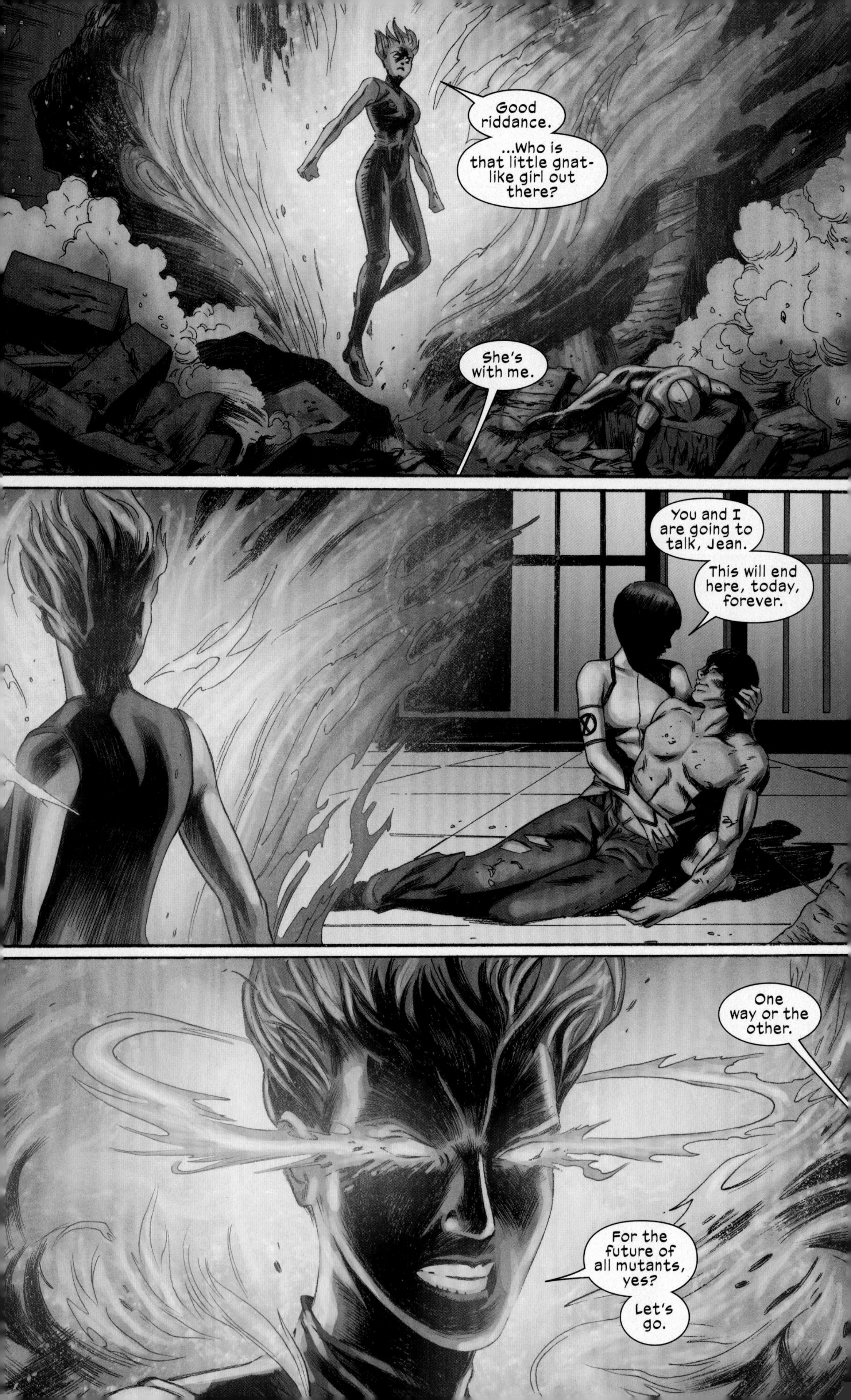
Good riddance.
...Who is that little gnat-like girl out there?
She's with me.
You and I are going to talk, Jean.
This will end here, today, forever.
One way or the other.
For the future of all mutants, yes?
Let's go.

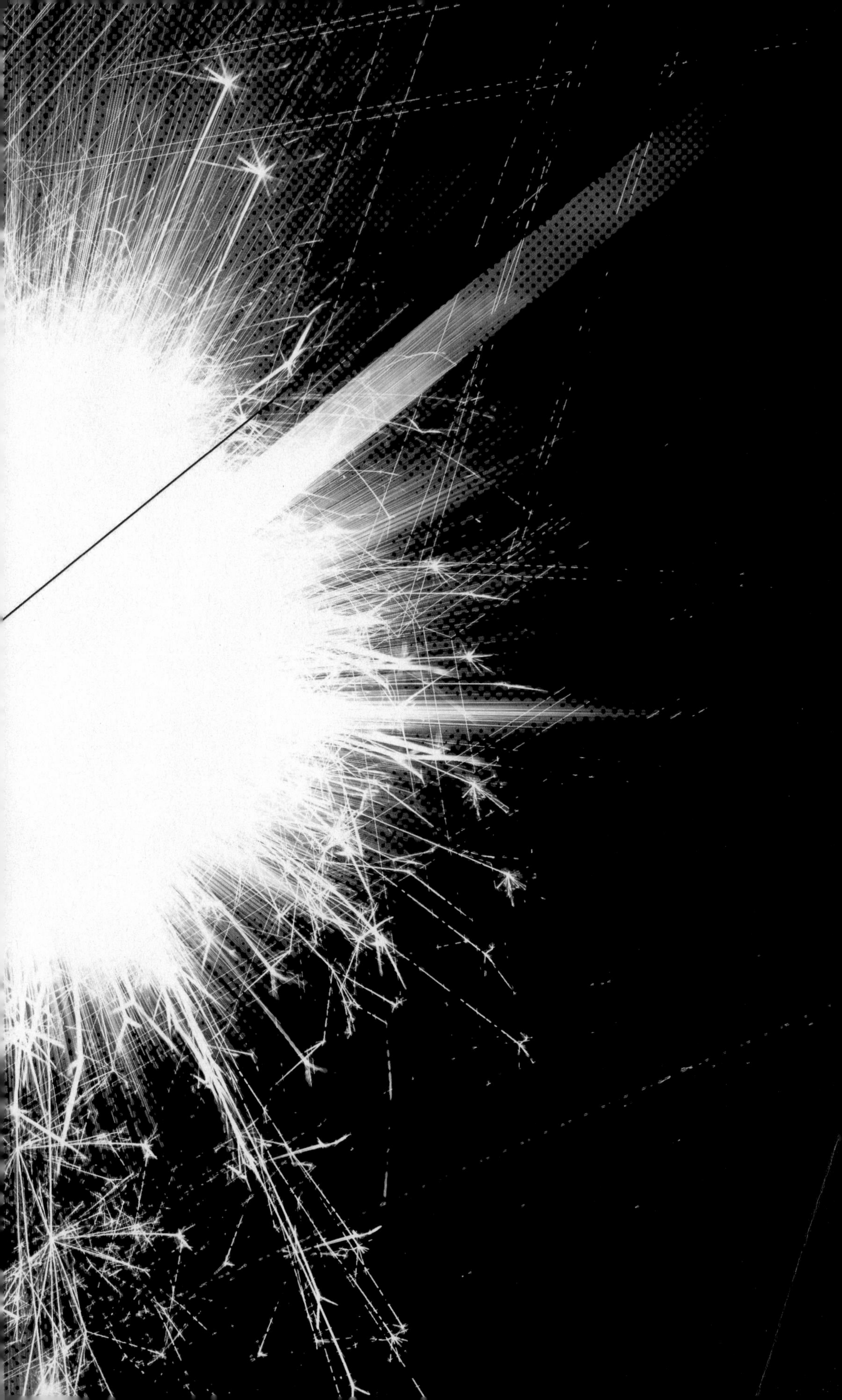

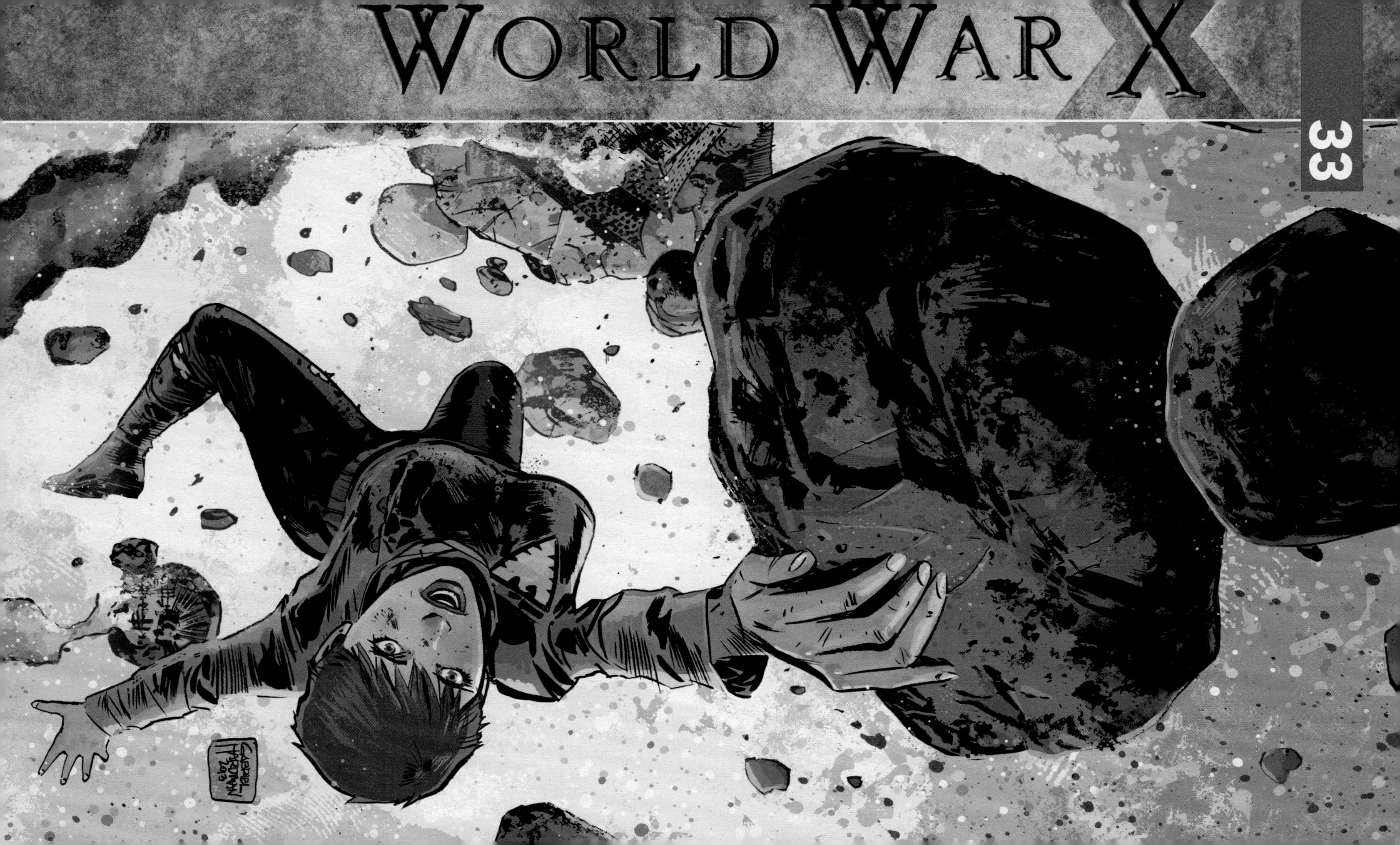
WORLD WAR X
33
GABRIEL HARDMAN 2013

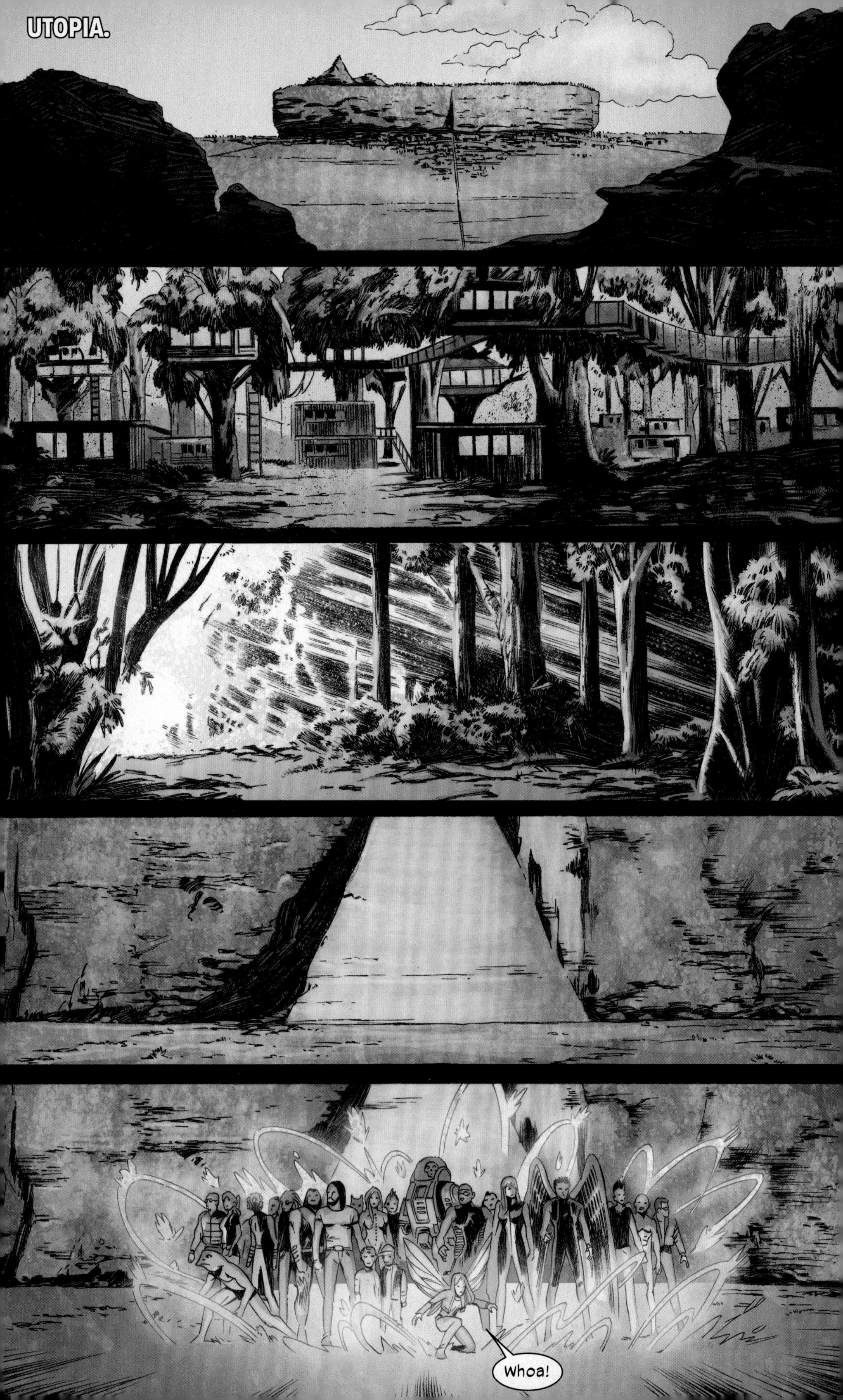
UTOPIA.
Whoa!

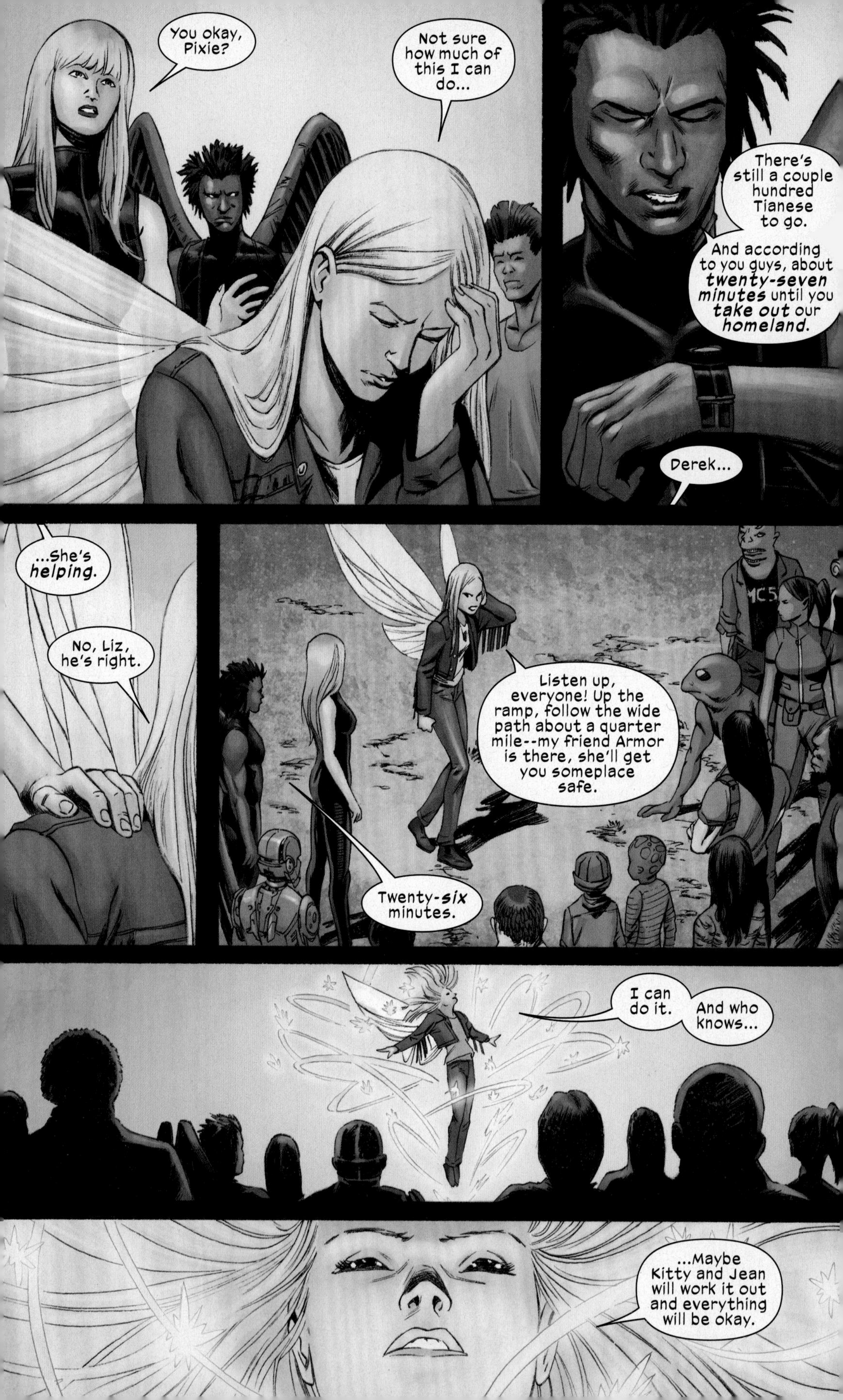
You okay, Pixie?
Not sure how much of this I can do...
There's still a couple hundred Tianese to go.
And according to you guys, about twenty-seven minutes until you take out our homeland.
Derek...
...She's helping.
No, Liz, he's right.
Listen up, everyone! Up the ramp, follow the wide path about a quarter mile--my friend Armor is there, she'll get you someplace safe.
Twenty-six minutes.
I can do it.
And who knows...
...Maybe Kitty and Jean will work it out and everything will be okay.

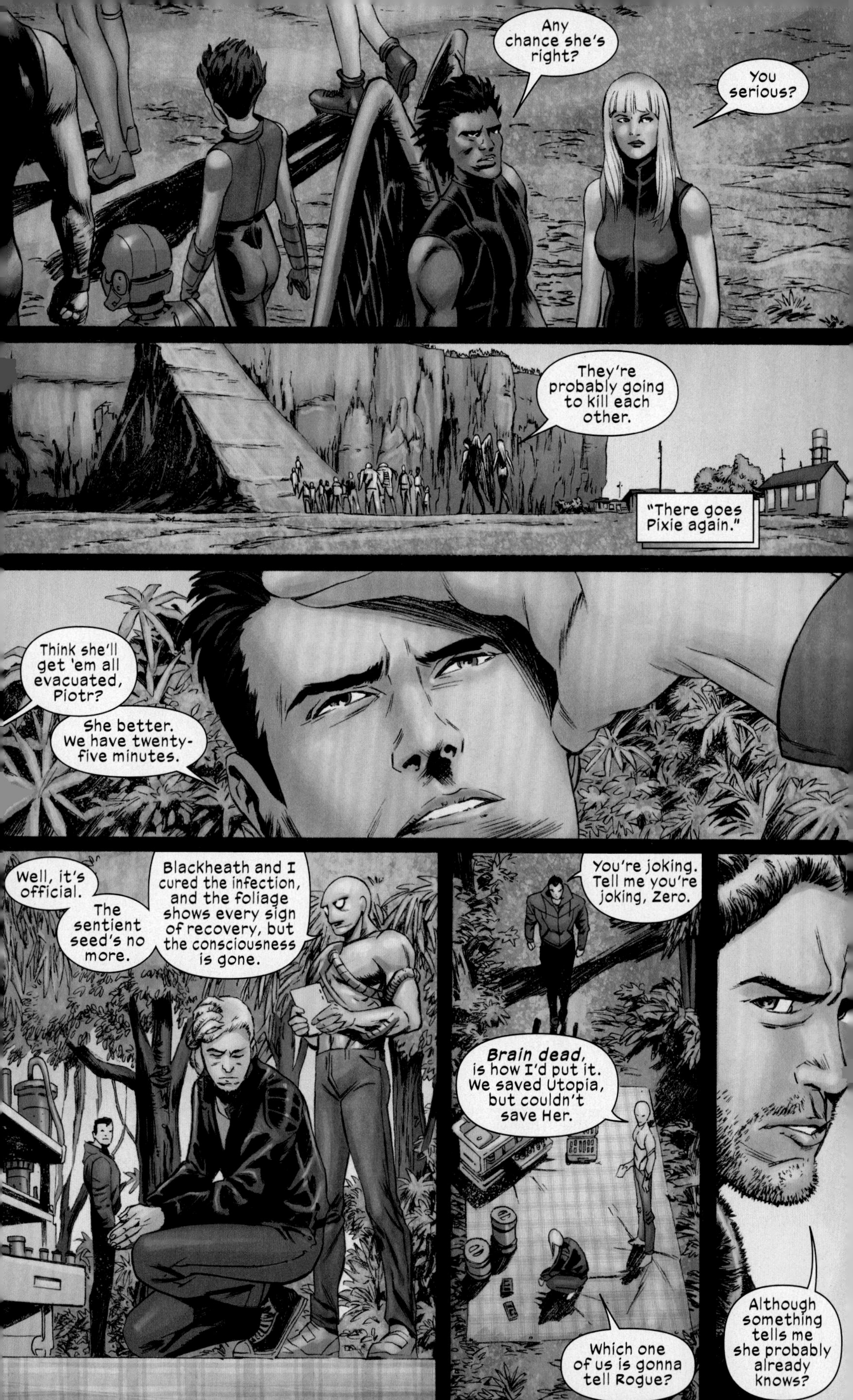
Any chance she's right?
You serious?
They're probably going to kill each other.
"There goes Pixie again."
Think she'll get 'em all evacuated, Piotr?
She better. We have twenty-five minutes.
Well, it's official.
The sentient seed's no more.
Blackheath and I cured the infection, and the foliage shows every sign of recovery, but the consciousness is gone.
You're joking. Tell me you're joking, Zero.
Brain dead, is how I'd put it. We saved Utopia, but couldn't save Her.
Which one of us is gonna tell Rogue?
Although something tells me she probably already knows?

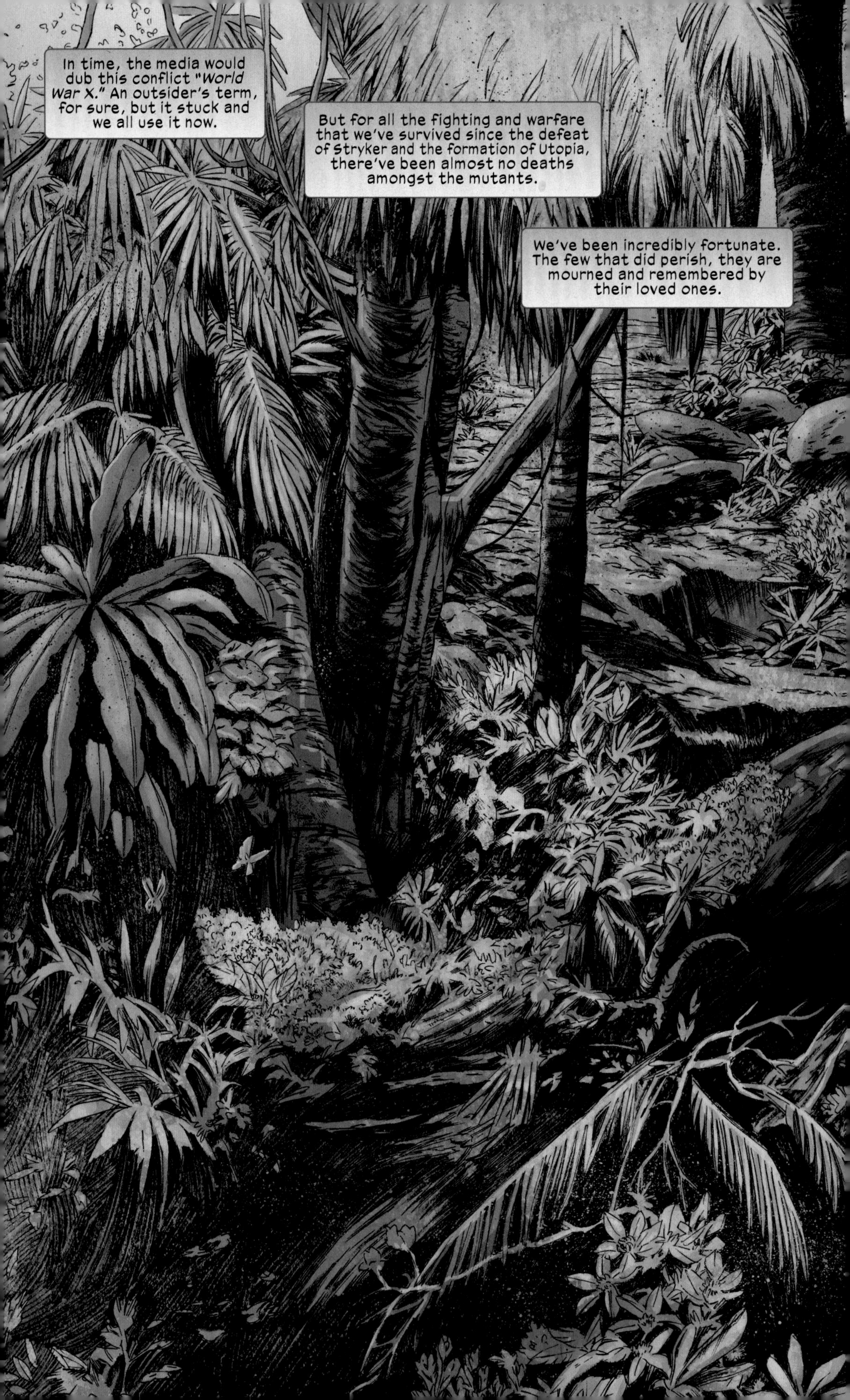
In time, the media would dub this conflict "*World War X*." An outsider's term, for sure, but it stuck and we all use it now.
But for all the fighting and warfare that we've survived since the defeat of Stryker and the formation of Utopia, there've been almost no deaths amongst the mutants.
We've been incredibly fortunate. The few that did perish, they are mourned and remembered by their loved ones.

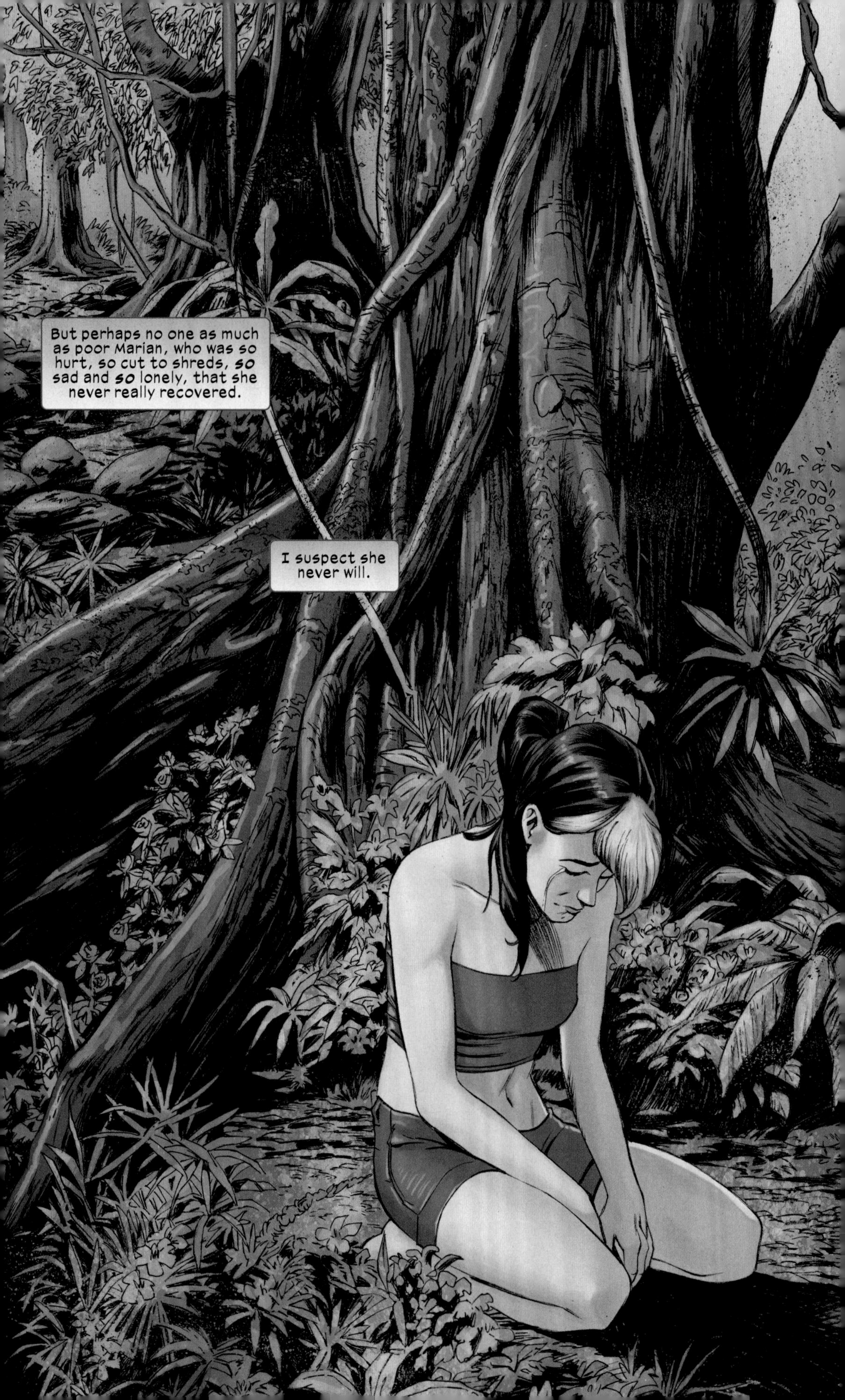
But perhaps no one as much as poor Marian, who was so hurt, so cut to shreds, *so* sad and *so* lonely, that she never really recovered.
I suspect she never will.

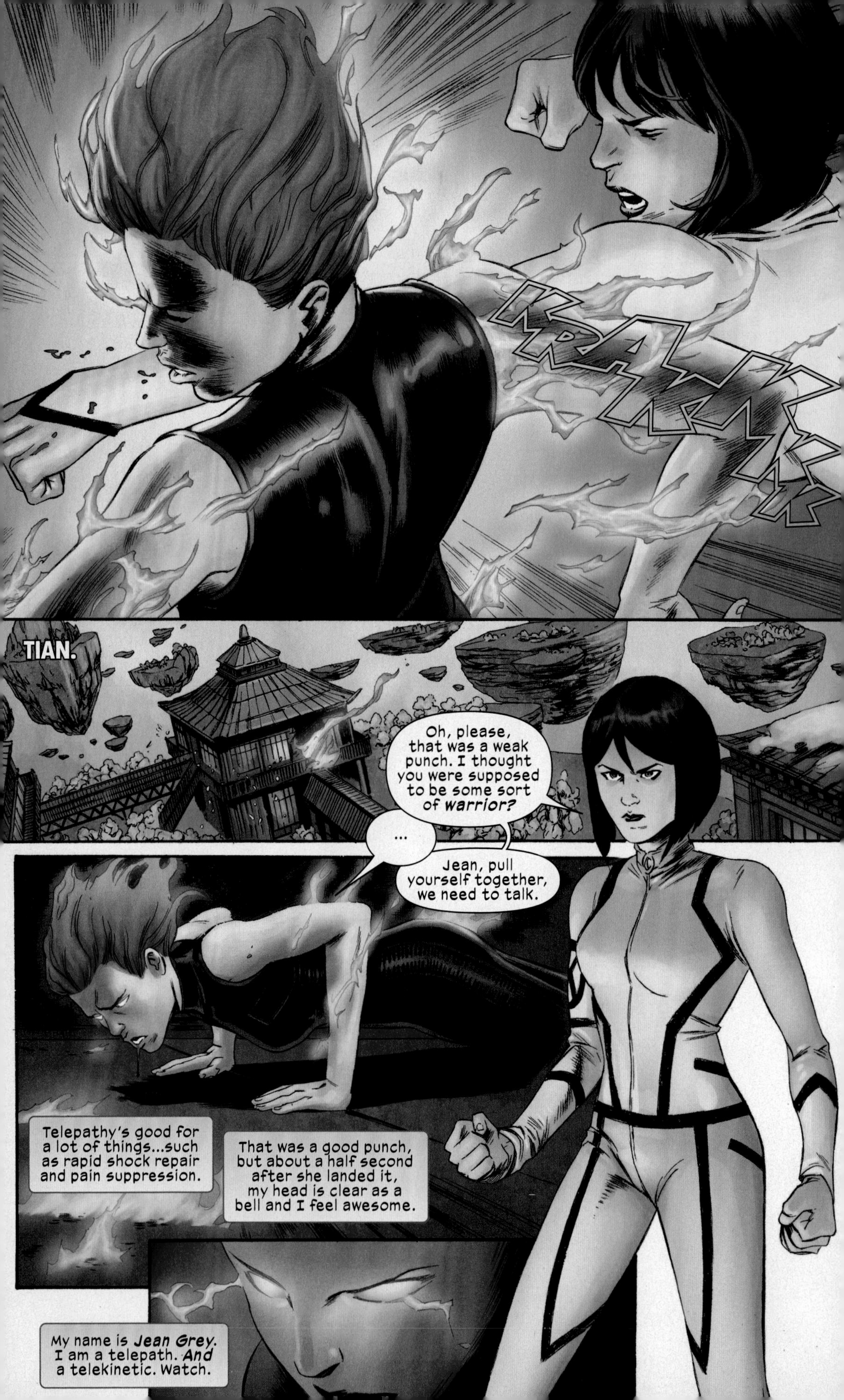
KRAKKK
TIAN.
Oh, please, that was a weak punch. I thought you were supposed to be some sort of *warrior?*
Jean, pull yourself together, we need to talk.
...
Telepathy's good for a lot of things...such as rapid shock repair and pain suppression.
That was a good punch, but about a half second after she landed it, my head is clear as a bell and I feel awesome.
My name is *Jean Grey.* I am a telepath. *And* a telekinetic. Watch.

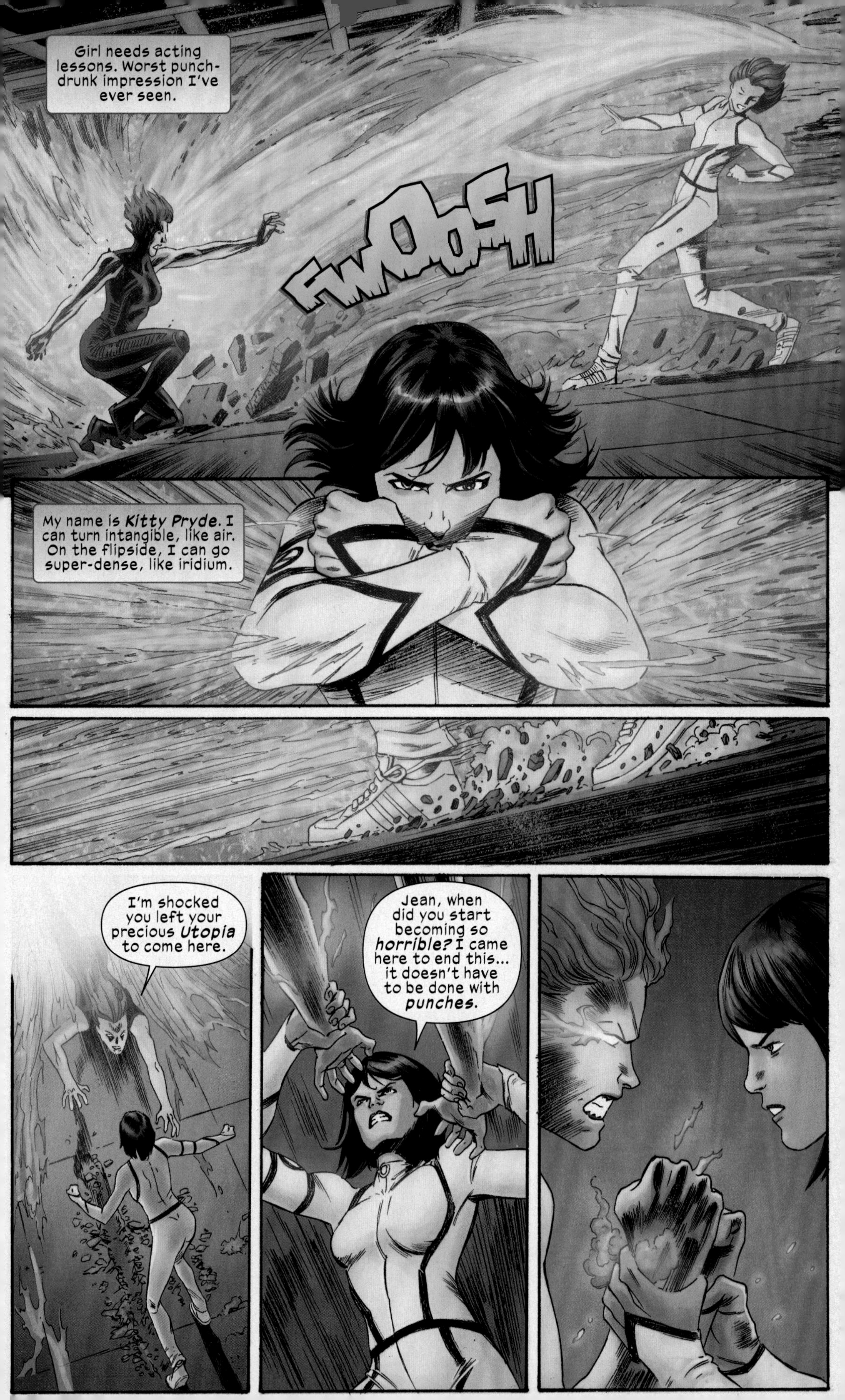
Girl needs acting lessons. Worst punch-drunk impression I've ever seen.
FWOOSH
My name is Kitty Pryde. I can turn intangible, like air. On the flipside, I can go super-dense, like iridium.
I'm shocked you left your precious Utopia to come here.
Jean, when did you start becoming so horrible? I came here to end this... it doesn't have to be done with punches.

Hah. I *gave* you a way out.

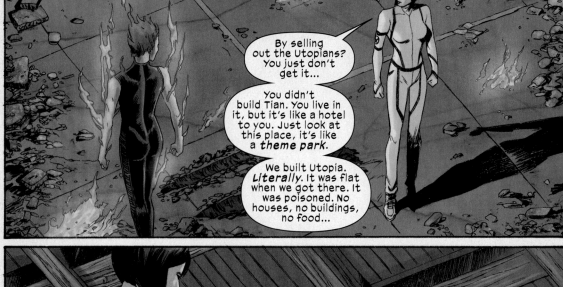

By selling out the Utopians? You just don't get it...

You didn't build Tian. You live in it, but it's like a hotel to you. Just look at this place, it's like a *theme park*.

We built Utopia. *Literally*. It was flat when we got there. It was poisoned. No houses, no buildings, no food...

...Someone's sick joke inside the government. But we sweated in the sun until we had something. Not a hotel. A *home*.

And you expect us to give that up?

Mutants need to be united.

I knew you'd say that. I thought about it on my way here. And I came to a conclusion.

Mutants *are* united.

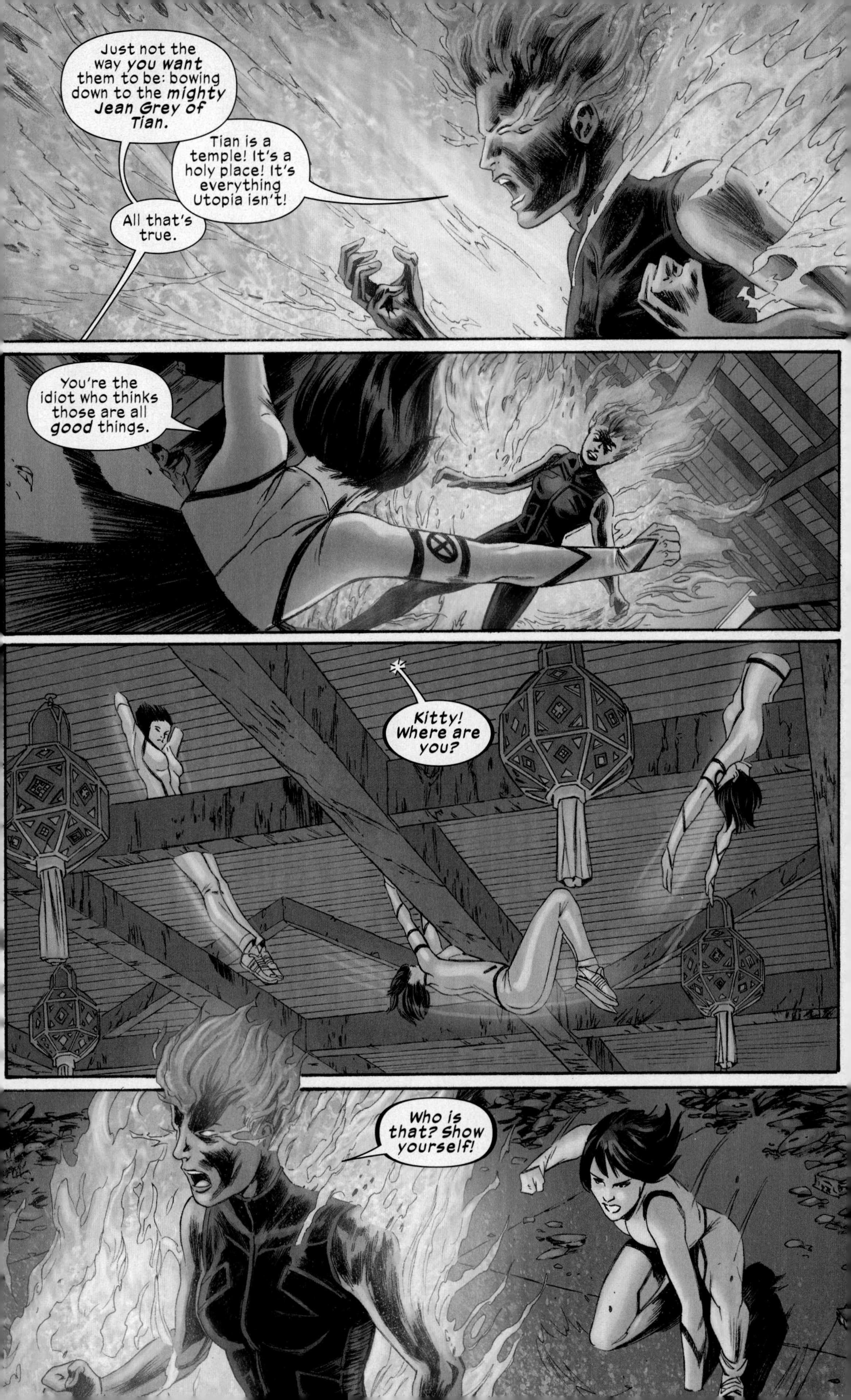

Just not the way you want them to be: bowing down to the mighty Jean Grey of Tian.
Tian is a temple! It's a holy place! It's everything Utopia isn't!
All that's true.
You're the idiot who thinks those are all good things.
Kitty! Where are you?
Who is that? Show yourself!

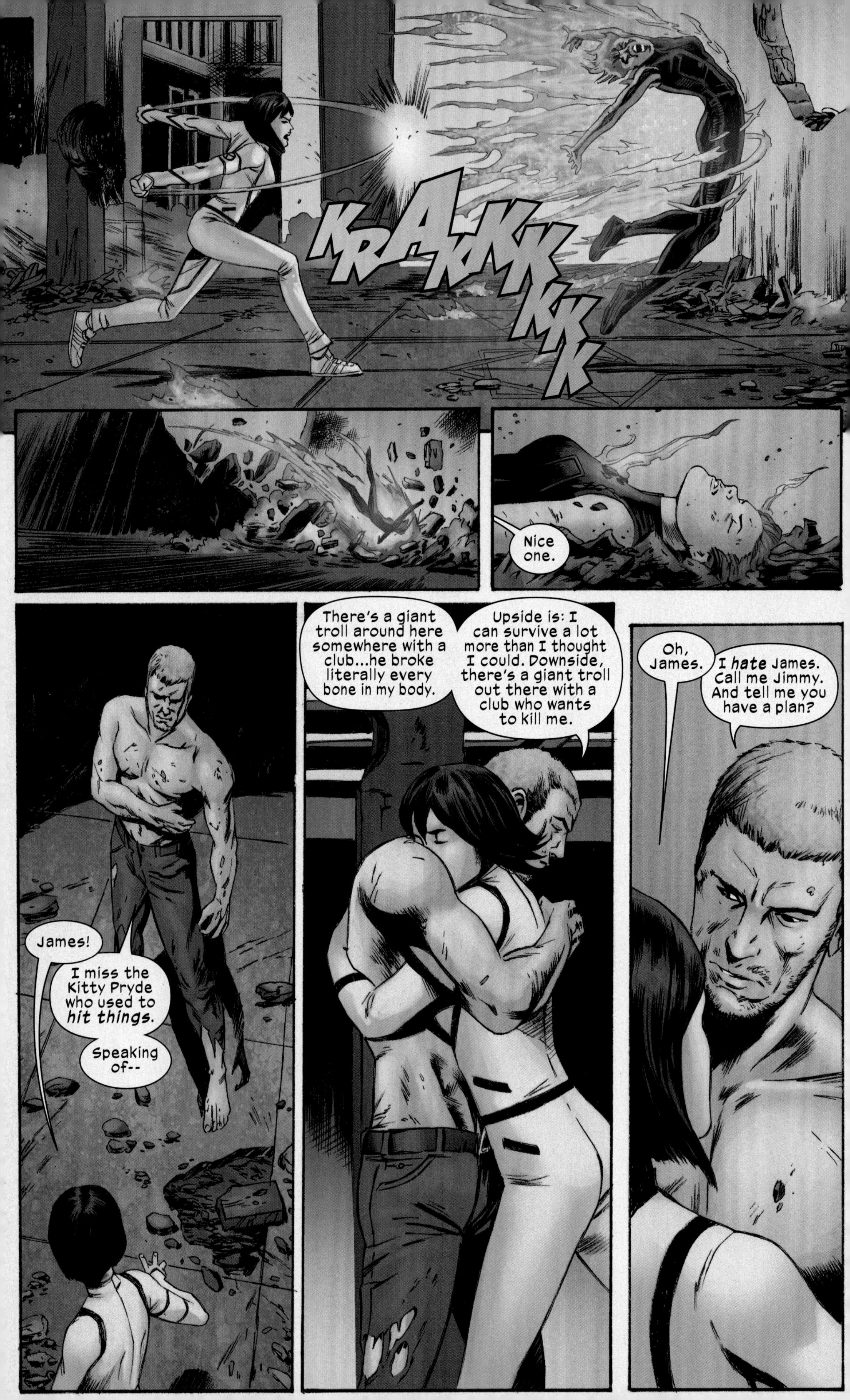
KRAKKKKK
Nice one.
James!
I miss the Kitty Pryde who used to *hit things*.
Speaking of--
There's a giant troll around here somewhere with a club...he broke literally every bone in my body.
Upside is: I can survive a lot more than I thought I could. Downside, there's a giant troll out there with a club who wants to kill me.
Oh, James.
I *hate* James. Call me Jimmy. And tell me you have a plan?

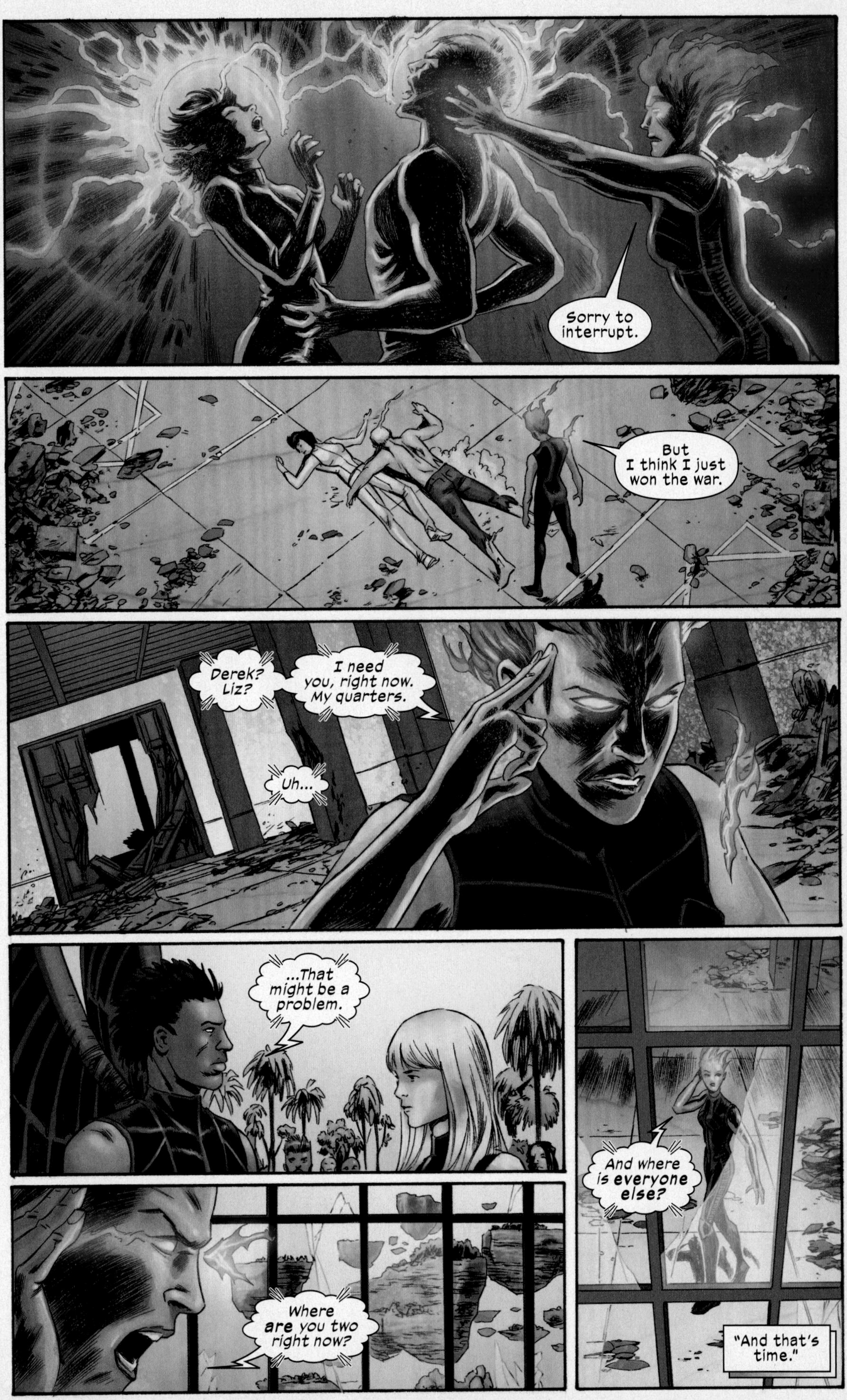

Sorry to interrupt.
But I think I just won the war.
Derek? Liz?
I need you, right now. My quarters.
Uh...
...That might be a problem.
Where are you two right now?
And where is everyone else?
"And that's time."

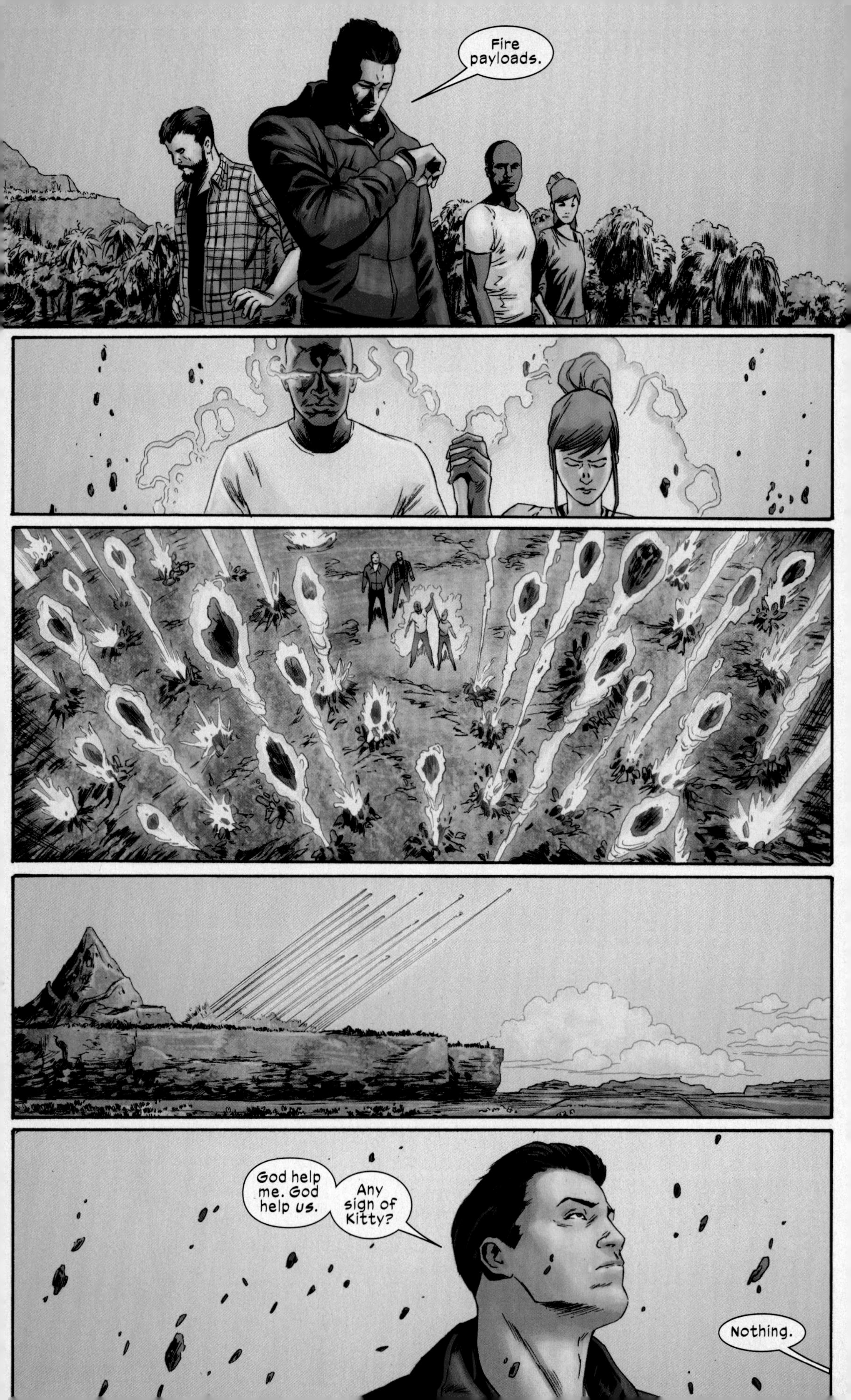
Fire payloads.
God help me. God help us.
Any sign of Kitty?
Nothing.

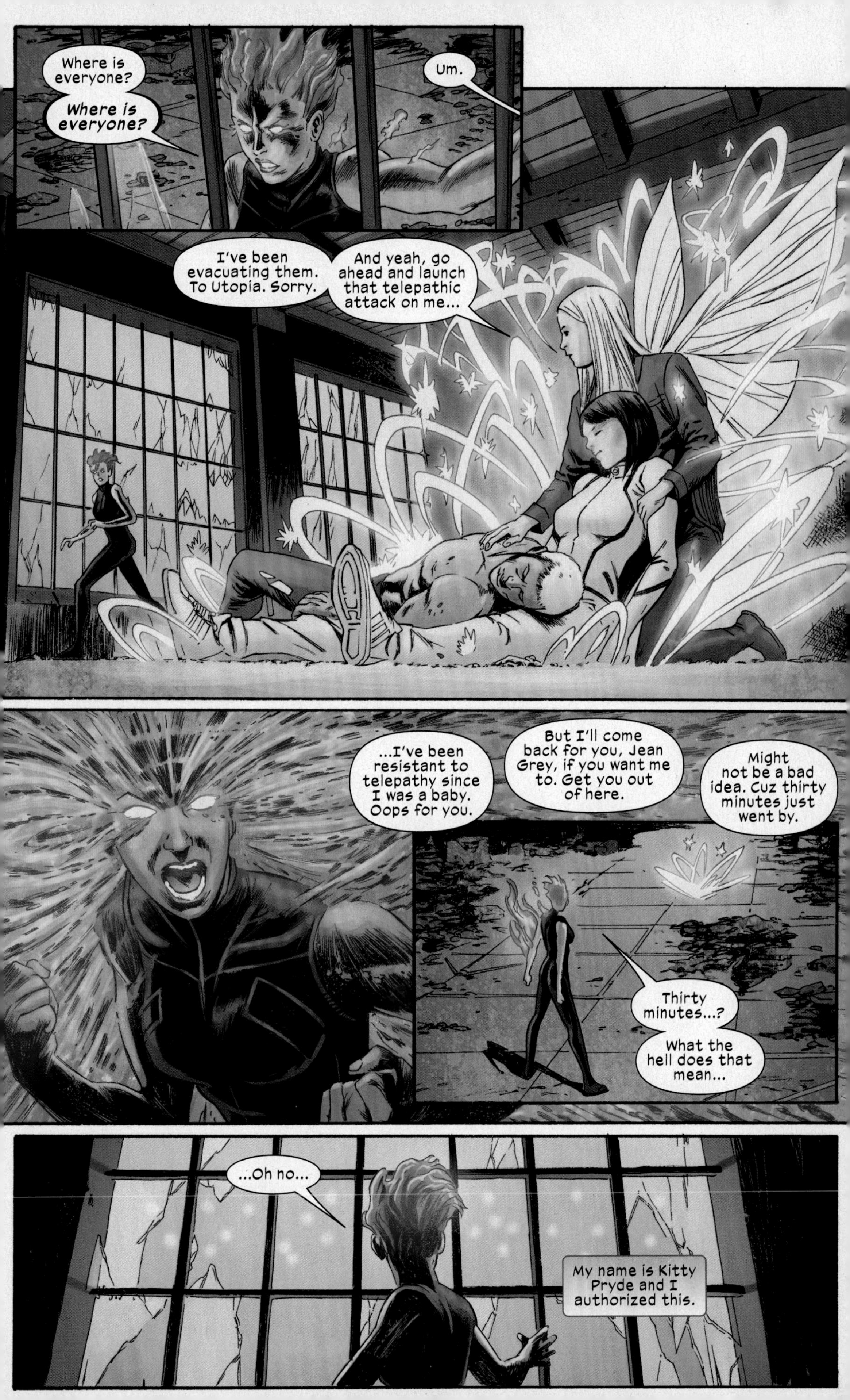

Where is everyone?
Where is everyone?
Um.
I've been evacuating them. To Utopia. Sorry.
And yeah, go ahead and launch that telepathic attack on me...
...I've been resistant to telepathy since I was a baby. Oops for you.
But I'll come back for you, Jean Grey, if you want me to. Get you out of here.
Might not be a bad idea. Cuz thirty minutes just went by.
Thirty minutes...?
What the hell does that mean...
...Oh no...
My name is Kitty Pryde and I authorized this.

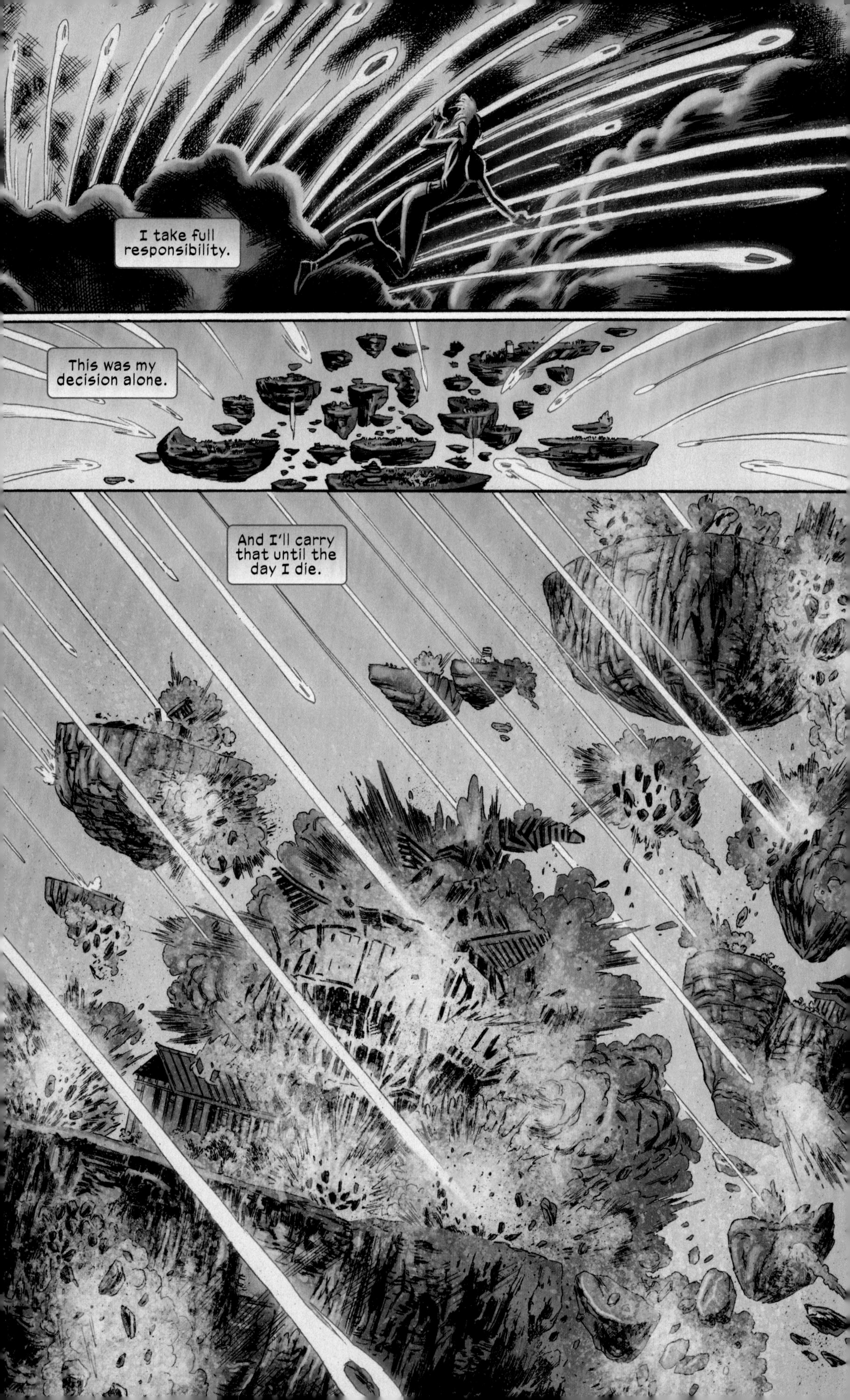
I take full responsibility.
This was my decision alone.
And I'll carry that until the day I die.

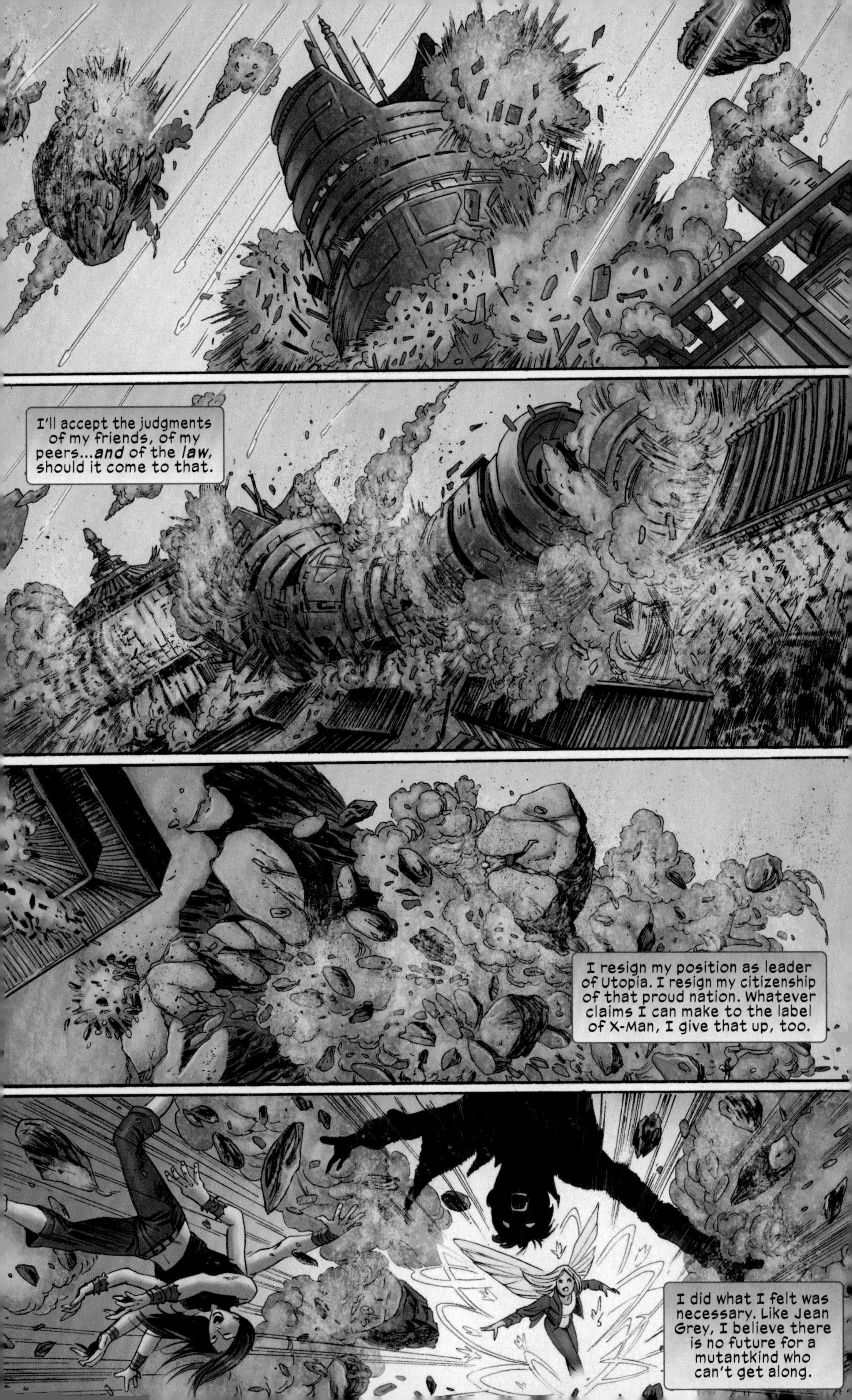
I'll accept the judgments of my friends, of my peers...*and* of the *law*, should it come to that.
I resign my position as leader of Utopia. I resign my citizenship of that proud nation. Whatever claims I can make to the label of X-Man, I give that up, too.
I did what I felt was necessary. Like Jean Grey, I believe there is no future for a mutantkind who can't get along.

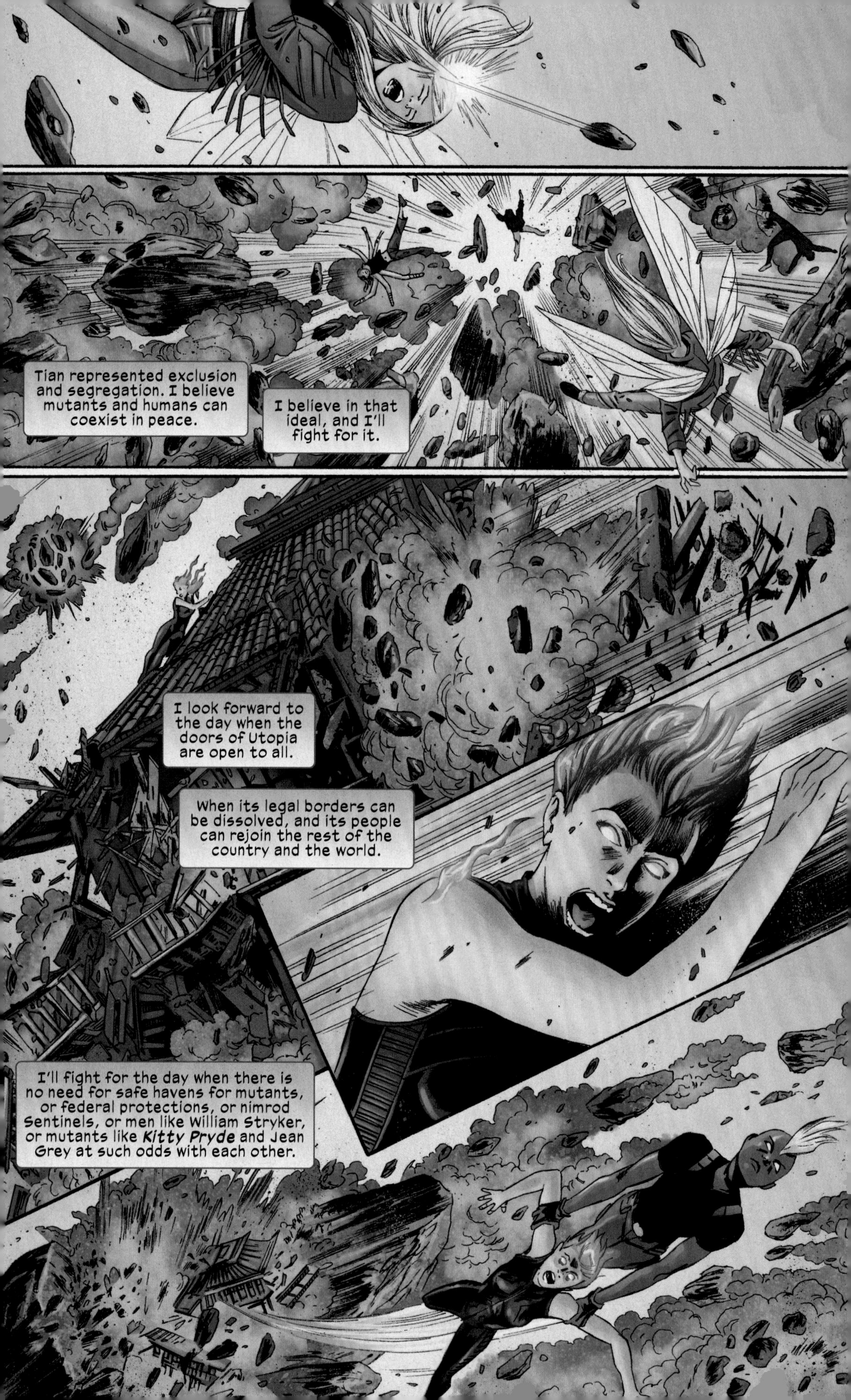
Tian represented exclusion and segregation. I believe mutants and humans can coexist in peace.
I believe in that ideal, and I'll fight for it.
I look forward to the day when the doors of Utopia are open to all.
When its legal borders can be dissolved, and its people can rejoin the rest of the country and the world.
I'll fight for the day when there is no need for safe havens for mutants, or federal protections, or nimrod Sentinels, or men like William Stryker, or mutants like *Kitty Pryde* and Jean Grey at such odds with each other.

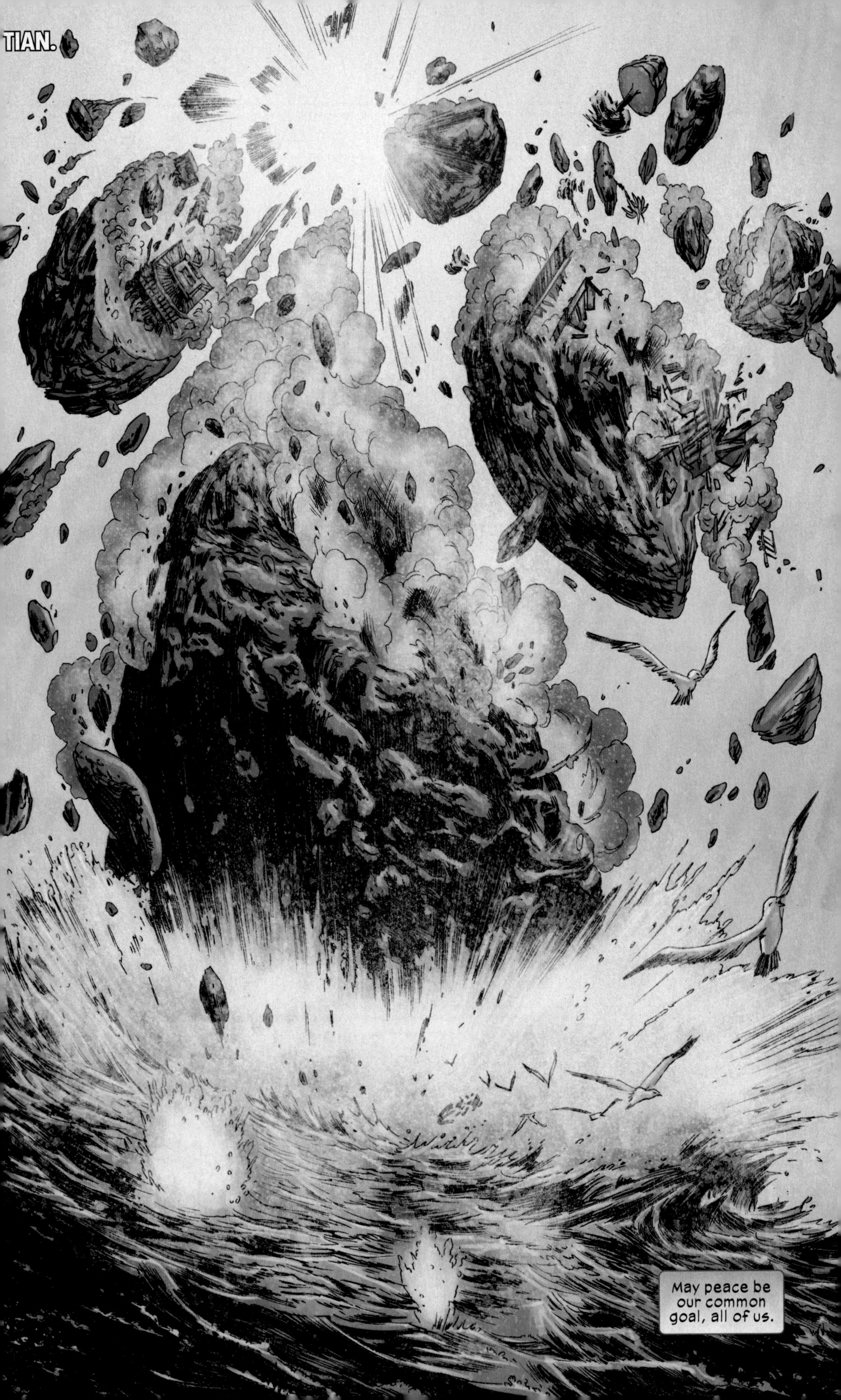
TIAN.
May peace be our common goal, all of us.

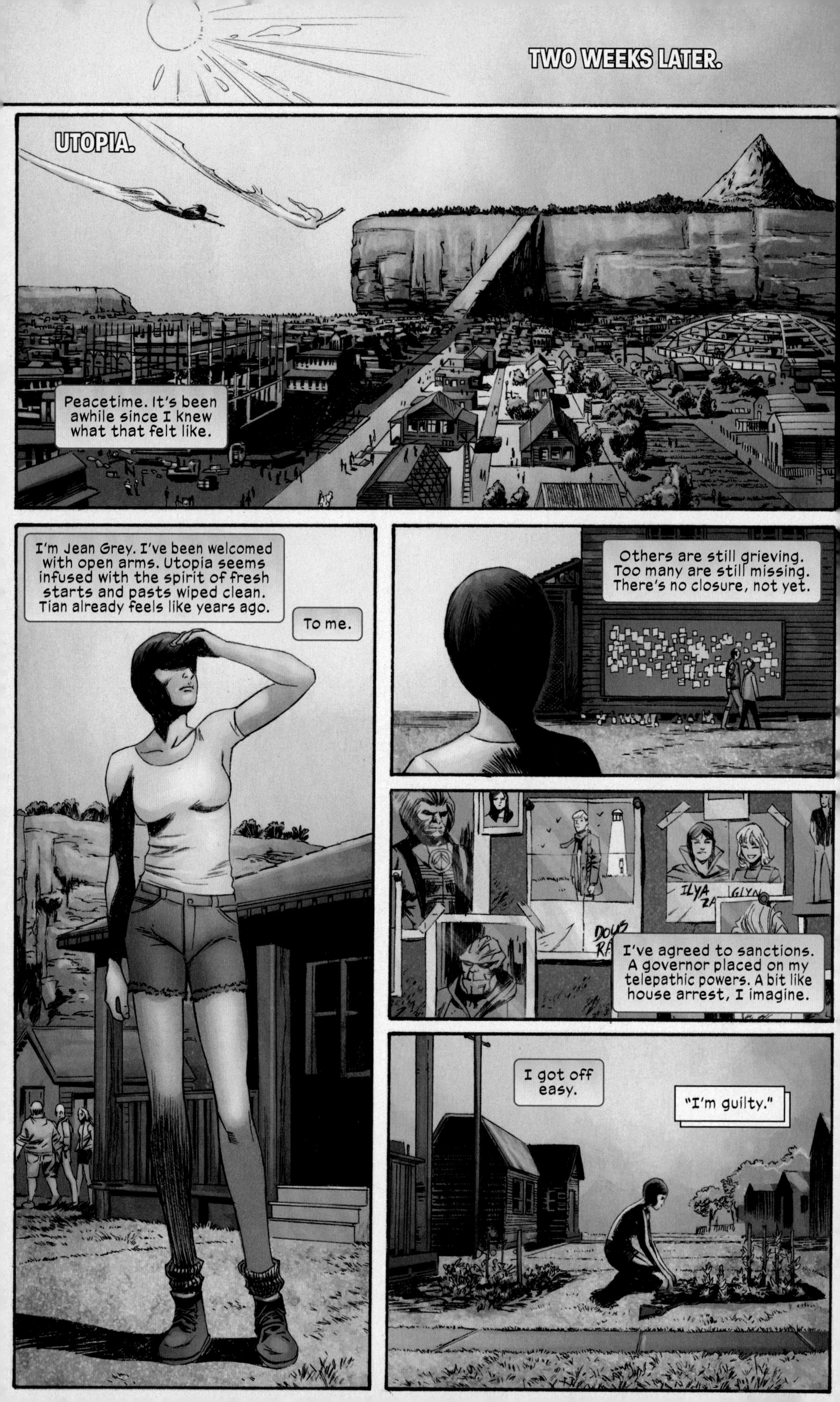
TWO WEEKS LATER.
UTOPIA.
Peacetime. It's been awhile since I knew what that felt like.
I'm Jean Grey. I've been welcomed with open arms. Utopia seems infused with the spirit of fresh starts and pasts wiped clean. Tian already feels like years ago.
To me.
Others are still grieving. Too many are still missing. There's no closure, not yet.
I've agreed to sanctions. A governor placed on my telepathic powers. A bit like house arrest, I imagine.
I got off easy.
"I'm guilty."

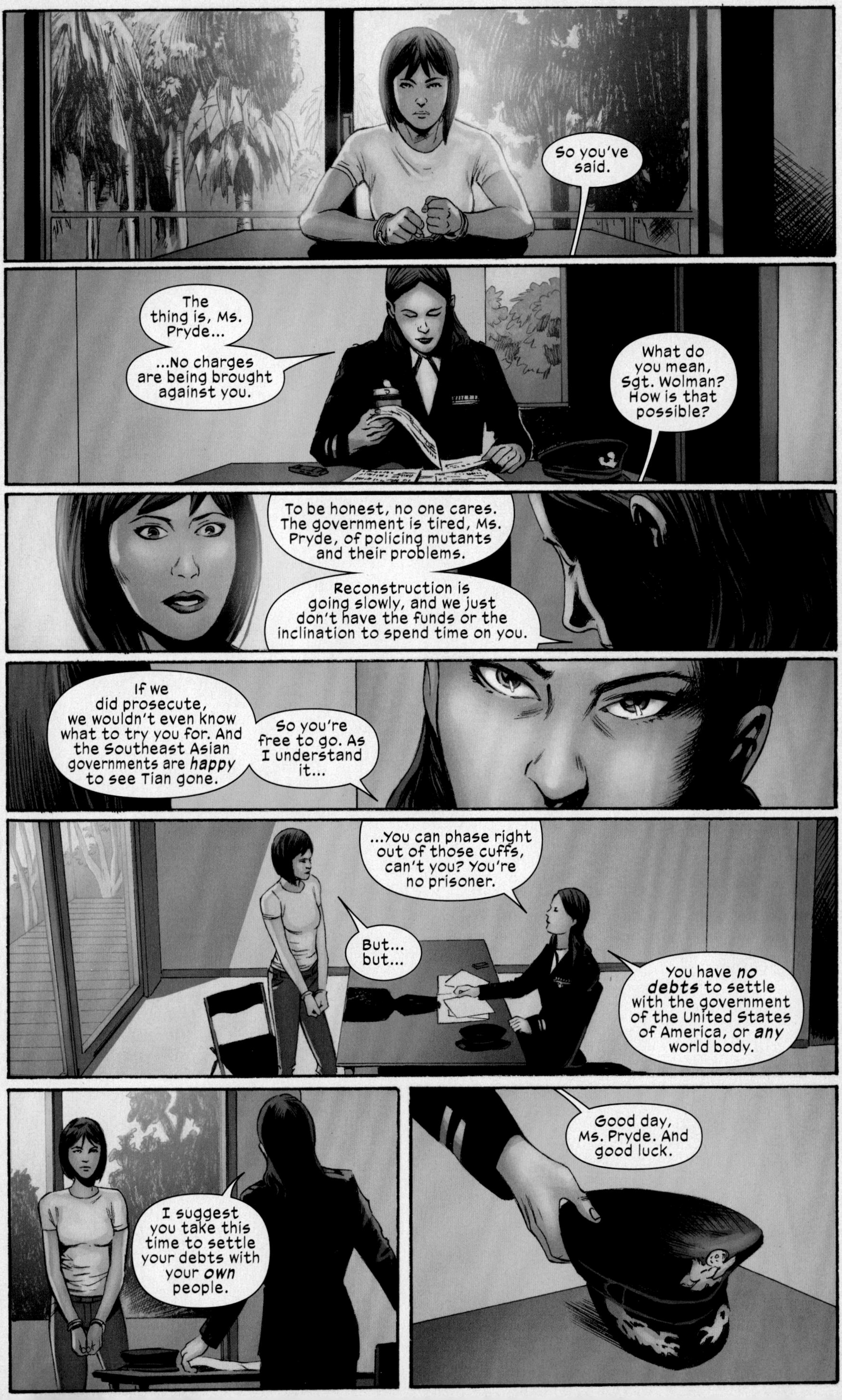
So you've said.
The thing is, Ms. Pryde...
...No charges are being brought against you.
What do you mean, Sgt. Wolman? How is that possible?
To be honest, no one cares. The government is tired, Ms. Pryde, of policing mutants and their problems.
Reconstruction is going slowly, and we just don't have the funds or the inclination to spend time on you.
If we did prosecute, we wouldn't even know what to try you for. And the Southeast Asian governments are *happy* to see Tian gone.
So you're free to go. As I understand it...
...You can phase right out of those cuffs, can't you? You're no prisoner.
But... but...
You have *no debts* to settle with the government of the United States of America, or *any* world body.
I suggest you take this time to settle your debts with your *own* people.
Good day, Ms. Pryde. And good luck.

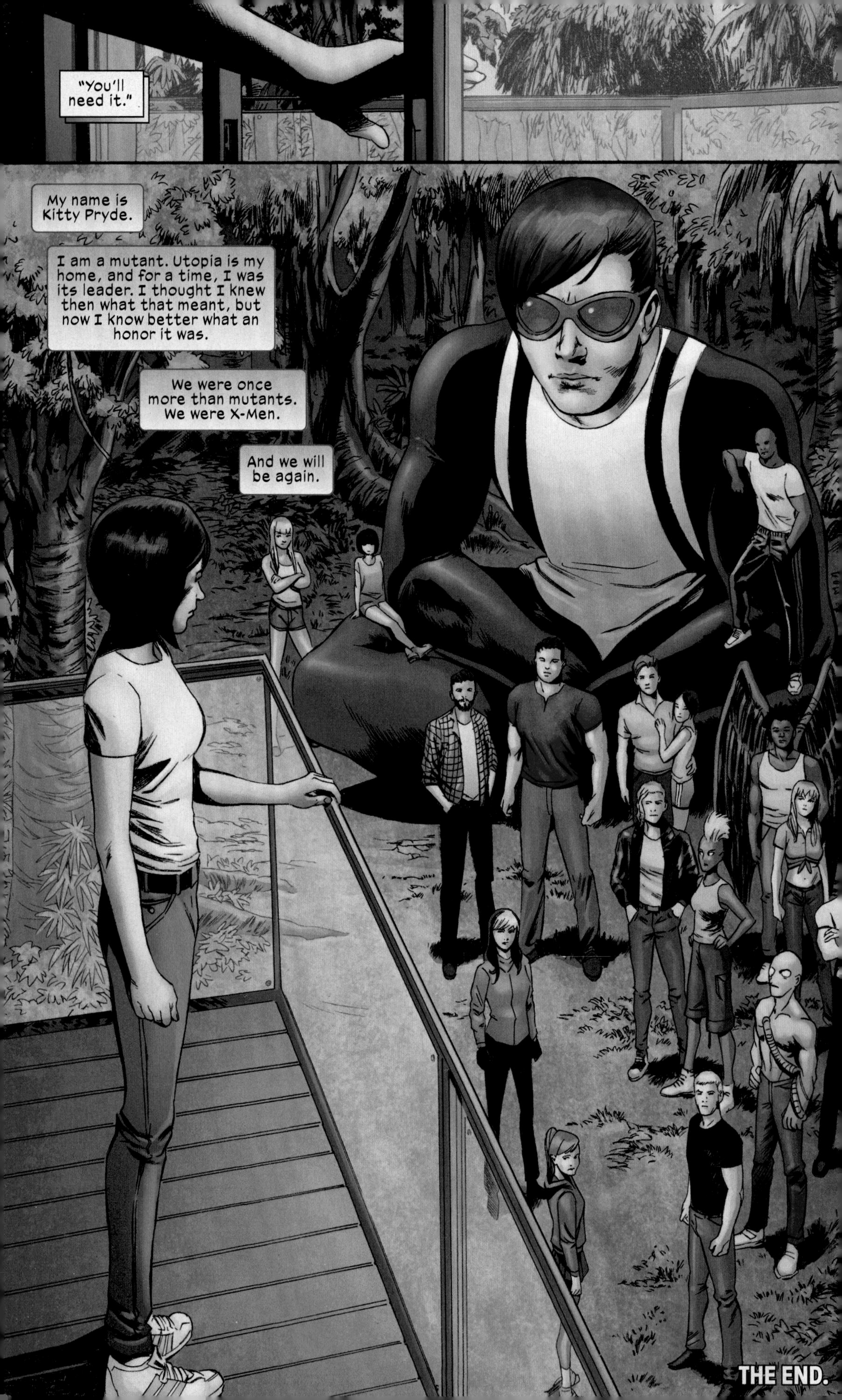
"You'll need it."
My name is Kitty Pryde.
I am a mutant. Utopia is my home, and for a time, I was its leader. I thought I knew then what that meant, but now I know better what an honor it was.
We were once more than mutants. We were X-Men.
And we will be again.
THE END.

29 VARIANT COVER BY CARLO PAGULAYAN

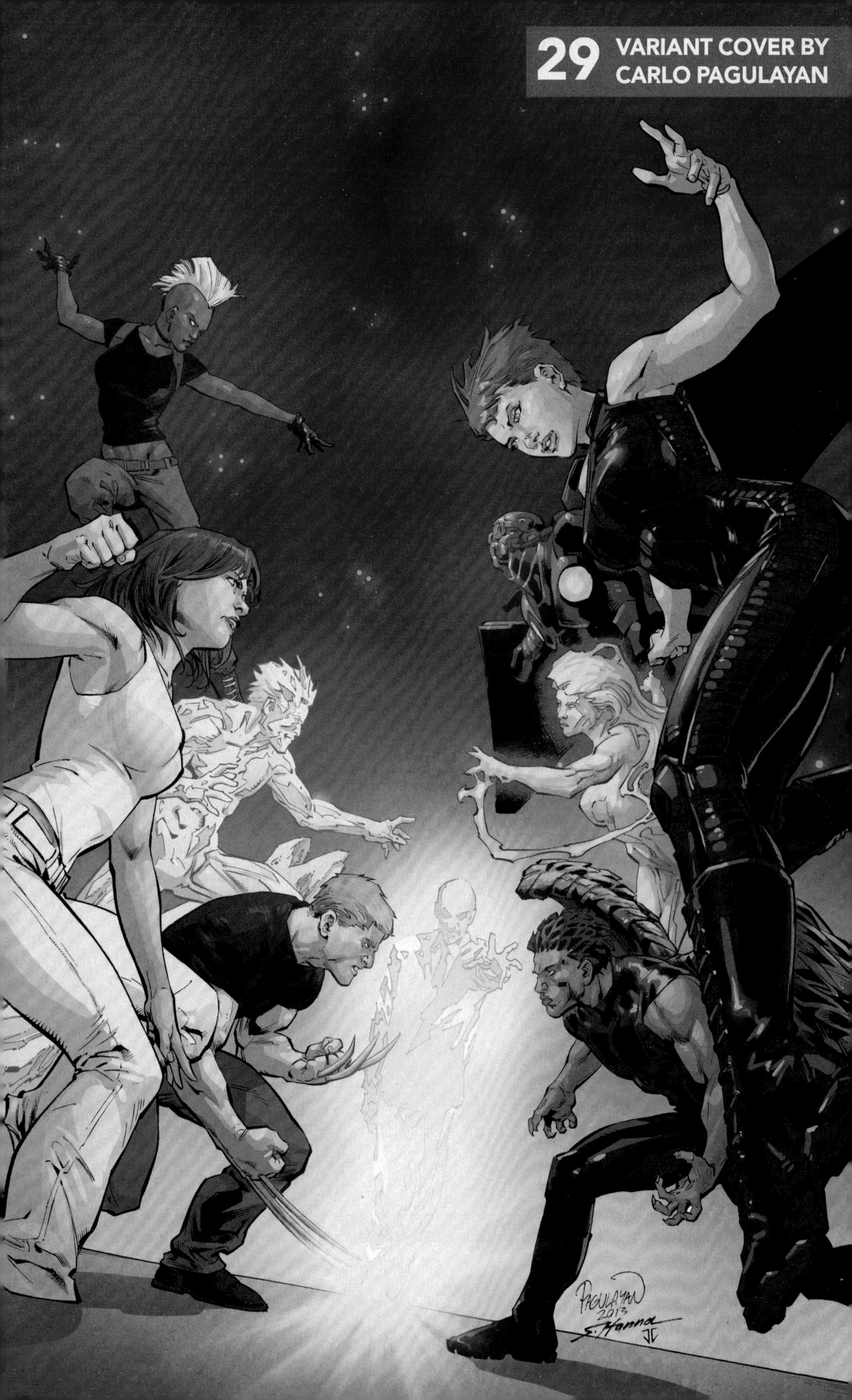
PAGULAYAN 2013
S. Hanna
JC

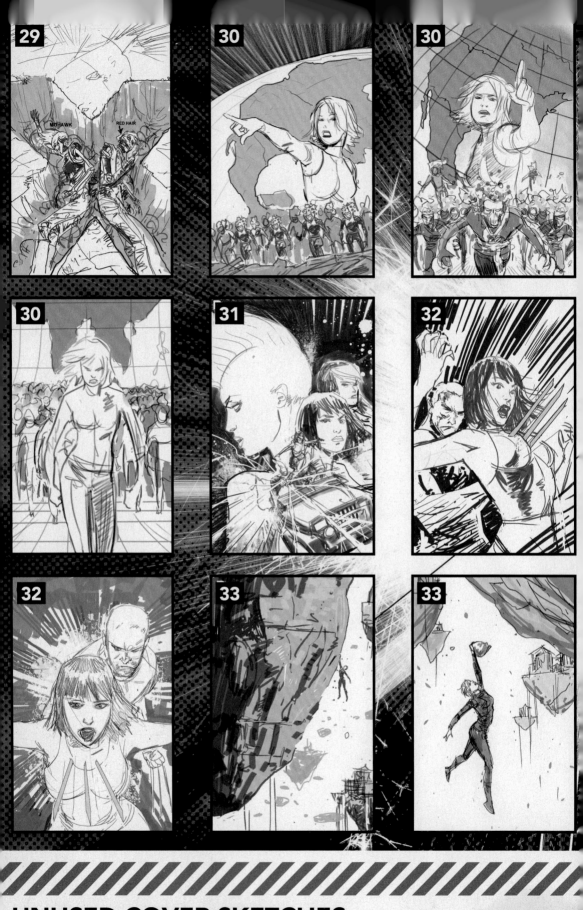

**UNUSED COVER SKETCHES
BY GABRIEL HARDMAN**